THE LANGUAGE GYM
ITALIAN TRILOGY I

THE LANGUAGE GYM
ITALIAN TRILOGY I

ITALIAN
SENTENCE BUILDERS
TRILOGY

A lexicogrammar approach

Beginner to Pre-Intermediate

PART I

About the authors

Gianfranco Conti taught for 25 years at schools in Italy, the UK and in Kuala Lumpur, Malaysia. He has also been a university lecturer, holds a Master's degree in Applied Linguistics and a PhD in metacognitive strategies as applied to second language writing. He is now an author, a popular independent educational consultant and professional development provider. He has written around 2,000 resources for the TES website, which have awarded him the Best Resources Contributor in 2015. He has co-authored the best-selling and influential book for world languages teachers, "The Language Teacher Toolkit" and "Breaking the sound barrier: Teaching learners how to listen", in which he puts forth his Listening As Modelling methodology. Gianfranco writes an influential blog on second language acquisition called The Language Gym, co-founded the interactive website language-gym.com and the Facebook professional group Global Innovative Language Teachers (GILT). Last but not least, Gianfranco has created the instructional approach known as E.P.I. (Extensive Processing Instruction).

Dylan Viñales has taught for 15 years, in schools in Bath, Beijing and Kuala Lumpur in state, independent and international settings. He lives in Kuala Lumpur. He is fluent in five languages, and gets by in several more. Dylan is, besides a teacher, a professional development provider, specialising in E.P.I., metacognition, teaching languages through music (especially ukulele) and cognitive science. In the last five years, together with Dr Conti, he has driven the implementation of E.P.I. in one of the top international schools in the world: Garden International School. This has allowed him to test, on a daily basis, the sequences and activities included in this book with excellent results (his students have won language competitions both locally and internationally). He has designed an original Spanish curriculum, bespoke instructional materials, based on Reading and Listening as Modelling (RAM and LAM). Dylan co-founded the fastest growing professional development group for modern languages teachers on Facebook, Global Innovative Languages Teachers, which includes over 12,000 teachers from all corners of the globe. He authors an influential blog on modern language pedagogy in which he supports the teaching of languages through E.P.I. Dylan is the lead author of Spanish content on the Language Gym website and oversees the technological development of the site. He completed the NPQML qualification in 2021 and is now planning to pursue a Masters in second language acquisition.

Christian Moretti has been teaching Modern Foreign Languages (Spanish and Italian) for over fifteen years in the UK and Ireland. He has been an Associate for Junior Cycle for Teachers, a Department of Education of Ireland agency and the National Council for Curriculum and Assessment of Ireland. He has been awarded a PhD in Comparative Literature (Spanish and Italian) by the University of Kent (UK). As a scholar, Christian has published numerous research papers in prestigious academic journals in the literary and medical humanities fields. He is currently a teacher of Modern Foreign Languages in Limerick Educate Together Secondary School (Ireland). Christian is passionate about language learning and teaching, wellbeing and equality, he is a fervent advocate for an inclusive education which is accessible to all. Christian has fully embraced Dr. Conti's research-based language teaching method from the beginning and is a very active resources creator. Christian is fluent in four languages.

Acknowledgements

We would like to thank our editor Giovanni Calandro for his tireless work, proofreading, editing and advising on this book. He is a multi-talented, accomplished professional who works at the highest possible level and adds value at every stage of the process. Not only this, but he is also a lovely, good-humoured colleague who goes above and beyond, and make the hours of collaborating a real pleasure.

Our sincere gratitude to all the people involved in the recording of the Listening audio files:
Ivano Confalone, Francesca Bonsignori, Giovanni Calandro & Giusi Serpi. Your energy, enthusiasm and passion comes across clearly in every recording and is the reason why the listening sections are such a successful and engaging resource, according to the many students who have been alpha and beta testing the book.

Our sincere thanks to Simona and Stefano for their ongoing support, since the very beginning of the Sentence Builder books project. Some important structural elements in this book, such as the inclusion of a listening element at the start of every unit, are inspired by their excellent work as lead authors of the Primary Sentence Builders series.

Finally, our gratitude to the MFL Twitterati for their ongoing support of E.P.I. and the Sentence Builders book series. In particular a shoutout to our team of incredible educators who helped in checking all the units: Angela Benedetti, Emanuela Bonardi, Barbara Borghi, Simona Gravina, Kim Louise Davis, Federica Mancusi, Diana Bonifaci, Tina Gallo, Eva Micheli, Sarah Milthorpe, Franka Maisano, Giovanna Matarazzo, Antonietta Maganuco, Sharon Mangion & Ilaria Agostini. It is thanks to your time, patience, professionalism and detailed feedback that we have been able to produce such a refined and highly accurate product.

Grazie a tutti,
Gianfranco, Dylan & Christian

DEDICATION

For Catrina
-Gianfranco

For Ariella & Leonard
-Dylan

For Gary, Adelaide, Damiano & Francesco
-Christian

Introduction

Hello and welcome to the first 'text' book designed to be an accompaniment to a Italian, Extensive Processing Instruction course. The book has come about out of necessity, because such a resource did not previously exist.

How to use this book

This book was originally designed as a resource to use in conjunction with our E.P.I. approach and teaching strategies. Our course favours flooding comprehensible input, organising content by communicative functions and related constructions, and a big focus on reading and listening as modelling. The aim of this book is to empower the beginner-to-pre-intermediate learner with linguistic tools - high-frequency structures and vocabulary - useful for real-life communication.

What's inside

The book contains 15 macro-units which concern themselves with a specific communicative function, such as 'Describing people's appearance and personality', 'Comparing and contrasting people', 'Saying what you like and dislike' or 'Saying what you and others do in your free time'. Each unit includes:

- a sentence builder modelling the target constructions;
- a set of listening activities to model and input-flood the target language
- a set of vocabulary building activities which reinforce the material in the sentence builder;
- a set of narrow reading texts exploited through a range of tasks focusing on both the meaning and structural levels of the text;
- a set of translation tasks aimed at consolidation through retrieval practice;
- a set of writing tasks targeting essential writing micro-skills such as spelling, functional and positional processing, editing and communication of meaning.
- a "Bringing it all together" section to recycle and interleave the target language seen in previous units

At the end of each term, there is also an End of Term - Question Skills unit. These units are designed to model asking and answering the key questions which have been studied throughout the term. This is also an additional opportunity for structured production as students move towards routinising the language and producing spontaneous speech by the end of the term.

Listening files

These can be accessed by going to **language-gym.com/listening** – access is free, and you can also share this link with students if you want to set a listening homework.

Each sentence builder at the beginning of a unit contains one or more constructions which have been selected with real-life communication in mind. Each unit is built around that construction <u>but not solely on it</u>. Based on the principle that each E.P.I instructional sequence must move from modelling to production in a seamless and organic way, each unit expands on the material in each sentence builder by embedding it in texts and graded tasks which contain both familiar and unfamiliar (but comprehensible and learnable) vocabulary and structures.

The point of all the above micro-units is to implement lots of systematic recycling and interleaving, two techniques that allow for stronger retention and transfer of learning.

Gianfranco, Dylan & Christian

SENTENCE BUILDERS TRILOGY
PART 1 - TABLE OF CONTENTS

* Units marked with an asterisk are optional

TERM 1 – OVERVIEW

This term you will learn:

Unit 0 - Register routine: saying how you are
• How to say your name
• How to say how you are feeling

Unit 1 - How to introduce yourself and say how you are
• How to say your name and age
• How to say someone else's name and age

Unit 2 - How to say when your birthday is
• When your birthday is
• Numbers from 15 to 31 / Months
• Where you and another person are from

Unit 3 - How to say where you live and are from
• What your apartment or house is like and where it is
• Renowned cities in Italy and Italian-speaking Switzerland

Unit 4 - OPTIONAL: How to talk about subjects & teachers
• Adjectives for describing people
• Masculine/feminine agreements

Unit 5 - How to talk about free time - likes / dislikes
• Three key verbs: fare / giocare / andare
• Activities that go with those verbs

KEY QUESTIONS

- Come ti chiami? — *What is your name?*
- Come stai oggi? — *How are you today?*
- Quanti anni hai? — *How old are you?*
- Quand'è il tuo compleanno? — *When is your birthday?*

- Hai fratelli o sorelle? — *Do you have any brothers or sisters?*
- Come si chiama tuo fratello/tua sorella? — *What is your brother/your sister called?*
- Quanti anni ha? — *How old is he/she?*
- Quand'è il suo compleanno? — *When is his/her birthday?*

- Di dove sei? — *Where are you from?*
- Dove abiti? — *Where do you live?*

- Quali materie studi? — *What subjects do you study?*
- Quale materia (**non**) ti piace? Perché? — *Which one do you (**not**) like? Why?*
- Ti piace l'italiano? Perché? — *Do you like Italian? Why?*

- Che cosa ti piace fare nel tuo tempo libero? — *What do you like to do in your free time?*

TERM 1

In this unit you will learn:

- How to introduce yourself
- Key questions: "Come ti chiami?" and "Come stai oggi?"
- How to say how you are feeling
- How to express your mental state

UNIT 0
EPI Register Routine

Come ti chiami?	*What is your name?*	**Mi chiamo** *My name is*	**Carlo** **Maria**
Come stai oggi?	*How are you today?*	**Sto bene, grazie** *I am well, thanks*	
Come va?	*How's it going?*		

					MASC	FEM
Ciao *Hello*						
Buongiorno *Good morning*		**benissimo** *great*			**ammalato** *sick*	**ammalata**
Buon pomeriggio *Good afternoon*		**molto bene** *very well*			**annoiato** *bored*	**annoiata**
Buona sera *Good evening*		**bene** *well*	**ma sono** *but I am (feeling)*	**abbastanza** *quite*	**arrabbiato** *angry*	**arrabbiata**
Buona notte *Good night*	**Oggi sto** *today I am*	**così-così** *so-so*			**emozionato** *excited*	**emozionata**
Salve *Hello*			**perché sono** *because I am (feeling)*	**un po'** *a bit*	**felice** *happy*	**felice**
Arrivederci *Goodbye*		**male** *(feeling) bad*		**molto** *very*	**nervoso** *nervous*	**nervosa**
Prego *You're welcome*					**stanco** *tired*	**stanca**
Grazie *Thank you*		**molto male** *(feeling) very bad*			**stressato** *stressed*	**stressata**
Piacere *Nice to meet you*					**tranquillo** *calm*	**tranquilla**
Va bene *OK*		**malissimo** *(feeling) awful*			**triste** *sad*	**triste**

Author's note: *"sto"* **means** *"I am".* *It is often used to talk about how you are feeling.* ***"sto male/malissimo"*** *should thus be translated as "I am <u>feeling</u> bad/awful"- not "I am a bad/awful person".* ***"Sono"*** *also means* ***"I am"*** *but it is used to talk about how you are.* ***"Sono annoiato"*** *means I am bored.*

1. Break the flow: draw a line between each word

a. Cometichiami?

b. CiaomichiamoPaola.

c. Comestaioggi?

d. Buongiornooggistobenissimo.

e. Oggisonoabbastanzastanca.

f. Sonounpo'arrabbiata.

g. Sonomoltofelice.

2. Faulty echo

a. Come ti chiami?

b. Mi chiamo Carlo.

c. Buongiorno, come stai?

d. Buonasera, sto malissimo.

e. Sono molto tranquillo.

f. Oggi sto benissimo, grazie.

g. Oggi sto male.

3. Arrange in the correct order

and quite calm.	
Today I am great	
What is your name?	
Good morning.	**1**
My name is Carlo.	
because I am very happy	
And you, how are you today?	

4. Fill in the blanks

a. C _ _ _   t _   c _ _ _ _ _ ?

b. C _ _ _   s _ _ _   o _ _ _ ?

c. B _ _ _ _ _ _ _ _ _ .

d. B _ _ _ _   n _ _ _ _ .

e. B _ _ _   p _ _ _ _ _ _ _ _ .

f. O _ _ _   s _ _ m _ _ _ _   b _ _ _ .

g. O _ _ _ s _ _ m _ _ _ .

h. S _ _ _   m _ _ _ _   f _ _ _ _ _ .

5. Listen and fill in the gaps

Francesco: Ciao, come ti _______?

Lucia: ______, mi chiamo Lucia.

Francesco: Piacere Lucia. Come stai ______?

Lucia: Oggi sto ___________ perché sono molto ______. E tu?

Francesco: Fantastico! Io sto ______ perché sono abbastanza ___________, grazie.

Lucia: Va bene Francesco, ______.

Francesco: Piacere ☺

tranquillo	felice	bene	oggi
benissimo	chiami	piacere	ciao

6. Listen and fill in the grid in Italian

		How are they?	Why?
e.g.	Luca	molto bene	felice
a.	Marco		
b.	Antonio		
c.	Paola		
d.	Dylan		
e.	Stefano		

Unit 0. EPI Register Routine: VOCABULARY BUILDING

1. Match

sto bene	I am (feeling) bad
sto male	I am sad
sto così-così	I am happy
sto malissimo	I am well
sto benissimo	I am stressed
sono stanco	I am so-so
sono felice	I am (feeling) awful
sono stressato	I am great
sono triste	I am tired

2. Faulty translation: some are correct!

a. sono felice: I am stressed

b. sono stanco: I am happy

c. sto bene: I am well

d. Sono stressato: I am sad

e. sono triste: I am tired

f. sto male: I am (feeling) bad

g. sto così-così: I am so-so

h. sto malissimo: I am (feeling) awful

i. oggi: now

j. buon pomeriggio: good afternoon

3. Break the flow

a. Stobeneperchésonofelice.

b. Stomaleperchésononervosa.

c. Stomoltobeneperchésonotranquilla.

d. Stomoltomaleperchésonostressata.

e. Stomaleperchésonotriste.

f. Stomaleperchésonoarrabbiata.

g. Stocosìcosìmasonostanca.

4. Fill in the gaps

a. ______, come ti ______?

b. Mi ________ Francesco, ______.

c. ______, come stai ______?

d. ______bene, grazie, e ______?

e. Sto bene ______.

f. …però_______ un poco ______.

chiamo	tu	Sto	stanco	Ciao
oggi	chiami	Piacere x 2	sono	grazie

5. Broken words

a. C_____ c_______ t__ c___________ ?
Hi, what's your name?

b. M__ c_______ L____, p_______ !
My name is Lily, nice to meet you!

c. C_____ s_______ o____?
How are you today?

d. O____ s_______ a_________ b______, g_______.
Today I am quite well (good), thanks.

e. S_______ c_________, p_______ s_______ u__
p_____ s_________.
I am so-so because I am a bit stressed (f).

6. Complete with a suitable word

a. __________, mi chiamo ____________.

b. E tu, come ti ____________?

c. ____ chiamo Francesco. _________.

d. _________, _________ stai oggi?

e. ________ abbastanza bene, _________.

f. E ____? Come stai ______?

g. Oggi sto male perché sono molto ________.

h. Sto ___________ perché sono felice.

i. Sto molto bene ___________ sono tranquillo.

Unit 0. EPI Register Routine: READING

Olga: Ciao, buongiorno. Come ti chiami?

Maria: Ciao, mi chiamo Maria, e tu?

Olga: Mi chiamo Olga. Come stai oggi Maria?

Maria: Sto benissimo, grazie. Sono felice e emozionata. E tu?

Olga: Oggi sto così-così.

Maria: Perché? Cosa c'è?

Olga: Sono molto stanca e un po' stressata.

Maria: Oh! Mi dispiace (*Oh! I am sorry*).

Olga: Sei molto gentile, grazie. Va bene, Maria, piacere.

Maria: Piacere mio *(my pleasure)*.

Olga: Arrivederci, Maria.

Enzo: Ciao, buon pomeriggio. Come ti chiami?

Giacomo: Ciao, mi chiamo Giacomo, E tu? Come ti chiami?

Enzo: Mi chiamo Enzo. Come stai oggi Giacomo?

Giacomo: Sto molto male.

Enzo: Perché? Cosa c'è?

Giacomo: Sono molto arrabbiato e anche (*also*) un po' triste. E tu?

Enzo: Oh, mi dispiace! *(sorry!)* Io sto abbastanza bene oggi perché molto tranquillo.

Giacomo: Mi fa piacere *(I'm glad)*.

Enzo: Va bene, Giacomo, piacere di conoscerti.

Giacomo: Piacere. Arrivederci Enzo!

---

1. Find the Italian for the following items in the Olga and María's dialogue

a. hello, good morning

b. what is your name?

c. my name is Maria

d. how are you today?

e. I am great, thank you

f. I am so-so

g. why?

h. what's up?

i. I am very tired

j. …and a bit stressed

k. you are very kind, thank you

l. I am sorry

m. OK

n. nice to meet you

o. my pleasure

p. goodbye

2. Answer the following questions about Olga and Maria

a. How is Maria feeling today?

b. What two reasons does Maria give to explain how she is feeling?

c. How is Olga?

d. What two reasons does Olga give to explain how she is feeling?

3. Find someone who…

a. …is feeling very tired

b. …is feeling very bad

c. …is feeling quite well

d. …is feeling a bit sad

e. …is feeling great

f. …is feeling a bit stressed

g. …is feeling very calm

h. …is feeling happy and excited

Unit 0. EPI Register Routine: WRITING

1. Faulty translation: spot and correct (in the English) any translation mistakes you find below

a. mi chiamo Dylan.   *your name is Dylan.*

b. come ti chiami?   *what are your like?*

c. come stai oggi?   *what are you today?*

d. sto così-cosi.   *I am great.*

e. sono molto felice.   *I am a bit happy.*

f. sono un po' stressato.   *I am very stressed.*

g. sto molto male.   *I am (feeling) very well.*

h. sto benissimo.   *I am OK.*

i. sono abbastanza stanco.   *I am quite tiring.*

j. piacere.   *nice to meet you..*

2. Translate into English

a. ciao, come ti chiami?

b. come stai oggi?

c. mi chiamo Pietro

d. sto abbastanza bene, grazie

e. e tu?

f. sto molto bene

g. oggi sono molto tranquillo

h. oggi non sto bene

i. sono molto felice

j. sono triste e arrabbiato

3. Anagram challenge: unscramble the words and then translate

a. ubgionroon

b. boun pimgogeiro

c. oecm sait?

d. onos etirts

e. soon ecifle

f. cmoe it cmhiai?

g. nsoo anastc

h. tso bsminsieo

i. sono ltoom rbatiaoarb

j. caipeer

4. Translate into Italian

a. hello

b. good morning

c. good afternoon

d. how are you today?

e. what's your name?

f. I am very well, thanks. And you?

g. I am so-so because I am a bit sad

h. I am very happy and calm

i. I am angry and nervous

j. I am a bit tired

UNIT 1
Talking about my age

In this unit you will learn:

- How to say your name and age
- How to say someone else's name and age
- How to count from 1 to 16
- A range of common Italian names
- The words for brother and sister

Ho dieci anni

Ho un anno

Ho sei anni

Ho quindici anni

UNIT 1
Talking about my age

Come ti chiami?		What is your name?						
Quanti anni hai?		*How old are you?*						

						un	1	**anno** *year*
Io *I*	**mi chiamo** *am called*	Alessio Antonio Anna Barbara Christian Davide Dylan Emanuela		**ho** *I have**	due	2		
					tre	3		
					quattro	4		
					cinque	5		
					sei	6		
					sette	7		
Mio fratello *My brother* **Mia sorella** *My sister*	**si chiama** *is called*	Filippo Gabriele Gianfranco Giulia Katia Mario Paolo Simona Stefano	**e** *and*	**ha** *he/she has**	otto	8	**anni** *years*	
					nove	9		
					dieci	10		
					undici	11		
					dodici	12		
					tredici	13		
					quattordici	14		
					quindici	15		

Author's notes:

1) The number **"uno"** becomes **"un"** when it goes before a noun. E.g. " Ho un fratello".

2) In Italian, we use the verb "to have" for age. So, we say "ho dieci anni" to say how old we are or how many years we completed as it means, literally "I have ten years". There are a few Latin languages (e.g. Spanish/French) that also do this :D

3) In Italian, you do not say 'my name is', you say: I am called.

"

1. Fill in the blanks

a. Mi _ _ _ _ _ _ Christian.

b. Ho _ _ _ _ _ _ _ _ _ anni.

c. Ho _ _ _ fratelli.

d. _ _ _ fratello minore si _ _ _ _ _ _ _ Roberto.

e. Mio _ _ _ _ _ _ _ _ _ maggiore _ _ chiama Gianfranco.

f. Come _ _ chiami?

g. Quanti _ _ _ _ hai?

2. Break the flow: draw a line between each word

a. MichiamoAntonio.

b. Hoquindicianni.

c. MiofratellosichiamaGabriele.

d. MiasorellasichiamaAnna.

e. Quantiannihai?

f. MiofratellosichiamaFilippo.

g. Cometichiami?

3. Arrange in the correct order

I am thirteen years old.	
Anna is fifteen years old.	
My name is Stefano.	**1**
My sister is called Anna.	
I have a brother and a sister.	
My brother is called Mario.	
Mario is fourteen years old.	

4. Spot the differences and correct the text

a. Ti chiamo anna.

b. Ho undici anni.

c. Ho due sorelle.

d. Mio fratello maggiore si chiama Giacomo.

e. Mio fratello maggiore si chiama Roberto.

f. Francesco ha quattordici anni.

g. Roberto ha otto anni.

h. Quanti anni ho?

5. Complete with the missing letters

a. Mi chiam_ Paolo.

b. Sono italian_.

c. Ho quindi_ _ anni.

d. Non ho fratell_.

e. ...ma ho un_ sorella.

f. Mia sorella si chiam_ Anna.

g. Anna h_ dodici a_ _ i.

h. E tu, come t_ chiami?

i. Quanti anni ha_?

6. Spot the missing words and write them in

a. Mi chiamo Paolo.

b. Sono italiano.

c. Ho tredici.

d. Ho un fratello una sorella.

e. Mio fratello chiama Roberto.

f. Sorella si chiama Isabella.

g. Roberto quattordici anni.

7. Listen, spot and correct the errors

a. Ho quattordici anno.

b. Mi chiama Carlo.

c. Mio fratello si chiamo Paolo.

d. Ho due fratello.

e. Ho uno fratello e una sorella.

f. Quanto anni hai?

8. Listen and fill in the grid

	Age	Brothers	Sisters
a. Maria			
b. Giacomo			
c. Anna			
d. Dylan			
e. Alice			
f. Franco			

9. Faulty translation: spot the translation errors and correct them

a. His name is Andrea.

b. I am Swiss.

c. I have three brothers.

d. My older sister is called Alice.

e. My younger sister is called Lucia.

f. Alice is ten.

g. Lucia is fourteen.

h. I am eleven.

10. Translate the sentences you hear into English

a.

b.

c.

d.

e.

f.

g.

h.

i.

11. Narrow listening: gap-fill

Mi chiamo ___________. Sono di Bari, in ______________. Nella mia famiglia ci sono quattro persone: ___________ madre, mio padre e i miei __________ fratelli. Mio fratello ___________ si chiama Michele e mio fratello ____________ si chiama Franco. Michele ha ___________ anni e mio fratello Franco ha ___________ anni. E tu, come ti ___________? ___________ anni hai?

chiami	Antonio	minore	maggiore	sei
mia	quindici	Italia	quanti	due

12. Narrow listening: gapped translation

(a) My name is ___________. I live in ___________, in Italy. In my family there are ___________ people: my mother, my father, my ___________ brother, my ________ brother and myself.

(b) My ________ brother is called ___________. He is ________ years old.

(c) My ___________ brother is called Angelo. He is ________ years old. How about you, what ____ ________ _______? How ________ ________ ________? How________ ________________ ________ ________ ________?

Unit 1. Talking about my age: VOCABULARY BUILDING

1. Match up

1. un anno	*a. seven years*
2. due anni	*b. four years*
3. tre anni	*c. five years*
4. quattro anni	*d. six years*
5. cinque anni	*e. eleven years*
6. sei anni	*f. ten years*
7. sette anni	*g. twelve years*
8. otto anni	*h. nine years*
9. nove anni	*i. two years*
10. dieci anni	*j. eight years*
11. undici anni	*k. one year*
12. dodici anni	*l. three years*

2. Complete with the missing word

a. Ho __________ anni.   *I am twelve years old.*

b. Mio fratello _____ chiama Sal.   *My brother is called Sal.*

c. Mi ____________ Roberto.   *My name is Roberto.*

d. Mio fratello _____ due anni.   *My brother is two years old.*

e. Mia sorella ha ________ anni.   *My sister is four years old.*

f. _____ chiamo Anna.   *My name is Anna.*

quattro	ha	si
mi	**dodici**	**chiamo**

3. Translate into English

a. ho tre anni

b. ho cinque anni

c. ho undici anni

d. ha quindici anni

e. ha tredici anni

f. ha sette anni

g. mio fratello

h. mia sorella

i. si chiama

4. Broken words

a. h____ *I have*

b. mi chia____ *my name is*

c. mia sor______ *my sister*

d. quin______ *fifteen*

e. sed______ *sixteen*

f. und_____ *eleven*

g. no______ *nine*

h. quatto________ *fourteen*

i. do________ *twelve*

5. Rank the people below from oldest to youngest as shown in the example

Michele ha quindici anni.	**1**
Giorgia ha tredici anni.	
Luca ha due anni.	
Piero ha quattro anni.	
Alex ha un anno.	
Roberta ha cinque anni.	
Benedetta ha nove anni.	
Dorotea ha tre anni.	

6. For each pair of people write who is the oldest, as shown in the example

A	B	OLDER
Ho undici anni.	Ho tredici anni.	**B**
Ho tre anni.	Ho sei anni.	
Ho undici anni.	Ho dodici anni.	
Ho quindici anni.	Ho tredici anni.	
Ho quattordici anni.	Ho undici anni.	
Ho otto anni.	Ho nove anni.	
Ho undici anni.	Ho sette anni.	

Unit 1. Talking about my age: READING

Ciao, mi chiamo Leo e ho dodici anni. Sto molto bene perché sono felice. Ho un fratello che si chiama Stefano. Stefano ha quattordici anni.

Buongiorno, mi chiamo Dita e ho dieci anni. Ho una sorella che si chiama Flutura e un fratello che si chiama Bledar. Flutura ha cinque anni. Bledar ha nove anni.

Mi chiamo Tian e ho tredici anni. Sto male, perché sono arrabbiato. Ho un fratello che si chiama Cheng. Cheng ha quindici anni.

Salve, mi chiamo Marine. Mi sento bene perché sono tranquilla. Sono francese e ho dieci anni. Ho una sorella che si chiama Fabienne. Fabienne ha undici anni. Ho **anche** *[also]* un fratello che si chiama Pierre. Pierre ha otto anni.

Mi chiamo Kaori e ho sette anni. Ho una sorella che si chiama Yoko. Yoko ha tredici anni. Ho anche un fratello che si chiama Hiroto. Hiroto ha dieci anni.

Ciao, mi chiamo Moritz e ho quattordici anni. Ho due fratelli. Mio fratello maggiore si chiama Patrick e mio fratello minore si chiama Philip. Patrick ha sedici anni e Philip ha quindici anni.

1. Find the Italian for the following items in Leo's text

a. I have a brother

b. my name is…

c. I feel very well

d. I am happy

e. who is called Stefano..

f. I am twelve

g. he is fourteen

2. Answer the following questions about Dita

a. What is the name of Dita's sister?

b. How old is Dita?

c. How many siblings does she have?

d. What's her brother called?

e. How old is he?

3. Complete the table below

	Age	How many siblings	Ages of siblings
Tian			
Leo			
Dita			

4. Moritz, Kaori or Marine?

a. Who has a 15- year-old brother?

b. Who has an 11-year-old sister?

c. Who is 11?

d. Who has an older brother aged 16?

e. Who is calm?

Unit 1. Talking about my age: TRANSLATION

1. Faulty translation: spot and correct (in the English) any translation mistakes you find below

a. mi chiamo Patrizia: *her name is Patrizia*

b. ho due sorelle: *I have two brothers*

c. mia sorella si chiama Marta: *my mother is called Marta*

d. mio fratello ha cinque anni: *my sister is 5*

e. ho quindici anni: *I am five*

f. mio fratello ha otto anni: *my brother is seven*

g. non ho fratelli: *I don't have a sister*

h. ho diciotto anni: *I am 17*

i. ho dodici anni: *I am 13*

j. mi chiamo Gianni: *my name is Gianni*

2. From Italian to English

a. mio fratello si chiama Dario

b. ho quindici anni

c. mio fratello ha sei anni

d. mia sorella si chiama Marina

e. ho sette anni

f. sto bene

g. mia sorella ha quattordici anni

h. ho un fratello e una sorella

i. Marta ha dodici anni

j. Annamaria ha nove anni

3. English to Italian translation

a. Hello, my name is Guido. I am six.

b. My brother is fifteen years old.

c. I am twelve. I am happy.

d. My sister is called Emanuela.

e. My name is Gianfranco. I am happy.

f. I have a brother and a sister.

g. My name is Filippo and I am fourteen.

h. My name is Gianfranco and I am eleven.

i. My name is Rossana. I am ten. I have a brother and a sister.

j. My sister is called Alberta. She is twelve.

k. I do not have a brother. I am sad.

Unit 1. Talking about my age: WRITING

1. Complete the words

a. M__ ch________ Roberto.

b. Ho quattor______ a______.

c. H__ un f__________o.

d. M___ f__________o si chi________ Giulio.

e. Mi ________mo Patrizio.

f. Mio ______tello s__ ______ma Marco.

g. ___o tr______ci anni.

h. Mia so__________a si ch________ Katia.

2. Write out the number in Italian

Nine = n__________________

Seven = s________________

Twelve = d________________

Five = c__________________

Fourteen = q______________

Sixteen = s______________

Thirteen = t______________

Four = q__________________

3. Spot and correct the mistakes

a. Mi ciamo Paolo.

b. Ho tredici anno.

c. Mio fratelo ha cinqe anni.

d. Mio fratello se chiama Gianmaria.

e. Me chiamo Patrizio.

f. Mi sorela si chiama Alessandra.

4. Complete with a suitable word

a. Mia sorella si ___________ Laura.

b. _____ fratello ha quindici anni.

c. Mi _________ Mario.

d. Ho un ____________ che si chiama Filippo.

e. Ho una ____________ che si chiama Annamaria.

f. Mio fratello ______ quattordici anni.

5. Guided writing – write 4 short paragraphs in the first person singular ['I'] each describing the people below

	Age	Feeling	Reason	Brother's name and age	Sister's name and age
Johann	12	well	happy	Franz 9	Martha 8
Flutura	15	very well	excited	Bledar 13	Luljeta 5
Michael	11	bad	sad	Thomas 7	Gerda 12
Kyoko	10	very bad	angry	Ken 6	Rena 1

6. Describe this person in the third person:

Name: Giovanni

Age: 12

Brother: Marco, 13 years old

Sister: Serena, 15 years old

Gianni: Ciao, come ti chiami?

Maria: Ciao, mi chiamo Maria e tu?

Gianni: Piacere, Maria. Mi chiamo Gianni, come stai oggi?

Maria: Sto bene, grazie. Sono molto felice. E tu Gianni? Come stai oggi?

Gianni: Anch' io sto abbastanza bene, ma un po' stanco, grazie. Di dove sei Maria?

Maria: Sono di Bologna, in Italia. E tu, Gianni?

Gianni: Sono di Bellinzona, in Svizzera.

Maria: Oh! Che bello! (Oh! How nice!). Quante persone ci sono nella tua famiglia?

Gianni: Ho una famiglia piccola. Ho una sorella e un fratello. E tu, Maria?

Maria: Ho una famiglia grande. Ho due fratelli ed una sorella. Quanti anni hanno i tuoi fratelli?

Gianni: Mia sorella minore ha cinque anni e si chiama Anna. Mio fratello maggiore si chiama Franco ed ha quindici anni. E i tuoi fratelli come si chiamano?

Maria: Mio fratello maggiore si chiama Filippo ed ha diciassette anni, mia sorella si chiama Carlotta ed ha dodici anni e mio fratello minore si chiama Tommaso ed ha otto anni.

Gianni: Ma dai! Che bello! Piacere, Maria.

Maria: Piacere mio Gianni. Arrivederci!

---

1. Gianni or Maria?

a. Is from Switzerland.

b. Is from Italy.

c. Is feeling well and. happy

d. Is feeling quite well but a bit tired.

e. Has a small family.

f. Has a big family.

g. Has three siblings.

h. Their siblings' ages add up to 20 years.

2. Complete with a suitable word

a. Ciao, come ti _______________?

b. Di dove _______________?

c. Come _______________ oggi?

d. Ho una famiglia _______________.

e. Ho un _______________.

f. Come si _______________ tuo fratello?

g. Quanti _______________ ha tua sorella?

h. Mio _______________ minore si chiama Gianni.

i. Mio fratello maggiore _______ chiama Carlo.

j. Mia sorella _______________ otto anni.

k. _______________, Gianni.

l. Piacere _______________.

3. Translate

a. What is your name?

b. Where are you from?

c. How are you today?

d. I have a big family.

e. I have a sister.

f. What is your brother called?

g. How old is your brother?

h. My sister is ten years old.

i. Nice to meet you.

j. Nice to meet you too.

UNIT 2
Saying when my birthday is

In this unit you will learn to say:

- When your birthday is
- Numbers from 15 to 31
- Months
- I am / He is / She is
- Names of Italian speaking locations
- Where you and another person (e.g. a friend) are from

UNIT 2
Saying when my birthday is

| Come ti chiami? | | | | What is your name? |
| Quand'è il tuo compleanno? | | | | When is your birthday? |

Mi chiamo Leonardo *My name is Leonardo*	**sono di Milano** *I am from Milan* *** ho x anni** *I am x years old*	**e** *and* **il mio compleanno è il/*l** *my birthday is the*	1 - uno/primo 2 - due 3 - tre 4 - quattro 5 - cinque 6 - sei 7 - sette 8 - otto 9 - nove 10 - dieci 11 - undici 12 - dodici 13 - tredici 14 - quattordici 15 - quindici	**gennaio** *January* **febbraio** *February* **marzo** *March* **aprile** *April* **maggio** *May* **giugno** *June*
La mia amica si chiama Caterina *My friend is called Caterina* **Il mio amico si chiama Francesco** *My friend is called Francesco*	**è di Bergamo** *he/she is from Bergamo* ***ha X anni** *he/she is X years old*	**e** *and* **e** **il suo compleanno è il/*l'** *his/her birthday is the*	16 - sedici 17 - diciassette 18 - diciotto 19 - diciannove 20 - venti 21 - ventuno 22 - ventidue 23 - ventitré 24 - ventiquattro 25 - venticinque 26 - ventisei 27 – ventisette 28 - ventotto 29 - ventinove 30 - trenta 31 - trentuno	**luglio** *July* **agosto** *August* **settembre** *September* **ottobre** *October* **novembre** *November* **dicembre** *December*

Author's notes: *(1) Don't forget! "Ho/Ha" actually means "I have" and "he/she has" in Italian. You use this verb for telling age. You will see it many times throughout this booklet!* ☺
(2) In Italian, numbers like "uno","otto" and "undici" use the article "lo" with an apostrophe to form "l'uno" "l'otto" and "l'undici."

1. Fill in the blanks

a. Mi _ _ _ _ _ _ _ Rocco e il mio compleanno è _ _ quindici _ _ _ _ _ _ _.

b. _ _ chiamo Tommaso e il _ _ _ _ compleanno è il _ _ _ _ _ _ _ _ _ _.

c. Mi chiamo _ _ _ _ _ e il mio compleanno è il _ _ _ _ _ _ _ _ _ _ _ _ _.

d. _ _ chiamo Alex e il mio _ _ _ _ _ _ _ _ _ _ è il _ _ _ _ _ _ _ _ _ _ _ _ _.

e. _ _ chiamo Paola e il mio compleanno _ il _ _ _ _ _ _ _ _ _ _ _ _ _ _ _ _.

2. Break the flow: draw lines between each word

a. Ilmiocompleannoèiltrediciottobre.

b. Ilmiocompleannoèilnovemaggio.

c. Quand'èiltuocompleanno?

d. Ilmiocompleannoèl'unoagosto.

e. Ilmiocompleannoèilsedicimaggio.

f. Quand'èilsuocompleanno?

g. Miofratellohaquattordicianni.

h. Ilsuocompleannoèilduegennaio.

3. Listen and spot the differences

a. Ti chiami Giorgio.

b. Non ho fratelli.

c. Sono figlia unica.

d. Sono di Pisa.

e. ...ma vivo in Italia.

f. Ho cinque anni.

g. Il mio compleanno è il quattordici giugno.

h. La mia ragazza Luisa ha tredici anni.

i. Il suo compleanno è il diciotto ottobre.

4. Listen, spot and correct the errors

a. Il mio compleanno il venti giugno.

b. La mia amica si chiama Patrizia. Ha dieci anni e il suo compleanno è il quindici maggio.

c. Il compleanno della mia amica è in il nove aprile.

d. Mia madre ho trentotto anni e il suo compleanno è il trenta noviembre.

e. Il mio amico si chiamo Roberto. Il suo compleanno è il quattordici octobre.

5. Listen and choose the option that you hear

a. **Andrea:** Età: 12 / 13 / 14 anni
Compleanno: 2 / 3 / 4 giugno

b. **Franco:** Età: 12 / 13 / 15 anni
Compleanno: 17 giugno/luglio/gennaio

c. **Nina:** Età: 8 / 9 / 10 anni
Compleanno: 10/11/12 novembre

d. **Dylan:** Età: 8 / 7 / 19 anni
Compleanno: 10/7/12 giugno

e. **Michele:** Età: 6 / 16 / 60 anni
Compleanno: 20/21/10 settembre

f. **Marta:** Età: 13 /14 / 4 anni
Compleanno: 14 / 4 / 12 dicembre

6. Narrow listening: gap-fill

a. Ciao, mi chiamo Silvia e __________ di Torino, Italia. Ho _________ anni. Il mio compleanno è il _________ maggio. Ho due fratelli, Filippo e Gianluca.

b. Filippo _________ quattordici anni e il suo compleanno è il ventuno marzo. Mio fratello Gianluca ha sedici anni e il _________ compleanno è il _________ giugno.

c. In _________ abbiamo anche un criceto. Si _________ Giorgio e ha due anni. La mia migliore _________ si chiama Chiara. Ha __________ anni. Il suo compleanno è il _________ gennaio.

7. Narrow listening: gapped translation

a. __ _______ is Ariella. I am _______ years old. I am from _________, in ________. My birthday is on the 16th of _______.

b. I have a _______ called _________. He is _____ years old. _____ birthday is on the _____ __ December.

c. My best friend is called ______. She is ______ years old and her birthday is on the ______ of _______.

d. My ______ is called Anita. She is ______ years old and her birthday is on the ______ of ______.

e. At home we have a pet. It is a ______. ______ _______ ___ Mac and it is ______ years old.

8. Listening slalom: follow the speaker from top to bottom and number the boxes accordingly

a. Giovanni	b. Leo	c. Alessandro	d. Gabriella	e. Carlo
My name is Giovanni	My brother is called Leo	My name is Alessandro	My name is Gabriella	My name is Carlo
I am from Vicenza	**I am from Brindisi**	I am from Bologna	He is from Savona	I am from Genova
He is 14	I am 21	**I am 13**	I am 9	I am 16
His birthday is on the 15th of March	**My birthday is on the 16th of July**	My birthday is on the 21st of May	My birthday is on the 23rd of June	My birthday is on the 30th of August
I have a friend	I have a hamster	I have a boyfriend	He has a girlfriend	**I have a sister**
His birthday is on the 12th	Her birthday is on the 7th of	**Her birthday is on the 1st**	His birthday is on the 2nd	Her birthday is on the 30th
of January.	of March.	of October.	of June.	of September.

9. Faulty translation: spot the translation errors and correct them

My name is Marco, I am italian. I am 13 years old. My parents are called Alessio and Marina. They are 38 years old. My mother's birthday is on 21st of March. My father's birthday is on 4th of August. I have two sisters, Raffaele and Ares. Raffaele is 10 years old and Ares is 12. Raffaele's birthday is on 11th of July. Ares' birthday in on 31st of April. At home we have a pet, a snake. Its name is Pablo and it is one year old. I have a girlfriend. Her name is Petra. She is 14. Her birthday is on 16th of September.

Unit 2. Saying when my birthday is: VOCABULARY BUILDING

1. Complete with the missing word

a. Mi __________ Gabriella.   *My name is Gabriella.*

b. La mia _______ si chiama Eva.   *My friend is called Eva.*

c. Il ____ amico si chiama Luca.   *My friend is called Luca.*

d. Il mio __________________ è il.   *My birthday is on the.*

e. Il __________ maggio.   *The 5th of May.*

f. L' __________ novembre.   *The 8th of November.*

g. Il quattro ____________.   *The 4th of July.*

h. Il _____ compleanno è il...   *His/her birthday is on...*

2. Match up

1. aprile	a. May
2. novembre	b. my birthday
3. dicembre	c. my friend (f)
4. maggio	d. April
5. gennaio	e. November
6. febbraio	f. s/he is called
7. il mio compleanno	g. December
8. il mio amico	h. I am called
9. la mia amica	i. February
10. mi chiamo	j. January
11. si chiama	k. my friend(m)

3. Translate into English

a. il quattordici gennaio =

b. l'otto maggio =

c. il sette febbraio =

d. il venti marzo =

e. il diciannove agosto =

f. il venticinque luglio =

g. il ventiquattro settembre =

h. il quindici aprile =

4. Add the missing letter

a. com__leanno   c. ma__zo   e. a__rile   g. ge__naio   i. lu__lio   k. d__cembre

b. feb__raio   d. mag__io   f. giug__o   h. ag__sto   j. novem__re   l. se__tembre

5. Broken words

a. i__ t______ g____________   *the 3rd of January*

b. i__ c________ l__________   *the 5th of July*

c. i__ n________ a__________   *the 9th of August*

d. i__ d________ m________   *the 12th of March*

e. i__ s__________ a________   *the 16th of April*

f. i__ d__________ d__________.   *the 19th of December*

g. i__ v________ o__________.   *the 20th of October*

h. i__ v____________ m______.   *the 27th of May*

i. i__ t________ s__________   *the 30th of September*

6. Complete with a suitable word

a. Mi ______________ Simona.

b. Il mio ____________ è il due marzo.

c. Ho nove ________.

d. Il mio __________ si chiama Gianni.

e. Gianni __________ dieci anni.

f. Il suo ____________ è il tre giugno.

g. Il mio____________ è il primo aprile.

h. La mia amica ____ chiama Claire.

i. Il ___ compleanno è il sei maggio.

j. Oggi è l'otto ________________.

k. ______ chiamo Leonardo Rossi.

Unit 2. Saying when my birthday is: READING

Mi chiamo Alberto. Ho dodici anni e il mio compleanno è il quindici settembre. La mia amica si chiama Gabriella e ha quattordici anni. Il suo compleanno è il ventotto maggio. Nel mio tempo libero suono sempre la chitarra con Gabriella! Il mio amico si chiama Carlo. Lui ha quindici anni ed è studente. Il suo compleanno è il ventuno giugno. Carlo ha un fratello maggiore. Il suo compleanno è l'otto gennaio.

Mi chiamo Mohamed. Ho ventidue anni e il mio compleanno è il dieci settembre. La mia amica si chiama Fatima e ha vent'anni. Il suo compleanno è il ventotto maggio. Nel mio tempo libero guardo sempre la televisione.

Mi chiamo Martina. Ho sette anni e il mio compleanno è il cinque dicembre. Ho due fratelli, Giulio ed Enrico. Giulio ha undici anni ed è molto bravo. Il suo compleanno è il trenta settembre. Enrico invece è cattivo. Ha tredici anni e il suo compleanno è il sette agosto.

Mi chiamo Gianluca. Ho otto anni e il mio compleanno è il nove agosto. Mia sorella minore ha quattro anni. È molto simpatica. Il suo compleanno è il nove agosto. Lo stesso giorno! Il mio amico si chiama Renzo e ha dieci anni. Il suo compleanno è il venticinque ottobre.

1. Find the Italian for the following items in Alberto's text

a. I am called:

b. I am 12 years old:

c. the eight of January:

d. my birthday is:

e. the 15th of:

f. her birthday is on:

g. in my free time:

h. my friend (m):

i. is called:

j. he is 15:

k. the 21st of June:

l. has an older brother:

3. Answer the following questions about Martina's text

a. How old is she?

____

b. When is her birthday?

____

c. How many brothers does she have?

____

d. Which brother is good?

____

e. How old is Enrico?

____

f. When is his birthday?

____

2. Complete with the missing words

Mi chiamo Anna. _____ tredici _____. _____ un gatto in casa. Il mio _____________ è il ventinove dicembre. Mio fratello _______ nove _______ e il suo compleanno è ___ dieci aprile.

4. Find Someone Who:

a. Has a birthday in December.

____

b. Is 22 years old.

____

c. Shares a birthday with a sibling.

____

d. Likes to play the guitar with his friend.

____

e. Has a friend who is 15 years old.

____

f. Has a birthday in September.

____

g. Has a little sister.

____

h. Has one good and one bad sibling.

____

Unit 2. Saying when my birthday is: WRITING

1. Complete with the missing letters

a. Mi chia_ _ Giorgio.

b. So_ _ d_ Torino.

c. I_ m_ _ complean_ _ è il die_ _ giu_ _o.

d. H_ quatt_ _ _ ici an _ _.

e. La mi_ ami_a si c_iam_ Carla.

f. Il mi_ amico _i chiama Gianfranco.

g. Il mi_ am_co s_ c_iama Michele.

h. Michele h_ und_ _ _ a _ _ i.

2. Spot and correct the mistakes

a. Il mia cumpleanno è il quattro gennaio.

b. Mi ciamo Giovanni.

c. Mi chiama Simona.

d. La mia amiga si chiamo Caterina.

e. Caterina ho undici anno.

f. Io ho cuattordici anni.

g. Il mio compleano e il primo de marzo.

h. Ho cuindici anni.

3. Answer the questions in Italian

a. *__Come__ ti chiami? Mi chiamo _______________________.

b.*__Quanti__ anni hai? Ho _______________ anni.

c. *__Quando__ è il tuo compleanno? Il mio compleanno è il

_____________ _______________________ .

d. __Quanti__ anni ha tuo fratello/sorella? Mio fratello ha ____anni.

*Author's note: * __Come__ means "what/how", *__Quanti__ means "how many", *__Quando__ means "when" ☺*

4. Write out the dates below in words as shown in the example

a. 15/05 = il quindici maggio

b. 10/06 =

c. 20/03 =

d. 19/02 =

e. 25/12 =

f. 01/01 =

g. 22/11 =

h. 14/10 =

5. Guided writing – write 4 short paragraphs in the 1st person singular ['I'] describing the people below

Name	Age	Birthday	Name of brother	Brother's birthday
Samuel	11	25/12	Nico	19/02
Francesca	14	21/07	Marco	21/04
Li	12	01/01	Wen	20/06
Andrea	16	02/11	Alfonso	12/10

6. Describe this person in the third person:

Name: Alessio

Age: 12

Birthday: 21/06

Brother: Leo, 16 years old

Birthday: 01/12

Unit 2. Saying when my birthday is: TRANSLATION

1. Faulty translation: spot and correct (in the English) any translation mistakes you find below

a. Il mio compleanno è il ventotto aprile:
My birthday is on the 27th April.

b. Mi chiamo Roberto: *His name is Roberto.*

c. Ho ventitré anni: *I am 22 years old.*

d. Il mio amico si chiama Paul:
I am called Paul.

e. Lui ha ventisei anni: *I have 26 years old.*

f. Il mio compleanno è il quattro luglio:
His birthday is on the 14th of July.

2. From Italian to English

a. l'otto ottobre.

b. il mio compleanno è…

c. il mio amico si chiama …

d. il suo compleanno è …

e. l'undici gennaio.

f. il quattordici febbraio.

g. il venticinque dicembre.

h. il sette luglio.

i. il primo giugno.

3. Phrase-level translation

a. my name is…

b. I am ten years old.

c. my birthday is the…

d. the 1st of May.

e. my friend is called Bella.

f. she is twelve years old.

g. her birthday is the…

h. the 23rd of August.

i. the 29th April.

Author's note: go back to e.
Did you make Bella a girl? "amica" Well done if
you did! ☺

4. Sentence-level translation

a. My name is Luigi. I am 30 years old. My birthday is on the 11th March.

b. My brother is called Piero. He is 14 years old. His birthday is on the 18th August.

c. My friend is called Simone. He is 22 years old and his birthday is on the 14th January.

d. My friend is called Angela. She is 18 years old and her birthday is on the 25th July.

e. My friend is called William. He is 20 years old. His birthday is on the 24th September.

TERM 1 - BRINGING IT ALL TOGETHER - 2

Pietro: Ciao! Come ti chiami?

Anna: Ciao, mi chiamo Anna e tu come ti chiami?

Pietro: Piacere Anna. Mi chiamo Pietro, di dove sei *(where are you from)*, Anna?

Anna: Sono di Lugano e tu?

Pietro: Io sono di Bologna. Come stai Anna?

Anna: Sto bene, grazie, però sono un po' stanca. E tu Pietro?

Pietro: Anche io sto bene, grazie, sei molto gentile. Sono molto felice. Quanti anni hai Anna?

Anna: Ho quattordici anni, e tu Pietro?

Pietro: Ho tredici anni. A proposito *(by the way)*, hai fratelli o sorelle, Anna?

Anna: Si, ho un fratello maggiore e una sorella minore. Mio fratello si chiama Luigi e mia sorella si chiama Marta. E tu Pietro?

Pietro: Anche io ho un fratello maggiore e una sorella minore. Si chiamano Tommaso e Paola.

Anna: Che bello! Quando è il tuo compleanno, Pietro?

Pietro: Il mio compleanno è il diciotto luglio, e il tuo?

Anna: Anche il mio compleanno è il diciotto luglio, che coincidenza!

Pietro: Si, è incredibile. Quando è il compleanno di tuo fratello Luigi?

Anna: Il compleanno di Luigi è il tredici gennaio. E il compleanno di tua sorella Paola?

Pietro: Il compleanno di Paola è il ventiquattro marzo.

Anna: Va bene, ora devo andare *(I've got to go)*, ciao Pietro.

Pietro: Ciao Anna!

1. Complete with the missing details

a. Anna is from __________, whilst Pietro is from ___________.

b. Anna is feeling a bit ________.

c. Anna is ________ years old, whilst Pietro is ___________.

d. Anna has an older ________ and a younger _________.

e. Anna's birthday is on _____________.

f. Pietro's birthday is on ____________.

g. Luigi is Anna's _____________.

h. Paola's birthday is on ____________.

i. ________ birthday is on 13th January.

2. Find someone...

a. Whose birthday is on 13th January.

b. Who has a sister called Marta.

c. Who has a brother called Luigi

d. Who is feeling a bit tired.

e. Who is from Bologna.

f. Who has a younger sister.

g. Whose birthday is on 24th March.

h. Who is from Lugano.

i. Whose birthday is on 18th July.

j. Who has a sister called Paola.

k. Who is thirteen.

3. Find the Italian equivalent in the text and write it in the spaces provided

a. my name is:

b. I am from:

c. I am thirteen:

d. when is your birthday?

e. I've got to go

f. Luigi's birthday

g. on 24th March:

h. your brother Luigi:

i. by the way:

j. my birthday is:

k. thanks for asking:

l. they are called:

Roberto: Ciao! Come ti chiami?

Ines: Ciao, mi chiamo Ines. E tu? Come ti chiami?

Roberto: Molto piacere, Ines. Mi chiamo Roberto. Di dove sei Ines?

Ines: Sono polacca *(Polish)*. E tu Roberto?

Roberto: Io sono di Ancona. Come stai, Ines?

Ines: Sto molto bene grazie, però sono un po' stressata. E tu?

Roberto: Sto abbastanza bene, grazie, sei molto carina. Sono molto felice. Quanti anni hai, Ines?

Ines: Ho dodici anni. E tu, Roberto?

Roberto: Anche io ho dodici anni. A proposito, hai fratelli o sorelle, Ines?

Ines: Si, ho due fratelli maggiori. I miei fratelli si chiamano Alberto e Paolo. E tu Roberto?

Roberto: Io ho un fratello maggiore e una sorella minore. Si chiamano Leonardo e Arianna.

Ines: Che bello! Quando è il tuo compleanno?

Roberto: Il mio compleanno è l'undici gennaio. E il tuo?

Ines: Il mio compleanno è l'undici febbraio.

Roberto: Che buffo! *(how funny)* L'undici è il mio numero preferito!

Ines: Anche il mio. Che coincidenza!

Roberto: Va bene, ora devo andare. Ciao, Ines.

Ines: A presto Roberto, ci vediamo.

---

4. Find in the text Italian words that look/sound like the English words below

a. pleasure

b. polish

c. stressed

d. proposed

e. major

f. minor

g. Leonard

h. preferred

i. coincidence

j. number

---

5. Translate into English

a. Di dove sei?

b. Sono di Ancona.

c. Sono un po' stressata.

d. Ho dodici anni.

e. Ho due fratelli maggiori.

f. ...si chiamano Alberto e Paolo.

g. Ho un fratello minore e una sorella minore.

---

6. The sentences below have been copied incorrectly. Can you fix them?

a. Ho dodichi anni.

b. I miei fratelli si chiama…

c. Ho due maggiori Fratelli.

d. Quando è il tuo complianno, Roberto?

e. Il mio compleanno è l'undici de febbraio.

f. Ke buffo!

g. Quanti ani hai?

---

7. Match questions and answers

Come ti chiami?	Si, ho due fratelli.
Di dove sei?	L'undici gennaio.
Come stai?	Sono polacco.
Hai fratelli?	Il numero undici.
Quando è il tuo compleanno?	Sto bene, grazie.
Qual è il tuo numero preferito?	Roberto.

UNIT 3
Saying where I live and am from

**In this unit you will learn
to talk about:**

- Where you live and are from
- If you live in an apartment or a house
- What your accommodation looks like
- Where it is located
- The names of renowned cities and countries in the Italian speaking countries
- The verb 'I am'

You will also revisit:
- Introducing yourself
- Telling age and birthday

UNIT 3

Saying where I live and am from

Come ti chiami?	*What is your name?*
Dove vivi?	*Where do you live?*
Di dove sei?	*Where are you from?*

Mi chiamo Paolo e… *My name is Paolo and…*	**vivo in** *I live in*	**un appartamento** *a flat* **un palazzo/ un edificio** *a building*	**antico** *old* **bello** *pretty* **brutto** *ugly* **confortevole** *comfortable* **grande** *big* **piccolo** *small* **moderno** *modern*		**in campagna** *in the countryside* **in centro** *in the centre* **nel centro della città** *in the city centre*
		una casa *a house* **una villa** *a villa*	**antica** **bella** **brutta** **confortevole** **grande** **piccola** **moderna**		**in montagna** *in the mountains* **in periferia** *on the outskirts* **sulla costa** *on the coast*
	sono di *I am from*	**Bari** **Bologna** **Cagliari** **Firenze** **Genova** **Lugano** **Milano** **Palermo** **Roma** **Torino**	**una città** *a city*	**in Emilia-Romagna** **nel Lazio** **in Liguria** **in Lombardia** **in Piemonte** **in Puglia** **in Sardegna** **in Sicilia** **in Svizzera** **in Toscana**	**nel centro (dell') Italia** *in the centre of Italy* **nel nord (dell') Italia** *in the north of Italy* **nel sud (dell') Italia** *in the south of Italy*

Author's note: *Italy surrounds two independent states: the Republic of San Marino and the Vatican City. In both states the official language is Italian. Italian is also an official language in Switzerland where it is spoken in the Cantons of Ticino and Grigioni.*

---

1. Fill in the blanks

a. Ciao. Mi _______ Davide. Vivo in una _______molto grande nel centro della _______.

b. Buongiorno. Mi chiamo Rossella. ____ di Matera. _____ in un appartamente piccolo in _______.

c. Come stai? ____ chiamo Maia. Sono ____Catania. Vivo in un ___________ carino sulla costa.

d. Ciao. Mi chiamo _______. Sono di Locarno, in _______. Vivo in una casa molto _______ in montagna.

e. Buon_____. Mi chiamo Daniele, vivo a Palermo in _______. Vivo in un edificio _______ nel centro della_________.

f. _______. Mi chiamo Beatrice. Vivo in ____casa grande però un po' ____ a Serravalle, San Marino.

---

2. Multiple choice quiz: select the correct location

	1	2	3
a. Giovanni	Bologna	Venezia	Genova
b. Samuele	Cagliari	Milano	Lugano
c. Giancarlo	Bellinzona	Locarno	Serravalle
d. Luca	Sassari	Roma	Bergamo
e. Serena	Modena	Bari	Napoli
f. Arianna	Torino	Verona	Parma
g. Patrizio	Potenza	Taranto	Reggio Calabria
h. Manuele	Perugia	Firenze	Savona

3. Spot the intruders: identify the words the speaker is NOT saying

Ciao. Mi chiamo Giacomo. Ho un quattordici anni e vivo già a Roma, il la capitale italiana. Nella mia famiglia siamo ci sono quattro persone: i miei genitori, mia sorella, mio fratello ed io. Mio fratello che si chiama Enzo. Vivo in una la casa piccola nel centro di Roma. La mia casa è molto carina.

---

4. Geographical mistakes: listen and correct

a. Mi chiamo Nino. Sono di Bologna. Bologna è in Umbria.

b. Mi chiamo Pietro. Sono di Savona. Savona è in Sicilia.

c. Mi chiamo Laura. Sono di Roma. Roma è nel Molise.

d. Mi chiamo Gianni. Sono di Lugano. Lugano è in Italia.

e. Mi chiamo Lorenzo. Sono di Napoli. Napoli è in Piemonte.

f. Mi chiamo Arianna. Sono di Bari. Bari è in Calabria.

5. Spelling challenge: which place names are being spelled out? Fill in the grid

a.	
b.	
c.	
d.	
e.	
f.	

6. Faulty translation: spot the translation errors and correct them

a. My name is Maia. I am Swiss. I am twelve.

b. I live in Bergamo, a region in the south of Italy.

c. I have blond hair and brown eyes. My hair is long and curly.

d. I live with my mother, Eugenia and my two brothers, Silvia and Paola.

e. ... in a small flat in the centre of Bergamo.

f. My flat is in an old building. It is beautiful.

g. My father lives in a small house in the mountains. His house is ugly and modern.

7. Spot the missing words and write them in

a. Vivo Bellinzona, la capitale Ticino. Bellinzona è una città bella. Vivo in un appartamento in un edificio moderno nel centro città.

b. Vivo con la mia famiglia a Milano, una città grande nord Italia. Vivo in casa moderna nella periferia città.

c. Vivo a Lugano, una città Svizzera. Vivo lì con la mia famiglia e il cane. Vivo in un appartamento grande brutto in un edificio.

d. Vivo a Venezia, Italia. Vivo in una casa grande e moderna costa.

8. Narrow listening: gapped translation

My name is Giulio. I am _________ years old and my birthday is on ________ August. I _________ in Bologna, in Emilia Romagna, in the _________ of Italy. I live in an _________ house on the _________. I have two _________, Marcella and Silvia. Marcella is very _________ but a bit silly. Silvia is a bit _________ but very _________ and funny. My friend Riccardo _________ in Bari but he is from Bologna like _________. He lives in a modern _________ in the _________. He has a big dog called _______. He lives in a big and _________ flat.

9. Listening slalom: follow the speaker from top to bottom and number the boxes accordingly

e.g.	a	b	c	d
I live	I am Swiss and	I live in Piemonte	I am Italian and	I live in Campania
I live in Rimini.	Near Torino.	I live near Lugano	near Napoli.	**in Abruzzo.**
I am 12 and	**I am 15 and**	I am 14 and	I am 16 and	I am 13 and
I live in a big house	I live in a small house	I live in a very small house	**I live in a small flat**	I live in a flat
in a modern building.	in an old building.	in the city centre.	near a lake.	on the coast.
I like my house	**My flat is ugly**	My house	My flat is cosy	My house is pretty
and pretty.	and spacious.	**but very big.**	is modern.	because it is big.

Unit 3. Saying where I live and am from: VOCABULARY BUILDING

1. Complete with the missing word

a. Vivo in __________ casa bella. *I live in a pretty house.*

b. Mi piace il mio ________________. *I like my flat.*

c. Sono ____ Firenze. *I am from Florence.*

d. ________ in una villa. *I live in a villa.*

e. Un appartamento in un ______________ moderno.
A flat in a modern building.

f. Sono di Roma, la____________ dell'Italia.
I'm from Rome, the capital of Italy.

g. Vivo in una casa molto ________________ in campagna.
I live in a very old house in the countryside.

h. Vivo in ____________________. *I live on the outskirts.*

2. Match up

1. il centro	*a. big*
2. bello	*b. small*
3. grande	*c. old*
4. palazzo	*d. pretty*
5. antico	*e. the centre*
6. la periferia	*f. the coast*
7. la costa	*g. i am from*
8. Italia	*h. the outskirts*
9. sono di	*i. ugly*
10. brutto	*j. i live in*
11. piccolo	*k. comfortable*
12. vivo in	*l. building*
13. confortevole	*m. Italy*

3. Translate into English

a. sono di Venezia =

b. vivo in una casa =

c. il mio appartamento è piccolo =

d. sono di Siena, in Toscana =

e. ...in un palazzo moderno =

f. sono di Cosenza, nel sud dell'Italia =

g. vivo in una villa a Positano sulla costa =

h. sono di Torino, nel nord dell'Italia =

4. Add the missing letter

a. Rom_ c. Mil_no e. Ital_a g. Ven_zia i. F_renze

b. Bar_ d. Sviz_era f. Cos_nza h. To_ino j. Tosc_na

5. Broken words

a. S____ d___ L__________, i___ S ____________.
I am from Lugano, in Switzerland.

b. V___ i___ u____ c______ v_________ .
I live in an old house.

c. S___ d___ R________, l___ c_________ dell' I__________.
I am from Rome, the capital of Italy.

d. V_____ i__ u___ c_____ s____ c_______ d__ Calabria.
I live in a house on the coast of Calabria.

e. V____ i___ u____ v_____ p______ i___ c____________.
I live in a small villa in the countryside.

6. Complete with a suitable word

a. Sono _____ Bologna.

b. Vivo _____ centro.

c. ...in un ______________ antico.

d. Vivo in una casa in ___________.

e. Roma è la capitale dell' _________.

f. Vivo in un appartamento ________.

g. Sono di _________________.

h. ....una __________ sulla costa.

i. Città di San ________, a San Marino.

j. Vivo a Positano sulla __________.

Unit 3. "Geography test": Using your own knowledge (and a bit of help from Google/your teacher) match the numbers to the city or region

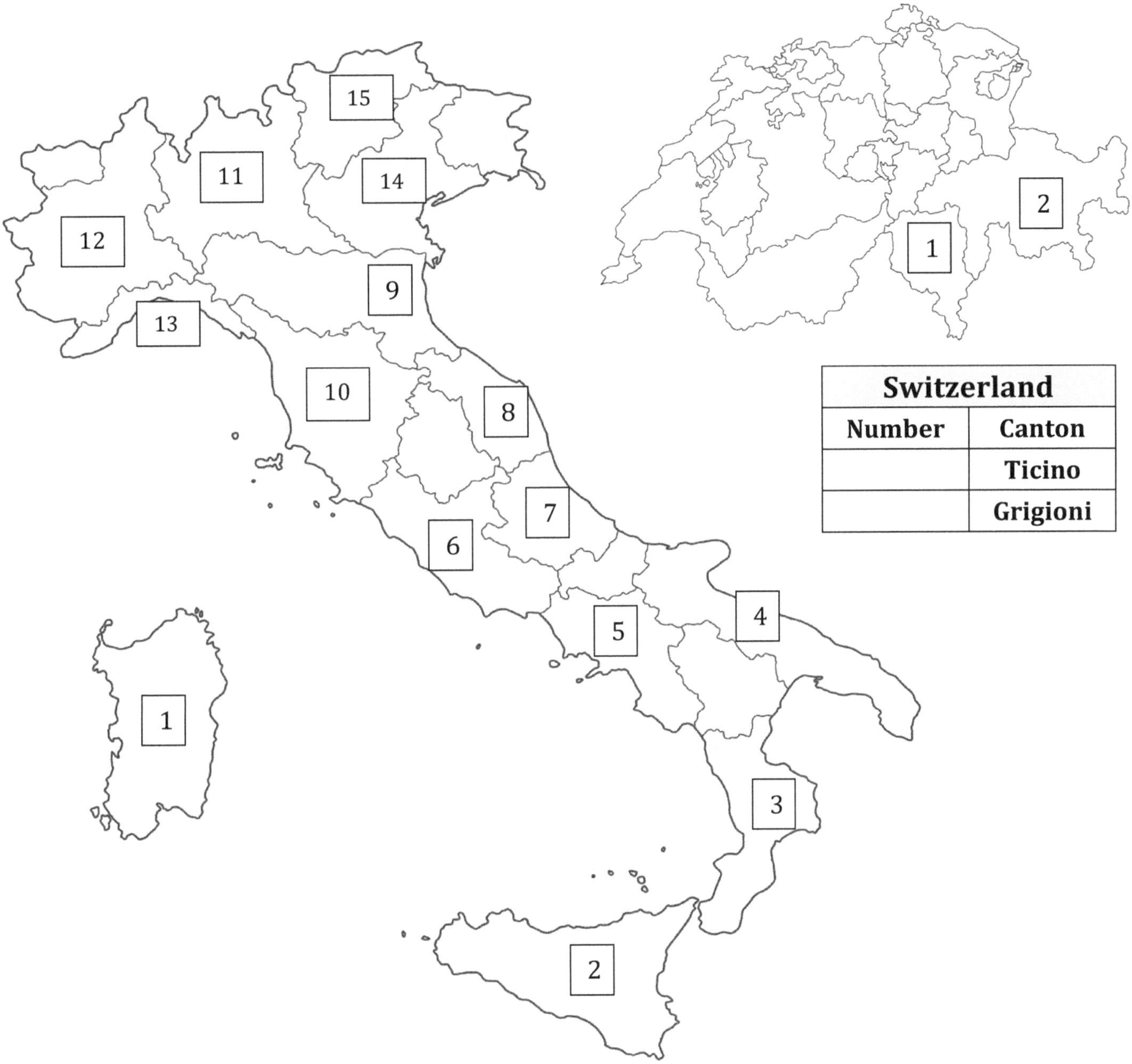

Switzerland	
Number	**Canton**
	Ticino
	Grigioni

Italy					
Number	**City / Region**	**Number**	**City / Region**	**Number**	**City / Region**
	Marche		Roma		Milano
	Bolzano		Sardegna		Napoli
	Calabria		Sicilia		Puglia
	Abruzzo		Torino		Bologna
	Genova		Venezia		Firenze

Mi chiamo Gianluigi. Ho ventidue anni e il mio compleanno è il nove agosto. Vivo a Borgo Maggiore, in San Marino. Vivo in una casa piccola in centro città.

Ho due fratelli, Edoardo e Dario. Mi piace molto Edoardo ma Dario non mi piace perché è stupidino.

Il mio amico Francesco vive a Siena, in Toscana. Lui vive in un appartamento in un palazzo abbastanza antico, in centro.

Mi chiamo Matilda. Ho quindici anni e vivo a Cagliari, in Sardegna. Nella mia famiglia siamo quattro persone: i miei genitori, mio fratello Giorgio ed io. Il mio compleanno è l'undici settembre, anche quello di Giorgio. Siamo gemelli! Mio zio vive a Malta.

Mi chiamo Stefania. Ho nove anni e vivo a Rimini, sulla costa adriatica in Italia. Vivo con la mia famiglia: i miei genitori, mia sorella maggiore Sara ed io. Il mio compleanno è il nove maggio e il compleanno di Sara è il trenta marzo. Lei ha undici anni. La mia casa è piuttosto grande e confortevole e si trova sulla costa. Mi piace troppo!

Mi chiamo Bella. Ho ventun' anni e vivo a Monte Carlo con la mia amica Marina. Abitiamo in un appartamento piccolo e moderno in periferia. Il mio compleanno è il due giugno e il compleanno di Marina è il dodici giugno.

Ho un cane che si chiama Buck. È molto grande e buono. Il suo compleanno è il primo aprile. Buck ha tre anni. Ho **anche** [also] un ragno, buono **ma** [but] brutto, che si chiama Aracno. Anche il compleanno del mio ragno è il primo aprile. **Quindi** [therefore] faccio una festa per i due animali lo stesso giorno. È **più** [more] pratico.

1. Find the Italian for the following in Bella's text

a. my name is

b. am 21 years old

c. I live in…

d. a small flat

e. on the outskirts

f. the 2nd of June

g. I have a dog

h. he is very big

i. his birthday is on the 1st April

j. he is 3 years old

k. I also have a spider

2. Complete the statements below based on Gianluigi's text

a. I am _______ years old.

b. My birthday is on the ______ of _______________ .

c. I live in a _______ house in the __________ of the city.

d. I have two _____________ .

e. I like Edoardo but Dario is ____________ .

f. My friend Francesco _________ in Siena.

g. He lives in a _______ in a quite old _______________ .

3. Answer the questions on the four texts above

a. How old is Matilda?

b. When is Matilda and Giorgio's birthday? What do you think '**gemelli**' means?

c. Who only likes one of his siblings?

d. Who has two pets that share a birthday?

e. Why is it convenient that they share a birthday?

f. Who has a friend that lives in a different city?

g. Who lives with their friend?

h. Who lives in Monte Carlo?

i. Whose birthday is on the 12th of June?

4. Correct any of the statements below [about Stefania's text] which are incorrect

a. Stefania vive a Napoli, nel sud Italia.

b. Nella famiglia di Stefania ci sono [there are] quattro persone.

c. Il suo compleanno è a marzo.

d. Il compleanno di Sara è il tre marzo.

e. Stefania vive in una casa piuttosto grande ma brutta sulla costa.

f. Le piace molto la sua casa.

Unit 3. Saying where I live and am from: TRANSLATION/WRITING

1. Translate into English

a. vivo in

b. una casa

c. un appartamento

d. confortevole

e. molto grande

f. in un palazzo

g. antico

h. moderno

i. in centro

j. in periferia

k. sulla costa

l. sono di

m. in Italia

n. in Svizzera

o. vivo a Glasgow

2. Gapped sentences

a. Vivo a Bari in una _______ antica.   *I live in Bari in an old villa.*

b. Una casa in ___________________.   *A house in the countryside.*

c. Vivo in un _________________ piccolo. *I live in a small flat.*

d. Una _______ in ________________.   *A house on the outskirts.*

e. _________ ____ Roma, la capitale dell' _________, ma vivo a Malta.
I am from Rome, the capital of Italy, but I live in Malta.

3. Complete the sentences with a suitable word

a. Sono _______ Borgo Maggiore, nella Repubblica di San Marino.

b. ________ di Firenze, il capoluogo della Toscana.

c. Sono argentino, vivo a __________ del Vaticano.

d. Vivo in un _________________ grande in ___________________.

e. Vivo a Bologna, in una casa nuova e ___________________ .

f. Vivo in un appartamento_________________ in centro.

g. Vivo a Grisignana, in Croazia, in _______ casa moderna.

4. Phrase-level translation [En to It]

a. I live in _______________________________

b. I am from _______________________________

c. a house _______________________________

d. a flat _______________________________

e. ugly (m) _______________________________

f. small (m) _______________________________

g. in an old building

____

h. in the centre _______________________________

i. on the outskirts _______________________________

j. on the coast _______________________________

k. in Tuscany _______________________________

5. Sentence-level translation [En to It]

a. I am from Pisa, in Tuscany in Italy. I live in a big and pretty house on the outskirts.

____

____

b. I am from Amalfi, in the south of Italy. I live in a small and comfortable apartment near the coast.

____

____

c. I am from Bellinzona, in Switzerland. I live in a big flat in a new building in the centre.

____

____

d. I am from Venice, in the north of Italy. I live in a flat in a building on the outskirts. I like my flat.

____

____

Unit 3. Saying where I live and am from: WRITING

1. Complete with the missing letters

a. Mi chia_ _ Angela.

b. Vi_ _ in una ca_ _ m_d _ rn_.

c. V_v_ in un ap_artam_nto grand_.

d. _ _vo a Pisa, in una _ _sa i_ cent_ _.

e. So_ _ di Mil_ no in Lom_ ard_a.

f. Io _ono d_ Rom_, la cap_tale d'Ital_a.

g. V_ _ o in una v_l_a grand_ in per_ feri_.

h. _ono di Firen_ e in T_ scan_.

2. Spot and correct the mistakes

a. Sono de Cosenza en Calabria.

b. Sono en Bari a Puglia.

c. Vivo in una casa piccolo a Malta.

d. Vivo in una appartamento grando.

e. Vivo a un palazzo nuovo.

f. Vivo en Roma con la mia famiglia.

g. Sono de Siena en Tuscana.

h. Vivo in una vila in campana.

3. Answer the questions in Italian

a. Come ti chiami? M__________________________________.

b. Quanti anni hai? H__________________________________.

c. *Di dove sei? Sono di __________________________________.

d. *Dove vivi? Vivo a __________________________________.

e. Vivi in una casa o in un appartamento? Vivo in ____________.

Author's note:
Di dove sei? = '*Where are you from?*'
Dove vivi ?= '*Where do you live?*'
Vivo <u>a</u> Edimburgo/Roma = *I live <u>in</u> Edinburgh/Rome*

4. Anagrams (regions of Italy and countries)

a. neVeto = *Veneto*

b. scanaTo =

c. gliaPu =

d. laCabria =

e. monPiete =

f. diaLombar =

g. noVacati =

h. razzeSvi =

i. noMariSan =

j. gnadeSar =

5. Guided writing – write 4 short paragraphs in the 1st person singular ['I'] describing the people below

Name	Age	Birthday	City	Country or region
Samuel	12	20/06	Roma	Lazio (Italia)
Alex	14	14/10	Lugano	Svizzera
Andrea	11	14/01	Monte Carlo	Monaco
Charles	13	17/01	Taormina	Sicilia (Italia)
Nina	15	19/10	Amalfi	Campania (Italia)

6. Describe this person in the third person:

Name: Alessio

Age: 16

Birthday: 15th May

Country of origin: Glasgow, Scotland *[Scozia]*

Country of residence: Lucca, Italy *[Italia]*

TERM 1 - BRINGING IT ALL TOGETHER – 3

Mi chiamo Vittorio. Sono svizzero. Ho undici anni e vivo a Bellinzona, la capitale del Canton Ticino. Oggi sto bene. Sono felice e molto tranquillo.

Il mio compleanno è il dodici settembre. Ho una sorella che si chiama Barbara e un fratello che si chiama Leo. Barbara ha cinque anni e Leo ha nove anni. Oggi Barbara non sta molto bene, è un po' triste. Però *(however),* Leo sta benissimo. É molto felice perché è il suo compleanno.

Io e la mia famiglia viviamo in un appartamento grande, carino e moderno nella periferia di Bellinzona. Mi piace il mio appartamento perché è grande e carino.

La mia amica si chiama Sofia e ha dodici anni. Il suo compleanno è il ventotto marzo. Vive in una casa piccola in montagna. La sua casa è molto piccola e brutta però è sempre pulita. Nel suo tempo libero suona il pianoforte.

Il mio migliore amico *(best friend)* si chiama Carlo. Ha dieci anni e anche lui vive a Bellinzona. Il suo compleanno è il sette febbraio. Carlo vive in un appartamento in un edificio moderno. Nel suo tempo libero suona l' ukelele.

1. Find the Italian equivalent in the text

a. I am Swiss

b. today

c. I am happy

d. I have a sister

e. who is called

f. (she) has

g. she is a bit sad

h. his birthday

i. in a big flat

j. on the outskirts

k. big and pretty

l. a small house in the mountains

2. Complete the sentences based on Vittorio's text

a. My name is Vittorio. Today I am feeling ________.

b. I am ________ and calm.

c. My sister is ______ years old.

d. Today Barbara is feeling a bit ______.

e. Today Leo is happy because it is _________.

f. Vittorio lives in a big, ______ and modern flat.

g. Sofía lives in a ______ house on the ________.

h. Carlo lives in a modern _________.

3. Answer the questions below in English

a. Who is feeling happy and calm today?

b. Who is Carlo?

c. Who lives in a small house?

d. Who plays musical instruments? (2)

e. Whose house is always clean?

f. Who lives on the outskirts of Bellinzona?

g. Whose birthday is on 28th March?

4. The second paragraph in Vittorio's text was copied incorrectly with EIGHT words missing. Can you spot them and add them in?

Il mio compleanno è il dodici settembre. Ho una sorella che chiama Barbara e fratello che si chiama Leo. Barbara ha cinque e Leo ha nove anni. Oggi Barbara non molto bene, un po' triste. Però *(however),* Leo benissimo. È felice perché il suo compleanno.

1. Mi chiamo Luca. Sono italiano. Ho nove anni e vivo a Roma, la capitale dell' Italia. Oggi sto molto bene. Sono felice e molto rilassato. Il mio compleanno è il tre agosto.

2. Ho una sorella che si chiama Lucia e un cugino *(cousin)* che si chiama Francesco. Lucia ha otto anni e Francesco ha undici anni. Oggi Lucia non sta molto bene, è molto stressata. Però *(however)*, Francesco sta benissimo. Oggi è molto felice.

3. Io e la mia famiglia viviamo in una casa grande e moderna, però è un po' brutta, ai Parioli, sulle colline *(hills)* di Roma. Mi piace la mia casa perché è vicino alla natura *(near the nature)*.

4. La mia amica si chiama Renata e ha undici anni. Il suo compleanno è il sedici aprile. Anche lei vive in una casa sulle colline. La sua casa è molto piccola, però molto moderna e carina. Normalmente è molto pulita. Nel suo tempo libero suona sempre il violino

5. Il mio migliore amico *(best friend)* si chiama Ivan. Ha otto anni e anche lui vive nel mio paese *(my town)*, vicino a Roma. Il suo compleanno è il ventidue gennaio. Ivan vive in un appartamento in un edificio antico. Nel suo tempo libero gioca sempre a calcio.

5. Spot the 9 mistakes in the following translation of Luca's first 2 paragraphs

My name is Luca. I am Italian. I am eight years old and live in Rome, the capital of Italy. Today I am quite well. I am happy and very excited. My birthday is on 3rd August. I have a sister who is called Lucia and a brother called Francesco. Lucia is nine and Francesco is twelve. Today Lucia is not very well. She is very tired. However, Francesco is OK. Today he is very calm.

6. Complete the following translation of paragraphs 3 and 4 in Luca's text

My family and I live in a _____ and modern, but a bit ugly house, in Parioli, on the _______ of Rome. I _______ my house because it is _____ the nature.

My friend is called Renata and is _______ years old. Her _______ is on _______ April. She _____ lives in a house on the _______. Her house is very _______, but very modern and _______. Normally it is very _______. In her _______ she _______ plays the violin.

7. Tick the words on the list below which are included in the text and translate them into English

a. oggi	h. mai
b. la sua	i. a volte
c. con	j. anche
d. di	k. amo
e. inoltre	l. suona
f. da	m. gioco
g. sempre	n. neanche

8. Answer the following questions in Italian, as if you were Luca. Note: you can use whole sections of the text, provided they are relevant

a. Come ti chiami?

b. Di dove sei?

c. Come stai oggi?

d. Come si chiama tuo cugino?

e. Come sta Lucia oggi?

f. Chi è Ivan?

g. Dove vive Renata?

h. Com'è la sua casa?

i. Quanti anni ha Ivan?

j. Che cosa fa Ivan nel suo tempo libero?

TERM 1 – MIDPOINT – RETRIEVAL PRACTICE

1. Answer the following questions in Italian

Come ti chiami?	
Come stai oggi?	
Quanti anni hai?	
Quando è il tuo compleanno?	
Hai fratelli o sorelle?	
Come si chiama tuo fratello/tua sorella?	
Quanti anni ha?	
Quando è il suo compleanno?	
Di dove sei?	
Dove vivi?	
Com'è la tua casa?	
Dov'è la tua casa?	

2. Write a paragraph in the first person singular (I) providing the following details

a. Your name is Fabio.

b. You are Italian and live in Como in the north of Italy.

c. You are 11 years old and your birthday is on 29th July.

d. You have an older brother called Mauro and a younger brother called Silvio.

e. Your older brother is 16 and your younger brother is 8.

f. Mauro's birthday in on 1st January and Silvio's birthday on 30th June.

g. You live in a house on the outskirts.

h. You like your house because it is always clean and quite spacious.

3. Write a paragraph in the third person singular (he/she) providing the following details about your best friend or a member of your family.

say:

a. their name

b. where they are from and live

c. how old they are and when their birthday is

d. how many siblings they have

e. say how old they are

f. say when their birthdays are

g. where their house/flat is located

h. why they like or dislike their house

UNIT 4
Things I like/dislike: school subjects & teachers

In this unit you will learn
to talk about:

- Which school subjects you study
- Which subjects you like/dislike
- Which subjects a friend likes/dislikes
- Adjectives for describing activities
- Reasons for liking or disliking a class

You will also revisit
- Adjectival agreements:
  masculine/feminine/plural

UNIT 4
Things I like/dislike: school subjects & teachers

Quali materie studi?	*What subjects do you study?*
Quale materia (non) ti piace? Perché?	*Which one do you (not) like? Why?*
Ti piace l'Italiano? Perché?	*Do you like Italian? Why?*

A scuola studio *At school I study*	**tedesco / scienze / storia / etc.**

Mi piace *I like*	**il**	**francese** *French* **tedesco** *German*				**è** *it is*	**complicato** *complicated* **divertente** *fun* **difficile** *difficult* **facile** *easy* **interessante** *interesting* **noioso** *boring* **stancante** *tiring* **utile** *useful*
Non mi piace *I don't like*	**lo**	**spagnolo** *Spanish*					
Al mio amico (gli) piace *My friend likes*	**l'**	**inglese** *English* **irlandese** *Irish* **italiano** *Italian*	**ma** *but*				
Alla mia amica (le) piace *My friend (f) likes*							
Al mio amico non (gli) piace *My friend (m) does not like*	**la**	**chimica** *chemistry* **geografia** *geography* **matematica** *maths* **storia** *history* **religione** *RE*		**perché** **perché** *because*	**non è** *it is not*	**complicata** **divertente** **difficile** **facile** **interessante** **noiosa** **stancante** **utile**
Alla mia amica non (le) piace *My friend (f) does not like*	**l'**	**arte** *Art* **educazione fisica** *PE* **informatica** *ICT*				
Mi piacciono *I like* **Non mi piacciono** *I don't like*	**le**	**lingue** *languages* **scienze** *science*			**sono** *are*	**complicate** **interessanti** **divertenti** **noiose** **difficili** **stancanti** **facili** **utili**

Inoltre,	**mi interessa** *it interests me*	**perché**	**è utile per il futuro** *it is useful for the future* **ho i miei amici nella classe** *I have my friends in class* **imparo molto** *I learn a lot*		
	mi interessano *they interest me*		**il professore è** *the teacher (m) is* **la professoressa è** *the teacher (f) is*	**abbastanza** *quite* **molto** *very* **un po'** *a bit*	**antipatico/a** *mean* **bravo/a** *good* **diligente** *diligent* **paziente** *patient* **simpatico/a** *nice*
	adoro *I adore*				

Author's note:** *If the noun being liked is a singular noun, we use* **piace** *(3rd person singular of* **piacere). If the noun being liked is a plural noun, we use* **piacciono** *(3rd person plural of* **piacere***). This is also valid for the expressions* **mi interessa/mi interessano***.*

e.g. • *Mi* **piace** *l'inglese (singular)* • *Mi* **piacciono** *le lingue (plural)*
      • *Mi* **interessa** *l'inglese (singular)* • *Mi* **interessano** *le lingue (plural)*

1. Underline the word you hear

a. La professoressa di francese è **noiosa/gentile/simpatica.**

b. La geografia è **divertente/interessante/difficile.**

c. Le scienze sono molto **difficili/complicate/utili.**

d. L'educazione fisica è **divertente/stancante/noiosa.**

e. **Mi piace/Mi interessa/Non mi piace** la musica.

f. Il professore di tedesco è **simpatico/antipatico/severo.**

g. La matematica è **interessante/difficile/noiosa.**

h. Il professore è un po' **simpatico/antipatico/severo.**

2. Break the flow

a. Mipiaceiltedescomaèdifficile.

b. Miinteressalospagnolo.

c. Nonmipiacelamatematica.

d. Mipiaceperchéimparomolto.

e. Èutileperilfuturo.

f. Hoimieiamicinellaclasse.

g. Laprofessoressaèmoltobrava.

3. Listening for detail: what subjects does Paola do each day? Tick the correct ones

Lunedì *Monday*	Spanish German	French Art
Martedì *Tuesday*	Maths Art	Science Geography
Mercoledì *Wednesday*	PE Religion	French ICT
Giovedì *Thursday*	Geography Art	History German
Venerdì *Friday*	Physics Spanish	Maths English

4. Complete with the missing words

a. Mi piace ____ spagnolo perché è ______.

b. Al mio amico piacciono ___ scienze.

c. Non mi ________ le lingue.

d. ...perché non ____ molto interessanti.

e. Mi piace ______ ho molti ________ in classe.

f. L' arte è un po' ______.

g. L' ______ è molto ______ per il futuro.

h. Il professore ____ molto ______.

5. Listen and fill in the grid

	Subject	Love/Like/Dislike	Reason
e.g.	*Italian*	*Like*	*Teacher is very good*
a.	**Maths**		
b.			**Learn a lot in class**
c.		**Dislike**	
d.	**Science**		
e.		**Like**	

6. Listen and correct the mistakes

a. La scuola studio storie.

b. Mi piacciono lo spagnolo perché è divertenti.

c. Mi piace perché ho amico in classe.

d. Non mi piacciono le scienze perché sono noioso.

e. Mio amico non piace la químicry.

f. La matematica sono molto utili.

g. Mi piace perché la professore è bravo.

h. Non mi piace perché imparo molto in classe.

7. Spot the difference and correct the text

Mi chiamo Giacomo Luci. Sono di Bari. A scuola studio inglese, spagnolo, tedesco e francese. Mi piace un po' lo spagnolo perché è facile e imparo molto a casa. É molto noioso e utile per il futuro. Inoltre, ho molti cani in classe. Il mio amico studia francese e spagnolo. Al mio amico piace molto il francese perché è abbastanza interessante.

8. Narrow listening - Gapped translation

My name is Roberto. I am _______ years old. I am _______ Bologna, in Emilia Romagna. At _______ I study English, Italian, French and _______. My favourite subject is _______ because the teacher is _______ _______ and because I _______ a lot in _______. My friend doesn't like _______ because he thinks that the _______ is a bit _______ and he doesn't have many _______ in class. However, it is an important subject because it is _______ for the _______. _____ also interests me, but it is quite _______.

9. Listening slalom: follow the speaker from top to bottom and number the boxes accordingly

a.	b.	c.	d.
At school,	I like art	On Mondays	My favourite
subject	I have	I study	because
IT class and	Spanish,	it is interesting	is German
because	and	it interests me	French
and history.	my teacher	I have	because
is very	My favourite	it is useful	many friends
good.	in class.	subject is history.	for the future.

Unit 4. Things I like/dislike: school subjects & teachers: VOCAB BUILDING

1. Match

mi piace	because
le scienze	boring
perché	I like
non mi piace	interesting
noioso	science
il mio amico	fun
divertente	I don't like
facile	my friend
interessante	easy

2. faulty translation: correct the english

a. mi piacciono le scienze — *I like maths*

b. l'inglese è noioso — *English is hard*

c. il francese è divertente — *French is easy*

d. la storia è interessante — *Drama is interesting*

e. al mio amico piace l'arte — *My friend hates art*

f. la matematica è difficile. — *Maths is complicated*

g. l'informatica è noiosa — *ICT is exciting*

h. imparo molto — *I listen a lot*

i. è utile per il futuro — *It is useless for the future*

3. spot the hidden word in each sequence of letters

a. *fun*   noiosofacilemoltopiacedivertentedifficileamicoscienze.

b. *easy*   scienzefacilemoltomatematicadivertentedifficileamico.

c. *boring*   mipiaceascoltoimparonoiosomiinteressainglese.

d. *because*   artecomplicatopiaceamicoperchéimparo.

e. *it is*   amicotedescocomplicatobravoèperchédivertentesono.

f. *science*   mipiaccionomoltolescienzeperché.

g. *friend (fem.)* allamiaamicanonpiaccionolescienze.

4. Translate into English

a. interessante

b. complicato

c. noioso

d. divertente

e. utile

f. bravo

g. facile

5. Complete the table

Italiano	English
noioso	
	useful
	fun
bravo	
	interesting
perché	
	easy
	complicated
ho i miei amici	
è utile	

6. Insert 'piace' or 'piacciono' as appropriate

a. Mi ________ l'arte.

b. Non mi _______ le scienze.

c. Mi _______ le lingue.

d. Mi _______ la chimica.

e. Mi _______ l'inglese.

f. Mi ________ la matemática.

g. Non mi _______ il francese.

h. Mi _______ l'italiano.

i. Non mi ______ la storia.

j. Mi ______ la musica.

k. Mi ________ i professori.

l. Mi ________ l'irlandese.

7. Complete the words

a. p_ _chè.

b. scie_ _ _.

c. le pi_ce l' ar_ _.

d. l' ing_ _s_.

e. non m_ pia_ _.

f. è divert_ _te.

g. la m_sic_.

h. le ling_ _.

i. il fran_ _ _ e

j. la sto_ _ _.

k. l' ital_ _ _ _.

l. br_ _o.

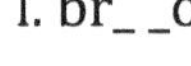

Unit 4. Things I like/dislike: school subjects & teachers: READING

Mi chiamo Enrico. Ho tredici anni. Vivo a Catania. Ho due fratelli e una sorella. Vado al Liceo Classico 'Virgilio', una scuola superiore abbastanza grande nella periferia della città. Mi piace molto la mia scuola perché i professori sono molto diligenti e simpatici. Mi aiutano sempre. Il mio professore preferito è il professore di italiano perché è molto bravo e mi aiuta sempre. Imparo molto nelle sue (his) lezioni e adoro l'italiano. Inoltre, mi piacciono molto le scienze e la matematica perché sono divertenti. Mi piace anche l'educazione física, ma è stancante. Non mi piacciono per niente la storia e la geografia perché sono noiose.

1. Find the Italian for the following in Enrico's text

a. I live: v____

b. school: s______

c. outskirts: p________

d. diligent: d______

e. they help me: m_ a______

f. good (sing.):   b______

g. I learn: i______

h. also: a______

i. tiring: s_______

2. Complete based on Enrique's text

a. He is _________.

b. He has __ siblings.

c. His Italian teacher is _____ and _____.

d. He adores ______.

e. Science is _____.

f. He _____ likes PE.

g. PE is ________.

h. History is _____.

Mi chiamo Ignazio. Ho quindici anni e il mio compleanno è l'otto giugno. Vivo a Cremona. Sono figlio unico. Vado al Liceo Alessandro Volta, una scuola superiore abbastanza grande nella periferia della città, vicino (near) allo stadio. Mi piace la mia scuola perché i professori sono molto bravi, diligenti e non sono severi. La mia materia preferita è l'informatica perché è molto interessante e utile e il professore è molto divertente e paziente. Imparo moltissimo nelle sue lezioni. Mi piacciono anche le lingue straniere, soprattutto (above all) il tedesco, perché i professori sono molto bravi e divertenti. Non mi piace per niente (at all) la matematica perché è complicata, noiosa e stancante.

3. Spot and correct the 11 mistakes in the following translation of Ignazio's text

My name is Ignazio. I am sixteen years old and my birthday is on the 8th June. I live in Cremona. I am unique. I go to the Liceo Alessandro Volta, a quite large secondary school in the centre of the city, near the stadium. I like my school because the teachers are very good, friendly and are not strict. My favourite teacher is ICT because it is very interesting and fascinating and the teacher is very friendly and patient. I listen very much in his lessons. I also like foreign languages, especially French, because the teachers are very interesting and fun. I don't like at all maths because it is complicated, boring and tiring.

4. Find the Italian for the following in Roberta's text

a. only child   e. diligent

b. school   f. I learn

c. port   g. friendly

d. good   h. English

Mi chiamo Roberta. Ho quattordici anni e il mio compleanno è il venti dicembre. Vivo ad Ancona. Sono figlia unica. Vado al Liceo Giacomo Leopardi. È una scuola superiore abbastanza piccola nel centro della città, vicina al porto. Non mi piace la mia scuola perché, anche se i professori sono bravi e diligenti, sono anche severi. La mia materia preferita è la storia perché la trovo (I find it) molto facile e il professore è molto simpatico. Imparo molto nelle sue lezioni. Mi piace anche l'inglese, perché è una lingua molto utile e la professoressa è brava e divertente. Non mi piacciono per niente (at all) le scienze, soprattutto la fisica, perché sono complicate e noiose. Non mi piace nemmeno (neither) la matematica perché il professore è molto severo e non capisco niente in classe.

5. Find someone who

a. ...doesn't like maths.

b. ...likes German.

c. ...has strict teachers.

d. ...likes ICT.

e. ...likes PE.

f. ...doesn't like science.

g. ...finds history easy.

6. Answer these questions about Roberta

a. Where is her school?

b. What are her teachers like?

c. Why does she like history?

d. What does she think about science?

Unit 4. Things I like/dislike: school subjects & teachers: TRANSLATION

1. Translate into English

a. Mi piace l'inglese

b. Il professore è bravo

c. Imparo molto

d. Non mi piace per niente

e. È complicato

f. È noioso

g. Mi piace molto la storia

h. Mi piacciono le scienze

i. Ho i miei amici in classe

j. È stancante

k. Mi piacciono molto le lingue

2. Gapped translation

a. Mi piace _______ l'inglese.　　*I like English a lot*

b. _______ molto　　*I learn a lot*

c. Mi interessano _______　　*I am interested in science*

d. Ho ______ amici in classe　　*I have my friends in class*

e. È ______ per il future.　　*It is useful for the future*

f. Il professore è _______　　*The teacher is good*

3. Tangled translation: into Italian

a. Mi piace l' **English** perché ho i miei **friends** in classe.

b. Non mi piace per **nothing** la **maths because** è **boring**.

c. **I don't like** le **science** perché la professoressa è **mean**.

d. Non mi piace l' **education** fisica **because** è **tiring**.

e. **I adore** l' italiano perché **the** professoressa **is funny** e **good**.

f. **I like** l' informatica **because** è **useful** per il **future**.

g. Non mi piace il **French** perché **it is** complicato.

4. Phrase level translation: English to Italian

a. I like sciences

b. I learn a lot

c. I have my friends

d. It is complicated (f)

e. They are boring (f)

f. They are useful

g. I adore French

h. In class

i. It is tiring

j. I like maths

k. For the future

l. I like history a lot

m. The teacher (m) is good

n. The teacher (f) is mean

5. Sentence level translation: English to Italian

a. I like French because I have my friends in class.

b. I don't like the sciences because the teacher is boring.

c. I adore Spanish because it is useful for the future.

d. I don't like maths because they are complicated.

e. I don't like history because the teacher is mean.

f. I don't like PE because it is tiring.

g. I like ICT because the teacher is good and fun.

Unit 4. Things I like/dislike: school subjects & teachers: WRITING

1. Anagrams

e.g. aL ecaip im grafiageo: Mi piace la geografia

a. eL znieecsi noos esoion.

b. L' glesine è tevniredet.

c. mproai lotom a iozelen.

d. oNn im ecpia al catematima.

e. iM pecia moolt li freasnce.

f. È litue rep li rotufu.

g. aL feproressoass è vraba.

h. oH i eeim imaic ni acless.

2. Broken words

a. Impa_ _ mo_ _ _ a le_ _ _ _ _ .

b. La mia professo_ _ _ _ _ è simp_ _ _ _ _.

c. N_n mi piac_ _ _ _ _ le scien_ _ .

d. _ ut_ _ _ per il fut_ _ _.

e. Il profes_ _ _ _ di art_ è simpa_ _ _ _.

f. H_ _ ami_ _ in classe.

g. il m_ _ professore è divert_ _ _ _.

h. Non m_ piace il fra_ _ _ _ _.

i. La mate_ _ _ _ _ _ è noio_ _.

3. Complete with the missing words

a. No mi _ _ _ _ _ _ _ _ _ le scienze.

b. Mi _ _ _ _ _ molto il francese.

c. Non _ _ piace _ _ matematica.

d. Mi piace _ inglese perché il _ _ _ _ _ _ _ _ _ _ è bravo.

e. Al mio amico _ _ _ _ _ l' arte _ _ _ _ _ _ è divertente.

f. Adoro _ _ spagnolo perché _ appassionante.

g. Mi piace l' informatica perché è _ _ _ _ _ per il futuro.

h. Ho i miei _ _ _ _ _ in classe.

4. Complete with *piace* or *piacciono* as appropriate

a. Non mi __________ la matematica.

b. Mi ________ molto il francese.

c. Al mio amico ________ le scienze.

d. A Marina _________ l' arte.

e. Alla mia amica ________ l' italiano.

f. Non ti ________ le lingue?

g. Mi ________ molto i miei professori.

h. A mio fratello non ________ la musica.

5. Guided writing: write 5 short paragraphs in the 1st person singular (I) describing the people below

Name	Subject they like	Reason	Subject they dislike	Reason
Samuele	French	Fun	Science	Boring
Ale	ICT	Useful	Maths	Teacher is not good
Andrea	English	Interesting	Art	Not fun
Carlo	Science	Interesting	PE	Tiring
Nina	Italian	Fun and interesting	History	Teacher is mean and no friends in class

6. Describe this person in the third person (he):

Name: Manuele

Age: 13

From: Switzerland

Lives in: Italy

Subjects he likes:

-French, because it is fun and useful for the future

- Maths, because it is exciting and the teacher is very good and funny

Subject he dislikes:

Geography because it is boring and the teacher is mean

TERM 1 - BRINGING IT ALL TOGETHER - 4

Mi chiamo Michele e ho dodici anni. Sono di San Marino ma vivo a Bellinzona, la capitale del Ticino. Oggi sto benissimo. Sono molto felice perché sono in vacanza *(on holiday)*. Inoltre, oggi è il mio compleanno!

Ho un fratello maggiore che si chiama Rodolfo. Rodolfo ha quindici anni ed è molto simpatico *(nice)*. Oggi Rodolfo sta così così perché è stanco.

Io e la mia famiglia viviamo in una casa grande nel centro di Bellinzona. Mi piace la mia casa perché è molto grande e ci sono molti negozi *(shops)* vicino. Nel mio tempo libero (in my free time) suono la chitarra (I play the guitar).

La mia migliore amica si chiama Alice e ha dodici anni, come me *(same as me)*. Il suo compleanno è il trenta aprile. Lei vive in un appartamento in un edificio antico nella periferia di Bellinzona. Le piace il suo appartamento perché è carino e ci sono molti ristoranti vicino.

Vado al liceo bilingue Nuovo Mondo, una scuola superiore molto grande vicino al centro della città. Mi piace la mia scuola perché i professori sono molto bravi, diligenti e non sono severi. È una scuola bilingue, quindi *(therefore)* studio alcune materie in inglese e altre in Italiano. Adoro l'inglese.

La mia materia preferita è la storia perché è interessante e il professore è divertente e mi aiuta sempre. Imparo sempre molto nelle sue lezioni. Mi piacciono molto anche le lingue, soprattutto *(above all)* l'inglese, perché le lezioni sono molto divertenti, imparo molto e ho i miei amici in clase.

Però (however), non mi piacciono per niente *(at all)* le scienze perché sono complicate, noiose e stancanti. Inoltre, il professore è un po' noioso e non ho amici in classe.

1. Find the Italian equivalent in the text

a. I am 12

b. today I am feeling great

c. I have an older brother

d. we live

e. I like my house

f. there are many shops nearby

g. in my free time

h. my best friend

i. on the outskirts of…

j. I go

k. a very big school

l. I like my school

m. the teachers are very good

n. hard–working

o. it is a bilingual school

p. I adore English

2. Arrange the information below in the same order as it occurs in the text

His name is Michele.	
He likes his school.	
Alice lives in the outskirts of Bellinzona.	
Michele is feeling great today.	
He likes his house.	
Michele loves English.	
There are many restaurants near Alice's house.	
Michele is on holiday.	
Alice's birthday is on 30th April.	

1. Mi chiamo Leonardo e ho quattordici anni. Sono svizzero e vivo a Locarno. Oggi sto così così. Sono un po' stressato perché ho molti compiti.

2. Ho un fratello minore che si chiama Gianni. Gianni ha tredici anni e normalmente è simpatico. Oggi Gianni è felice perché è il suo compleanno.

3. Vivo con la mia famiglia in una casa abbastanza grande e un po' antica nella periferia di Locarno. Mi piace la mia casa anche se è *(although it is)* un po' brutta. Ci sono molti ristoranti vicino. Nel mio tempo libero suono sempre il flauto.

4. Il mio migliore amico si chiama Antonio e ha quindici anni, quasi come me *(nearly the same as me)*. Il suo compleanno è il tredici febbraio. Vive in un appartamento enorme in un edificio moderno nel centro di Locarno. Gli piace il suo appartamento perché è grande e carino e c'è un centro sportivo *(sports centre)* vicino.

5. Vado al Liceo Federale, una scuola superiore molto buona vicino al centro della città. La scuola è storica: è stata istituita *(it was established)* nel 1898. Mi piace la mia scuola perché i professori sono molto intelligenti e sono molto pazienti. Studio molte materie differenti, come la storia, la geografia e la musica. Adoro l'italiano.

6. La mia materia preferita è l'italiano perché è molto interessante e utile *(useful)* per il futuro. La professoressa si chiama Paola ed è molto intelligente e divertente. Mi aiuta sempre e non mi sgrida mai, è molto paziente. Mi piace anche la musica perché le lezioni sono molto interessanti e ho il mio migliore amico nella classe.

7. Però, odio *(I hate)* la matematica perché è difficile *(hard)*, e noiosa. So *(I know)* che è importante, ma non mi importa *(I do not care)*! Inoltre, il professore è molto impaziente. A volte ci sgrida.

3. Faulty translation: correct the 10 mistakes found in the translation below of paragraphs 1, 2 and 3 of Leonardo's text

1. My name is Leonardo and I am fifteen years old. I am Swiss and live in Locarno. Today I am unwell. I am a bit agitated because I have a lot of homework.

2. I have an older brother whose name is Gianni. Gianni is thirteen and usually is very mean. Today Gianni is very sad because it is his birthday.

3. I live with my family in a quite small and old house in the center of Locarno. I like my house even though it is a bit small. There are many restaurants nearby. In my free time I occasionally play the drums.

4. Complete the translation of paragraph 4

My _____ friend is called Antonio and is ___ years old, nearly the _______ as me. His birthday is on ___ February. He lives in a a huge _____ in the centre of Locarno. He ______ his flat because it is very ______ and ______and there is a sports centre _____.

5. Complete the sentences below based on paragraphs 5 to 7

a. Leonardo's school is located_______________.

b. He likes his school because the teachers are (1) ___________ and (2) __________.

c. His favourite subject is ________ because it is (1) ___________ and (2) ___________ _______.

d. His Italian teacher is very (1) __________ and (2) ____________.

e. She always ______ him and never ______ him off.

f. He also enjoys music because the lessons are ________ and he has ______________ in class.

g. He hates maths because they are _______ and _________. Also, the teacher is very ________.

UNIT 5
Things I like/dislike: free time

**In this unit you will learn
to talk about:**

- What sports and activities you do in your free time
- The "mi piace + infinitive" structure with "giocare", "fare" & "andare"
- Different places you can go to – using the verb "andare"
- Who you do the activities with
- Reasons for liking/disliking an activity

You will also revisit
- Previously seen adjectives, applied to a different context

UNIT 5
Things I like/dislike: free time

Che cosa ti piace fare nel tuo tempo libero?				*What do you like to do in your free time?*
Quando ho tempo *When I have free time* **Nel mio tempo libero** *In my free time*	**amo** *I love* **mi piace** *I like* **non mi piace** *I don't like*	**giocare** *to play*	a calcio a carte al computer a pallacanestro alla Play a scacchi a tennis ai videogiochi	*soccer* *cards* *on the computer* *basketball* *Playstation* *chess* *tennis* *videogames*
		fare *to do*	ciclismo equitazione escursionismo footing nuoto sport	*cycling* *horse riding* *hiking* *jogging* *swimming* *sport*
		andare *to go*	al centro commerciale al centro sportivo a passeggio al parco in palestra a pesca in piscina in spiaggia	*to the shopping mall* *to the sports centre* *going for a walk* *to the park* *to the gym* *fishing* *to the pool* *to the beach*

con *with*	**la mia amica Anna** **il mio amico Pietro** ***i miei amici** **le mie amiche**	*my friend Anna* *my friend Pietro* *my friends* *my friends (f)*	**mia sorella** **mio fratello** **i miei fratelli**	*my sister* *my brother* *my siblings*

mi piace *I like it* **non mi piace** *I don't like it*	**perché** *because*	**è** *it is* **non è** *it is not*	divertente emozionante interessante noioso sano stancante	*fun* *exciting* *interesting* *boring* *healthy* *tiring*

***Author's note:** Use **"i miei amici"** for a group of friends that are either **all boys, or a mix of boys & girls**. Use **"le mie amiche"** for a group of friends that are made up of **girls only**.

1. Select the correct answer

a. Mi piace giocare a tennis/pallacanestro/calcio.

b. Mi piace fare sport/i compiti/equitazione.

c. Mi piace giocare a scacchi/a carte/a golf.

d. Mi piace fare footing/passeggiate/escursionismo.

e. Mi piace andare al parco/in palestra/al cinema.

f. Mi piace andare a passeggio/in spiaggia/a pesca.

g. Mi piace perché è divertente/noioso/stancante.

h. Non mi piace perché è noioso/inutile/divertente.

2. Break the flow: draw a line between each word

a. Neltempoliberomipiacegiocare.

b. Mipiacegiocareapallacanestro.

c. Nonmipiacel'equitazione.

d. Mipiaceandareinspiaggia.

e. Mipiaceperchéèinteressante.

f. Nonmipiaceperchéèstancante.

g. Mipiaceandareapasseggio.

3. Listening for detail: what activities does Christian do each day? Tick the correct ones

Lunedì *Monday*	Cycling Sport	Jogging Horse riding
Martedì *Tuesday*	Chess Cards	Go for walk Football
Mercoledì *Wednesday*	Swimming Cycling	Hiking Sport
Giovedì *Thursday*	Pool Fishing	Videogames Park
Venerdì *Friday*	Tennis Golf	Chess Shopping mall

4. Complete with the missing words

a. Mi piace giocare a ___________________

b. Non mi piace andare al ___________________

c. Non mi piace fare ___________________

d. Mi piace molto andare a ___________________

e. Non mi piace fare ___________________

f. Mi piace giocare a ___________________

g. Mi piace perché è ___________________

h. Mi piace andare in ___________________

5. Listen and fill in the grid

	Opinion	Activity	Reason
e.g.	*Dislikes*	*Jogging*	*Not fun*
a.			
b.			
c.			
d.			
e.			

6. Listen and correct the mistakes

a. Mi piace andare passeggio.

b. Mi piace giocare a nuoto.

c. Mi piace perché divertente.

d. Mi piace molto andare in parco.

e. Non mi piacciono fare sport.

f. Mi piace abbastanza andare a palestra.

g. Mi piace perché emozionante.

h. Non mi piace giocare ciclismo.

7. Spot the differences between the sentences you hear and those written down and make changes to the latter. Don't make any changes if identical.

a. Non mi piace giocare a carte.

b. Mi piace molto andare a pesca.

c. Mi piace giocare a tennis.

d. Mi piace andare in piscina.

e. Non mi piace fare niente.

f. Mi piace molto perché è divertente.

g. Non mi piace fare equitazione.

h. Mi piace molto fare shopping.

i. Non mi piace fare sport.

8. Narrow listening: gapped translation

Ciao, __ _______ Anna e sono di Milano. Ho _______ anni. Nella mia famiglia ci sono _______ persone: mia madre, mio padre, mio fratello _______, Roberto, e mio fratello _______, Pietro. Il mio compleanno è il _______ luglio. Non mi piace _______ studiare. A _______ studio molte materie, ma mi piacciono solo l' _______ e l' educazione fisica. Odio fare ___ _______! Nel mio tempo libero mi piace fare _______. Mi piace molto giocare a _______, andare in _______ e fare _______. Mi piace giocare a pallacanestro perché è _______. Non mi piace fare _______ perché è noioso e _______.

9. Listening slalom: follow the speaker from top to bottom and number the boxes accordingly

a	b	c	d
Nel tempo libero	Quando ho	Non mi piace	Mi piace
molto	andare	mi piace	tempo
in palestra	andare	mi piace giocare	giocare
ai	a scacchi	perché è	a pesca
e	videogiochi	perché	noioso
con	fare	e	è
interessante.	mio padre.	nuoto.	stancante.

Unit 5. Things I like/dislike: free time – VOCABULARY BUILDING

1. Match

andare a pesca	to go for a walk
fare nuoto	to go fishing
giocare a scacchi	to play soccer
andare a passeggio	to go to my friend's house
giocare a calcio	to go swimming
fare sport	to go hiking
andare in palestra	to go to the beach
fare footing	to play chess
andare in spiaggia	to go to the gym
fare escursionismo	to go jogging
andare a casa del mio amico	to do sport

2. Faulty translation

a. fare equitazione: *to do horse riding*

b. fare sport: *to do jogging*

c. andare a pesca: *to go to the cinema*

d. fare footing: *to do cycling*

e. andare in spiaggia: *to do climbing*

f. fare escursionismo: *to go swimming*

g. andare in palestra: *to go for a walk*

h. giocare a scacchi: *to play basketball*

i. andare a passeggio: *to go for a wal.*

j. giocare a calcio: *to play basketball*

k. fare nuoto: *to do horse riding*

3. Sentence puzzle: rewrite the jumbled up Italian

a. tempo Nel amo mio libero andare in palestra.　　*In my free time I love to go to the gym.*

b. Mi divertente perché è molto piace.　　*I like it because it is a lot of fun.*

c. miei amici Mi piace fare footing con molto i.　　*I like a lot to go jogging with my friends.*

d. perché Mi piace rilassante molto è.　　*I like it because it is very relaxing.*

e. Non a scacchi giocare mi piace.　　*I don't like to play chess.*

f. mi è noioso Non piace perché.　　*I don't like it because it is boring.*

4 Translate into English

a. passeggio

b. equitazione

c. scacchi

d. footing

e. spiaggia

f. andare

g. mi piace

h. amo

i. giocare

j. piscina

k. amici

l. casa

m. rilassante

n. stancante

5. Tick all the adjectives

a. rilassante

b. casa

c. stancante

d. equitazione

e. emozionante

f. passeggio

g. divertente

h. fantastico

6. Complete with the correct option

a. Mi piace andare a ______ con i miei amici.

b. Non mi ______ giocare a calcio.

c. Amo _______ footing.

d. Mi piace molto fare __________.

e. Mi piace perché è __________.

f. _______ piace giocare a scacchi.

g. Mi piace ________ è divertente.

h. Mi piace giocare _______ pallacanestro.

piace	divertente	passeggio	nuoto
a	mi	fare	perché

7. Complete the table

English	Italiano
friends	
	scacchi
	pallacanestro
i love	
because	
	passeggio
	pesca
to do	
to play	

8. Gapped translation

a. Nel tempo libero mi piace fare escursionismo: _____________ *I like to go* ___________.

b. Mi piace perché è molto rilassante: *I like it because it is* __________ __________.

c. Mi piace molto fare footing con i miei amici: *I like* ________ *to go* ________ *with my friends.*

d. Mi piace perché è molto rilassante: *I* ________ *it because it is very* __________.

e. Non mi piace giocare a scacchi. È noioso: *I don't like to play* __________. *It is* ________.

f. Non mi piace perché è stancante: *I* __________ *it because it is* ____________.

g. Amo andare a pesca perché è divertente: *I love to go* ________ *because it is* ________.

9. Find the Italian for the words/phrases below

p	e	b	d	r	a	m	p	e	r	c	h	è	o
s	a	p	a	s	s	e	g	g	i	o	m	a	m
r	p	r	s	l	n	r	d	o	i	s	s	e	s
h	i	m	c	d	o	e	l	r	e	m	u	a	i
a	s	y	a	p	a	l	e	s	t	r	a	m	n
g	c	a	c	s	t	a	n	c	a	n	t	e	o
o	i	i	c	r	n	m	i	e	h	n	s	l	i
t	n	y	h	r	i	o	n	r	s	g	i	a	s
a	a	s	i	f	a	r	e	i	m	t	s	p	r
p	a	l	l	a	c	a	n	e	s	t	r	o	u
o	g	b	e	n	o	i	o	s	o	d	o	u	c
a	p	e	m	o	z	i	o	n	a	n	t	e	s
f	r	i	ü	m	a	z	e	l	m	a	n	i	e

a. walk

b. chess

c. to do

d. basketball

e. hiking

f. exciting

g. tiring

h. because

i. boring

j. pool

k. gym

Unit 5. Things I like/dislike: free time: READING

- *Come ti chiami?*
- Mi chiamo Carlo.
- *Che cosa ti piace fare nel tempo libero?*
- Nel tempo libero mi piace fare sport. Mi piace giocare a pallacanestro con i miei amici, andare in piscina e in palestra con mio fratello e fare ciclismo. Mi piace anche fare escursionismo con mio padre il fine settimana. È emozionante.
- *Che cosa non ti piace fare nel tempo libero?*
- Non mi piace per niente giocare a calcio, è noioso.

- *Come ti chiami?*
- Mi chiamo Stefania.
- *Che cosa ti piace fare nel tempo libero?*
- Nel tempo libero mi piace giocare ai videogiochi con il computer o con il telefonino. Amo anche fare nuoto con i miei amici. È divertente.
- *Che cosa non ti piace fare nel tempo libero?*
- Non mi piace andare a pesca con mio padre il fine settimana.

- *Come ti chiami?*
- Mi chiamo Isabella.
- *Che cosa ti piace fare nel tempo libero?*
- Nel tempo libero mi piace fare shopping e andare a passeggio con le mie amiche. Mi piace anche giocare a scacchi con mia sorella maggiore e andare in piscina con la mia famiglia. Mi piace perché è rilassante.
- *Che cosa non ti piace fare nel tempo libero?*
- Non mi piace per niente fare sport perché è noioso e stancante.

1. find the italian for the following in isabella's text

a. in my free time

b. to go shopping

c. also

d. to play chess

e. older

f. to go to the pool

g. relaxing

h. what you do not like…?

i. I don't like at all

j. to do sport

k. tiring

2. Complete the statements below based on Carlo's text

a. In my free time I like to do

__________.

b. I like to play __________ with my friends.

c. I like to go to the __________ and to the __________ with my brother and to go __________.

d. At the weekend I enjoy to go __________ with my father because it is __________.

e. I don't like at all to __________ __________ because it is __________.

3. Tick or cross? Tick the 9 words on the list below which are included in Stefania's text and cross the remaining ones out

a. free

b. video games

c. female friends

d. bike

e. shopping centre

f. fun

g. weekend

h. computer

i. swimming

j. jogging

k. i don't like

l. because

m. fishing

n. time

o. saturday

p. walk

4. Find someone who…

a. …likes to play videogames.

b. …doesn't like football.

c. …likes to play chess.

d. …thinks sport is tiring.

e. …likes to go cycling.

f. …doesn't like to fish with their father.

g. …likes to go hiking with their father.

h. …has an older sister.

i. …likes to play on their mobile phone.

Unit 5. Things I like/dislike: free time: WRITING

1. Transl-Anagrams: unjumble the words and translate them into English

a. è veretedint

b. im aicep olotm

c. è sionoo

d. regaioc a sicacch

e. eraf smoesrucsioin

f. riocage ia deviogoichi

g. refa tuono

2. broken words

a. passegg_ _   *walk*

b. pes_ _   *fishing*

c. a_ _   *i love*

d. and_ _ _ in spia_ _ _ _   *to go to the beach*

e. escursio_ _ _ _ _   *hiking*

f. equi_ _ _ _ _ _ _   *horse riding*

g. cal_ _ _   *soccer*

h. pallaca_ _ _ _ _ _   *basketball*

3. Complete the sentences with FARE, ANDARE or GIOCARE as appropriate

a. Mi piace _______ a tennis.

b. Mi piace _______ escursionismo.

c. Mi piace _______ a passeggio.

d. Mi piace _______ in spiaggia.

e. Mi piace _______ nuoto e equitazione.

f. Mi piace _______ a calcio.

g. Mi piace molto _______ footing.

h. Mi piace _______ a pallacanestro.

i. Mi piace _______ a pesca.

j. Amo_______ ai videogiochi.

4. Translate into Italian

a. videogames.

b. horse riding.

c. swimming.

d. fishing.

e. hiking.

f. tiring.

5. Translate into Italian

a. I like to do hiking.

b. I don't like to go swimming.

c. I love to play videogames.

d. it is tiring.

e. I like to go fishing.

f. it is exciting.

6. Translate into Italian

a. I love to play basketball with my friends. I like it because it is fun.

b. I don't like to go hiking with my family. I don't like it because it is boring.

c. I like to go to the swimming pool with my friends. It is fantastic!

d. I don't like to go to the beach with my father and my brother. It is tiring.

e. I love to go for a walk with my best (female) friend. It is very relaxing.

f. I like a lot to go shopping with my friends. It is exciting!

g. I don't like to go fishing with my family. It is boring.

Mi chiamo Marta e ho dieci anni. Il mio compleanno è l'otto settembre. Sono Italiana ma vivo a Bellinzona, la capitale del Ticino. Oggi sto benissimo. Sono molto felice perché dopo vado a giocare a calcio con le mie amiche.

Ho una sorella maggiore che si chiama Carolina. Carolina ha sedici anni ed è molto gentile (*kind*). Oggi sta così così perché un po' ammalata (*sick*).

Io e la mia famiglia viviamo in un appartamento accogliente (*cosy*) nel centro di Bellinzona. Mi piace molto il mio appartamento perché è comodo e ci sono molti parchi vicino. Il mio cane si chiama Merlino ed è molto affettuoso (*affectionate*).

Il mio migliore amico si chiama Andrea e ha dieci anni, come me. Il suo compleanno è il venti giugno. Lui vive in una casa nella periferia di Bellinzona. Gli piace la sua casa perché è tranquilla e ci sono molti alberi (*trees*) intorno (*all around*).

Vado alla scuola Elementare San Gottardo, una scuola piccola nel centro della città di Bellinzona. Mi piace la mia scuola perché i professori sono molto bravi e gentili. Non sono severi. Adoro l'educazione fisica, ma è un po' stancante. La mia materia preferita è la letteratura perché è molto interessante e mi aiuta (*helps me*) a sviluppare (*develop*) la mia immaginazione. Inoltre, il professore è divertente e mi aiuta sempre.

Nel tempo libero mi piace fare shopping e andare a passeggio con le mie amiche. Mi piace anche giocare ai videogiochi con mia sorella maggiore e andare in piscina con la mia migliore amica. Mi piace perché è rilassante. Non mi piace molto giocare a scacchi perché è un po' noioso. Però, la mia migliore amica ama gli scacchi. Lei pensa (*thinks*) che è molto interessante ed emozionante.

1. Complete the sentences, based on Marta's text

a. Marta is _______ years old.

b. Today she is feeling ________.

c. Carolina is her __________________.

d. Carolina is a bit _________ today.

e. Near her flat there are many _________.

f. Her dog is very __________.

g. Andrea is her ___________.

h. Marta attends a _________ school in the centre of Bellinzona.

i. She likes her school because her teachers are _____________ and _____________.

j. She adores PE but it is a bit ___________.

k. Her literature teacher is ___________.

l. In her free time she enjoys going shopping and ___________ with her friends.

m. She also plays videogames with her _________ sister and goes to the ___________ with her ________ friend.

2. Find and correct the 8 mistakes in the below translation of the second last paragraph

I go to Scuola Elementare San Gottardo, a large school in the centre of the city of Bellinzona. I like my school because the teachers are very hard-working and kind. They aren't silly. I love physics, but it is a bit boring. My favourite subject is literature because it is very fascinating and helps me develop my imagination. Also, the teacher is competent and always listens to me.

3. Find the Italian equivalent in the last paragraph

a. free time

b. going shopping

c. older sister

d. best friend

e. relaxing

f. chess

g. boring

h. exciting

1. Mi chiamo Dylan e ho sedici anni. Il mio compleanno è il nove febbraio. Sono spagnolo ma vivo in Veneto, nel nord Italia. Oggi sto male perché sono molto stanco e stressato. Il mio cavallo (*horse*) è ammalato (*sick*)!

2. Ho una sorella minore che si chiama Lucia. Lucia ha quindici anni ed è molto divertente. Oggi sta benissimo. È felice perché è il compleanno della sua migliore amica, Claudia.

3. Io e la mia famiglia viviamo in un appartamento carino a Jesolo. È un paese molto carino sulla costa. Mi piace molto il mio appartamento perché è abbastanza grande e ci sono molte spiaggie vicino. Nel tempo libero, mi piace nuotare (*swim*) nel mare. Il mio cavallo si chiama Fulmine ed è molto grande e forte. Mi piace anche andare a pesca.

4. Il mio migliore amico si chiama Raffaele e ha quindici anni, un anno in meno rispetto a me (*compared to me*). Il suo compleanno è il ventisette luglio. Lui vive in una casa sulle montagne. Gli piace la sua casa perché è tranquilla e c'è un lago (*lake*) carino vicino.

5. Vado al liceo linguistico Dante Alighieri, una scuola grande nel centro di Jesolo, vicino alla laguna (*lagoon*). A scuola impariamo *(we learn)* in italiano, in spagnolo, la mia lingua madre (*mother tongue*) e anche in inglese. Amo le lingue *(languages)* perché sono molto utili.

6. Mi piace la mia scuola perché i professori sono molto simpatici e pazienti. Amo le scienze, però a volte sono un po' complicate. La mia materia preferita è la geografia perché è molto interessante e mi aiuta *(helps me)* a capire *(understand)* meglio il mondo.

7. Nel tempo libero mi piace andare al cinema e al centro commerciale con i miei amici. Mi piace anche giocare a calcio con mia sorella minore e andare in spiaggia con il mio migliore amico Raffaele. Mi piace perché è molto divertente. Ci facciamo sempre un sacco di risate *(we laugh a lot)*. Mi piace molto leggere libri perché è molto interessante. Però, il mio migliore amico adora suonare la chitarra. Lui pensa *(thinks)* che è divertente.

4. Answer the following questions on Dylan's text (paragraphs 1 to 4)

a. How old is Dylan?

b. Where in Italy is Veneto?

c. Why is he not feeling good today?

d. What is wrong with his horse?

e. Why is his younger sister happy?

f. Why does Dylan like his flat? (2)

g. What is his horse like? (2)

h. Where is Raffaele's house located?

i. Why does he like his house? (2)

5. Complete the following translation of paragraph 5

I attend liceo linguistico Dante Alighieri, a ______________ school in the _________ of Jesolo, near the _________. In my school we learn in ___________, in Spanish, my _________ tongue and in _________ too. I _______ languages because they are very _________.

6. Find the Italian equivalent in paragraphs 6

a. I like my school

b. friendly

c. sometimes

d. subject

e. helps me understand

f. better

g. the world

7. Translate into English the following phrases from paragraph 7

a. nel tempo libero

b. con i miei amici

c. mi piace giocare

d. è molto divertente

e. leggere libri

f. adora suonare la chitarra

TERM 1 - BRINGING IT ALL TOGETHER – QUESTION SKILLS

1. Fill in the missing words

a. Come ti _ _ _ _ _ _ ?

b. C_ _ _ s_ _ _ oggi?

c. Q _ _ _ _ _ anni hai?

d. Q _ _ _ _ _ è il tuo compleanno?

e. H_ _ fratelli o sorelle?

f. C_ _ _ si c_ _ _ _ _ tuo fratello?

g. Q _ _ _ _ _ anni ha?

h. Q _ _ _ _ è il suo compleanno?

i. D _ d_ _ _ sei?

j. D_ _ _ vivi?

k. Q _ _ _ _ materie studi?

l. Q _ _ _ _ ti p_ _ _ _ ?

m. P_ _ _ _ _ ?

n. C _ _ cosa ti p _ _ _ _ fare nel tempo libero?

2. Listen and choose the option that you hear

a. Mi chiamo **Matteo / Ivano / Carlo**.

b. Oggi sto **benissimo / malissimo / così così**.

c. Ho **ventisei / sei/ seidici** anni.

d. Il mio compleanno è il **trenta / tredici / tre** settembre.

e. Sì, ho **un fratello/ una sorella / un cugino** minore.

f. Mio **fratello / padre / zio** si chiama Giuseppe.

g. Ha **otto / nove / dieci** anni.

h. Il suo compleanno è il ventidue **gennaio / febbraio / marzo**.

i. **Sei / Siamo / Sono** italiano.

j. Vivo a Catania, nel **sud /centro / nord** Italia.

k. Studio **inglese / matematica / scienze**.

l. Non mi piacciono le **scienze / lingue / professoresse**.

m. Nel tempo libero mi piace fare **sport / nuoto / equitazione**.

3. Listen and write in the missing information

a. _________ ti chiami? — *Mi _______ Paola.*

b. _________ stai oggi? — *Oggi _______ benissimo.*

c. _________ anni hai? — *Ho _______ anni*

d. _________ è il tuo compleanno? — *Il mio compleanno è il _______ _______.*

e. _______ fratelli o sorelle? — *Si, ho __ _______ minore.*

f. _______ si chiama tuo fratello? — *Mio _______ si _______ Giuseppe.*

g. _______ anni ha? — *Ha _______ anni.*

h. _______ è il suo compleanno? — *Il suo _______ è il ventidue _______.*

i. ___ _______ sei? — *Sono _______.*

j. _______ vivi? — *_______ a Catania, nel _______ Italia.*

k. _______ materie _______? — *_______ le scienze, la_______, la geografia, e l'educazione _______.*

l. _______ non ti piace? Perché? — *Non mi _______ le scienze _______ sono troppo _______.*

m. __ _______l'italiano? Perché? — *Amo l'_______ perché è _______ e molto _______ per il _______.*

n. ___ _______ti piace fare nel tempo libero? — *Nel _______ libero mi piace _______ sport e andare a _______ con i miei _______.*

TERM 1 - BRINGING IT ALL TOGETHER – QUESTION SKILLS

4. Fill in the grid with your personal information

Question	
1. Come ti chiami?	
2. Come stai oggi?	
3. Quanti anni hai?	
4. Quando è il tuo compleanno?	
5. Hai fratelli o sorelle?	
6. Quando è il suo compleanno?	
7. Di dove sei?	
8. Dove vivi?	
9. Quale materia studi?	
10. Quale (non) ti piace?	
11. Ti piace ___ _____________?	
12. Che cosa ti piace fare nel tempo libero?	

5. Survey two of your classmates using the same questions as above– write down the main information you hear in Italian

Q.	Person 1	Person 2
1.		
2.		
3.		
4.		
5.		
6.		
7.		
8.		
9.		
10.		
11.		
12.		

No Snakes No Ladders

TERM 1

1	Good morning
2	How are you today?
3	I am well thanks
4	Today I am great
5	I am bad because I am tired
6	I am a bit stressed and angry.
7	Nice to meet you.
8	My name is Diego
9	I am ten years old
10	My brother is called Roberto
11	He/she is twelve years old
12	He/she is thirteen years old
13	He/she is fourteen years old
14	He/she is fifteen years old
15	I am from Rome, the capital of Italy
16	My friend is called Luisa
17	His/her birthday is the 10th of January
18	His/her birthday is the 18th of August
19	His/her birthday is the 20th of October
20	I live in a pretty house on the coast.
21	I live in an ugly flat in the centre
22	I am from Como, in Lombardia
23	I am from London, the capital of England
24	At school I study history.
25	I like Italian because it is fun
26	I don't like ICT because it is boring
27	I like it because the teacher (f) is good
28	I like it because I have friends in class
29	I like it because it is useful for the future
30	I like it because I learn a lot

START

FINISH

No Snakes No Ladders

PARTENZA	1 Buongiorno.	2 Come stai oggi?	3 Sto bene, grazie.	4 Oggi sto benissimo.	5 Sto male perché sono stanco.	6 Sono un po' stressato e arrabbiato.	7 Piacere.
15 Sono di Roma, la capitale d'Italia	14 Ha quindici anni	13 Ha quattordici anni	12 Ha tredici anni	11 Ha dodici anni	10 Mio fratello si chiama Roberto	9 Ho dieci anni	8 Mi chiamo Diego
16 La mia amica si chiama Luisa	17 Il suo compleanno è il dieci gennaio	18 Il suo compleanno è il diciotto agosto	19 Il suo compleanno è il venti ottobre	20 Vivo in una casa carina sulla costa	21 Vivo in un apartamento brutto nel centro	22 Sono di Como in Lombardia	23 Sono di Londra, la capitale dell' Inghilterra
ARRIVO	30 Mi piace perché imparo molto	29 I piace perché è utile per il futuro	28 Mi piace perché ho i miei amici in classe	27 Mi piace perché la professoressa è brava	26 Non mi piace l'informatica perché è noiosa	25 Mi piace l'italiano perché è divertente	24 A scuola studio storia

PYRAMID TRANSLATION

Unit 5 Recap – Free Time

Translate each part of the pyramid out loud with your partner, then write it into the spaces provided below.

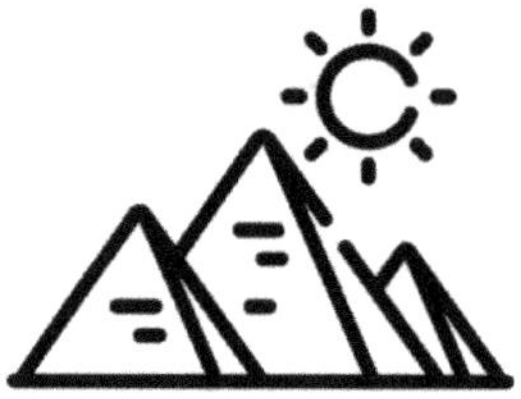

a. In my free time...

b. In my free time I love to play videogames...

c. In my free time I love to play videogames with my friends...

d. In my free time I love to play videogames with my friends and to do jogging in the park with my brother.

e. In my free time I love to play videogames with my friends and to do jogging in the park with my brother. I also like to go to the shopping centre with my sister.

f. In my free time I love to play videogames with my friends and to do jogging in the park with my brother. I also like to go to the shopping centre with my sister. However, I don't like to go fishing. It is too boring.

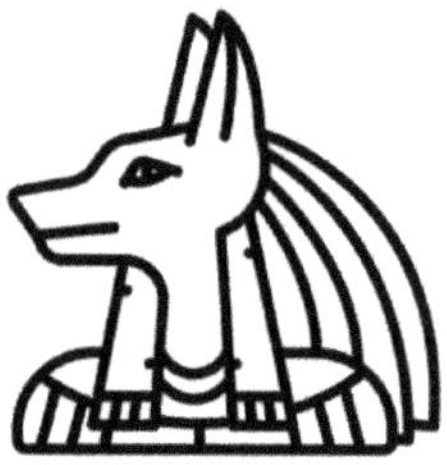

Write your translation here:

SOLUTION: Nel tempo libero amo giocare ai videogiochi con i miei amici e fare footing nel parco con mio fratello. Mi piace anche andare al centro commerciale con mia sorella. Però non mi piace andare a pesca. È troppo noioso.

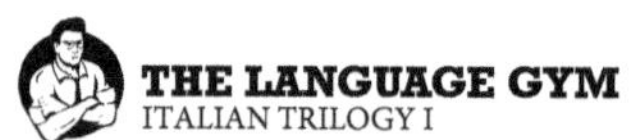

One pen One dice

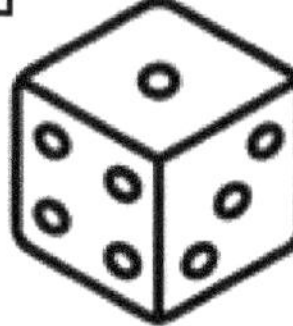

Play in pairs. You only have 1 pen and 1 dice.

One person has the pen and starts translating the sentence into **English.** The other person rolls the dice until they roll a 6, they swap the pen and translate. The winner is the person who finishes translating all the sentences first.

1. Buona sera, come stai oggi?	
2. Oggi sto così così perché sono stanco/a.	
3. Piacere.	
4. Mio fratello si chiama Luca.	
5. Il suo compleanno è il 19 luglio.	
6. Sono di Bari, in Italia.	
7. Mi piace la storia perché è interessante.	
8. Mi piace perché ho amici/che in classe.	
9. Nel tempo libero gioco a calcio con i miei amici	
10. Mi piace anche fare equitazione.	

One pen One dice

Play in pairs. You only have 1 pen and 1 dice.

One person has the pen and starts translating the sentence into **Italian.** The other person rolls the dice until they roll a 6, they swap the pen and translate. The winner is the person who finishes translating all the sentences first.

1. Good afternoon, how are you today?	
2. Today I am so-so because I am tired.	
3. Nice to meet you.	
4. My brother is called Luca.	
5. His birthday is the 19th July.	
6. I am from Bari, in Italu.	
7. I like history because it is interesting.	
8. I like it because I have friends in class.	
9. In my free time I play football with my friends.	
10. I also like to do horseriding.	

TERM 2 – OVERVIEW

This term you will learn:

Unit 6 - How to talk about your family
- Who is in your family
- How old they are
- How you get on with them

Unit 7 - OPTIONAL: Describing my hair and eyes
- What colour your hair and eyes are
- What your hair style is like

Unit 8 - Describing myself and another family member
- How to say what your immediate family members are like
- How to describe physical and personality traits
- All the persons of the verb 'Essere' in the present indicative

Unit 9 - Comparing people's appearance & personality
- How to use comparatives: more/less than
- New adjectives to describe people

Unit 10 - Describing my teachers
- How to talk about teachers using adjectives
- Review school subjects
- How to describe positive/negative behaviours

Unit 11 - Saying what I and others do in our free time
- What activities you do and when
- The verbs 'giocare', 'fare' and 'andare'
- Other free time activities

KEY QUESTIONS

- Quante persone ci sono nella tua famiglia?	*How many people are there in your family?*
- Con chi vai d'accordo nella tua famiglia?	*Who do you get on well with in your family?*
- Non vai d'accordo con qualcuno?	*Do you get on badly with anyone?*
- Perché (non) vai d'accordo con tuo padre?	*Why do you (not) get on with your father?*
- Quanti anni ha tuo fratello/tua sorella?	*How old is your brother/sister?*
- Com'è tuo fratello/tua sorella?	*What is your brother/sister like?*
- Come sono i tuoi capelli?	*What is your hair like?*
- Di che colore sono i tuoi occhi?	*What colour are your eyes?*
- Quanti anni ha?	*How old is he/she?*
- Quando è il suo compleanno?	*When is his/her birthday?*
- Ti piace il professore di inglese?	*Do you like your English teacher?*
- Qual è il tuo professore/la tua professoressa preferito/a?	*Which is your favourite teacher?*
- C'è un professore che non ti piace? Quale?	*Is there any teacher you do not like? Which one?*
- Quale professore ti aiuta sempre?	*Which teacher always helps you?*
- Qual è la tua materia preferita?	*Which is your favourite subject*
- Che cosa fai nel tuo tempo libero?	*What do you do in your free time?*
- Quale sport fai?	*What sports do you do?*
- Che cosa fai quando fa bel/cattivo tempo?	*What do you do when the weather is good/bad?*

UNIT 6
Talking about my family members, saying their age and how well I get on with them. Counting to 100.

In this unit you will learn to talk about:
- How many people there are in your family and who they are
- If you get on well with them
- Words for family members
- What their age is
- Numbers from 31 to 100

You will also revisit
- Numbers from 1 to 31
- Hair and eyes description

Talking about my family members, saying their age and how well I get on with them. Counting to 100

Quante persone ci sono nella tua famiglia?	*How many people are there in your family?*
Con chi vai d'accordo nella tua famiglia?	*Who do you get on well with in your family?*
Non vai d'accordo con qualcuno?	*Do you get on badly with anyone?*
Perché vai/non vai d'accordo con tuo padre?	*Why do you get on well/badly with your father?*
Perché vai/non vai d'accordo con tua madre?	*Why do you get on well/badly with your mother?*

			un *1*	anno *(year old)*
Ci sono quattro persone nella mia famiglia *There are four people in my family…*	**mio nonno Alfonso** *my grandfather Alfonso*		Due *2*	
	mio padre Giuseppe *my father Giuseppe*		tre *3*	
			quattro *4*	
	mio zio Luciano *my uncle Luciano*	**Lui ha** *He has*	cinque *5*	
			sei *6*	
			sette *7*	
	mio fratello maggiore /minore *my older/younger brother*		otto *8*	
Nella mia famiglia siamo in quattro *We are a family of four…*			nove *9*	
			dieci *10*	
	mio cugino Marco *my cousin Marco*		venti *20*	
			ventuno *21*	
			ventidue *22*	
			ventitré *23*	
			trenta *30*	
			trentuno *31*	
Vado d'accordo con… *I get on well with…*	**mia nonna Rosa** *my grandmother Rose*		trentadue *32*	**anni** *(years old)*
			trentatré *33*	
			trentaquattro *34*	
	mia madre Lina *my mother Lina*		trentacinque *35*	
			trentasei *36*	
			trentasette *37*	
Non vado d'accordo con… *I do not get on well with…*	**mia zia Anna** *my aunt Anna*	**Lei ha** *She has*	trentotto *38*	
			trentanove *39*	
			quaranta *40*	
	mia sorella maggiore /minore *my older/younger sister*		cinquanta *50*	
			sessanta *60*	
			settanta *70*	
			ottanta *80*	
	mia cugina Lara *my girl cousin Lara*		novanta *90*	
			cento *100*	

*Author's note: the number 1, **uno**, becomes shortened to '**un**' before a noun. After 20 in Italian simply put numbers together, no space, no hyphen. i.e. 25 **venticinque**. The final vowel of the tens number disappears when you add **uno**(1) or **otto**(8); i.e. 41 **quarantuno**, 48 **quarantotto**. When you add the number **tre** (3) the final vowel becomes é: 53 **cinquantatré***

1. Fill in the blanks

a. Nella mia _ _ _ _ _ _ _ ci sono _ _ _ _ _ _ persone.

b. Mio nonno ha _ _ _ _ _ _ _ anni.

c. Nella _ _ _ famiglia _ _ _ _ _ sei _ _ _ _ _ _ _ .

d. Mio _ _ _ _ _ si chiama _ _ _ _ _ .

e. Vado d' _ _ _ _ _ _ _ con _ _ _ fratello _ _ _ _ _ _ _ _ .

f. Non _ _ _ _ d'accordo con mia _ _ _ _ _ .

g. Vado _ _ _ _ _ d'accordo _ _ _ mio _ _ _ _ _ .

2. Break the flow

a. Cisonoseipersonenellamiafamiglia.

b. Vadod'accordoconimieigenitori.

c. Miononnohaottant'anni.

d. Mioziohaquarant'anni.

e. Miofratellomaggioresichiamagianni.

f. Nellamiafamigliacisonotrepersone.

g. Miopadrehaquarantadueanni.

3. Multiple choice quiz: select the correct age

	1	2	3
a. Giacomo	40	50	60
b. Silvia	90	80	70
c. Gianni	30	40	60
d. Pietro	60	70	100
e. Marina	36	46	56
f. Carolina	65	85	95
g. Enrico	33	63	73
h. Paolo	72	21	41
i. Manuela	57	67	47

4. Spot the intruders: identify the word(s) in each sentence the speaker is NOT saying

a. Nella mia famiglia ci sono sei mila persone.

b. Mio zio Pietro ha quarantuno anni.

c. Vado molto d'accordo con i miei genitori.

d. Mio cugino Ian ha come cinquant'anni.

e. I miei nonni materni hanno ottant'anni.

f. Io non vado d'accordo con mio cugino Giulio.

5. Faulty translation: spot the translation errors and correct them

a. My name is Francesco. I am 16 years old.

b. I have blond and long hair.

c. I have green eyes.

d. In my family there are 4 people: my father, my mother, my cousin, my brother and I.

e. My father is 54, my mother is 34.

f. My sister is 9 and my brother is 7.

g. My grandparents are called Roberta and Raffaele.

h. My aunt is 51 years old and my uncle is 70.

i. My maternal grandparents are 80 years old.

j. My paternal grandfather is 76.

6. Spot and write in the missing words

a. Ciao chiamo Christian.

b. Vivo Roma.

c. Ho fratello.

d. Il mio compleanno il venti marzo.

e. Nella mia famiglia cinque persone.

f. C'è mio padre, mia madre, i miei fratelli e io.

g. Io ho trentasette anni. Mia madre ha sessantadue e mio padre sessantatrè anni.

h. Mio fratello ha quarant' anni e mio fratello ha trentacinque anni.

i. Vado d'accordo i miei genitori.

7. Narrow listening: gapped translation

My name is Damiano. I am from __________. I am ____________ years old. My birthday is on ____ _____

______________. I have __________, long and __________ hair. I have __________ eyes. In my family there are

__________ people: my stepfather, my __________ and my two sisters. My older sister is ____________ years

old. My younger sister is ___________ years old. I ____ ___ ______ _____ with my parents. My maternal

___________ lives with us. He is _____________ years old. I get on well with him.

8. Listening slalom: follow the speaker from top to bottom and number the boxes accordingly

a. Elena	b. Filippo	c. Matilde	d. Lorenzo	e. Max
My name is Elena	My name is Filippo	My name is Matilde	My name is Lorenzo	My name is Max
and I am 17.	and I am 16.	and I am 20.	and I am 11.	and I am 30.
My birthday is on 25th October.	My birthday is on 20th June.	My birthday is on 31st December.	My birthday is on 15th March.	My birthday is on 7th January.
My mother is 50	My mother is 48	My mother is 44	My mother is 39	My mother is 62
and my father is 49.	and my father is 43.	and my father is 53.	and my father is 64.	and my father is 52.
My grandad is 81	My grandad is 75	My grandad is 76	My grandad is 73	My grandad is 90
and my grandma is 68.	and my grandma is 80.	and my grandma is 81.	and my grandma is 72.	and my grandma is 79.

9. Narrow listening: listen and fill in the missing details on the grid

Name	Age	Birthday	Family size	Older sibling's age	Mother's age	Father's age
a. Andrea		20th June		16		41
b. Mario	14		4			44
c. Sofia		15th Sept			43	
d. Eugenio	13		5		39	
e. Miriam	28			31		55

Unit 6. Talking about my family + Counting to 100: VOCAB BUILDING

1. complete with the missing word

a. nella mia f____________ c'è — *in my family there is*

b. ci sono __________ persone — *there are five people*

c. mio __________ alfonso — *my grandfather Alfonso*

d. mio nonno ________ ottant'anni — *my grandfather is 80 years old*

e. mia ________ Lina — *my mother Lina*

f. lei __________ cinquant'anni — *she is 50 years old*

g. vado d' __________ con mio fratello — *I get on well with my brother.*

2. Match up

1. sedici	*a. 66*
2. sessantasei	*b. 48*
3. ventuno	*c. 13*
4. dieci	*d. 16*
5. trentatré	*e. 10*
6. tredici	*f. 21*
7. quarantotto	*g. 15*
8. cinquantadue	*h. 5*
9. cinque	*i. 33*
10. quindici	*j. 52*

3. Translate into English

a. Non vado d'accordo con

b. Mia nonna Luigina

c. Mio zio

d. Ci sono quattro persone.

e. Nella mia famiglia.

f. Vado d'accordo con.

g. Mio padre.

h. Ha vent'anni.

4. Add the missing letter

a. fami _lia   c. p _rsone   e. frat _llo   g. ma_re   i. vado _'accordo   k. tren_adue

b. z_o   d. n_nno   f. ma_giore   h. cugi _o   j. n_lla   l. nov_nta

5. Broken words

a. C__ s______ s____ p__________ n____ m__ f__________.
There are 6 people in my family.

b. M___ s__________ h__ d________ a______.
My sister is 12 years old.

c. N____ m___ f__________ c'__. *In my family there is.*

d. M__ c________ s__ c________. *My male cousin is called.*

e. M__ p________ h____ q__________________ a______.
My father is 46 years old.

f. N___ v_____ d' a__________ c___ m__ f____________ m__________. *I do not get on well with my older brother.*

g. V___ d'a__________ c___. *I get on well with.*

6. Complete with a suitable word

a. nella mia __________________

b. ci__________ tre persone

c. mia sorella __________________

d. ha quattordici ____________

e. mia __________ Gina ha trentacinque anni

f. __________ d'accordo con mio padre

g. _____ mia famiglia ci sono ...

h. non vado d'__________ con mia zia

i. mio zio _____ quarantasei anni

j. mio __________ ha trentanove anni

k. vado d'accordo ______ mio nonno

Unit 6. Talking about my family + Counting to 100: VOCABULARY DRILLS

1. Match up

nella mia	there are
famiglia	in my
ci sono	with
sette	I get on well
persone	seven
vado d'accordo	family
con	people

2. complete with the missing word

a. Ci _______ cinque persone — *There are five people*

b. Mio ______ John ha sessant' anni — *My uncle john is 60*

c. Vado ____________ con mia cugina — *I get on well with my cousin*

d. ____ vado d'accordo ____ mia zia — *I don't get on well with my aunt*

e. Mia zia Anna _____ quarantasette anni — *My aunt Anna is 47*

f. Lui ha _______________ anni — *He is 18*

g. Lei ________ ventinove anni — *She is 29*

h. Mia _______ Luigina ha ottant' anni — *My grandmother Luigina is 80*

3. Translate into English

a. Lui ha settantacinque anni.

b. Lei ha quarant' anni.

c. Mio padre ha cinquantatré anni.

d. Non vado d'accordo con mio nonno.

e. Vado d'accordo con mia sorella.

f. Mia sorella minore ha cinque anni.

g. Ci sono sei persone nella mia famiglia

h. Vai d'accordo con tua sorella?

4. complete with the missing letters

a. Mio fratello m_ _giore
My older brother

b. Nella mia fa_ _ _lia ci s_ _ _ tre persone
In my family there are 3 people

c. Mio cugino h_ dici_ _nove anni
My cousin is 19

d. Vado molto d' acc_ _do con mio fratello
I get on very well with my brother

e. Mio z_ _ ha quaranta_ _ _ anni
my uncle is 46 years old

f. _ _ _ _ _ molto d'accordo con mi_ cugin_
I get on very well with my female cousin

g. Mio cug_ _ _ ha q_ _ndici anni
My male cousin is 15 years old

h. Vado abbastanza d'accordo con _ _ _ sorella
I get on quite well with my sister

5. Translate into Italian:

a. In my family:____________________

b. There are: ______________________

c. My father: ______________________

d. Is 40 years old:________________

e. I get on well with my brother:

____

6. Spot and correct the errors.

a. nella mi famiglia ci sono tre persona

b. mia nona Carla

c. mio fratello a nove ani

d. vado dacordo con mio cugino

e. mia cugino ha otto anni

f. mia sorrela maggior Benedetta

Unit 6. Talking about my family + Counting to 100: TRANSLATION

1. Match up

1. venti	*a. 30*
2. cinquanta	*b. 70*
3. settanta	*c. 100*
4. trenta	*d. 50*
5. sessanta	*e. 20*
6. novanta	*f. 80*
7. ottanta	*g. 40*
8. quaranta	*h. 60*
9. cento	*i. 90*

2. Write out in Italian

a. 35 = trentacinque

b. 63 = s______________________

c. 89 = o______________________

d. 74 = s______________________

e. 98 = n______________________

f. 100 = c______________________

g. 82 = o______________________

h. 24 = v______________________

i. 17 = d______________________

3. Write out with the missing number

a. Io ho t______________________ anni.
I am 32.

b. Mio padre ha c______________________ anni.
My father is fifty-seven.

c. Mia madre ha q______________________ anni.
My mother is forty-eight.

d. Mio nonno ha c____________ anni.
My grandfather is one-hundred years old.

e. Noi abbiamo t____________ anni.
We are thirteen.

f. Loro hanno n______________ anni.
They are ninety.

g. I miei cugini hanno q______________________ anni.
My cousins are forty-four.

h. Lei ha s______________ anni?
Is she seventy?

4. Correct the translation errors

a. My father is forty = mio padre ha quattordici anni

b. My mother is fifty = mia madre ha cinquantadue anni

c. We are forty-eight = noi abbiamo quarantadue anni

d. I am forty-two = ho quarantuno anni

e. They are thirty-four = loro hanno trentadue anni

5. Translate into Italian (please write out the numbers in letters)

a. In my family there are six people:______________________.

b. My mother is called Sara and she is 43:______________________.

c. My father is called Mohamed and he is 48:______________________.

d. My older sister is called Fatima and she is 31:______________________.

e. My younger sister is called Carmen and she is 18:______________________.

f. I am called Ariana and I am 27: ______________________.

g. My grandfather is called Antonio and he is 87:______________________.

Unit 6. Talking about my family + Counting to 100: Writing

1. Spot and correct the spelling mistakes

a. querenta = *quaranta*

b. trentoono = ___________________________

c. otantadue = ___________________________

d. veintuno = ___________________________

e. novente = ___________________________

f. ciento = ___________________________

g. septenta =___________________________

h. sedicci = ___________________________

3. Rearrange the sentence below in the correct word order

a. mia Nella quattro famiglia persone sono ci.
In my family there are four people.

b. vado con mio d'accordo Non fratello.
I don't get on well with my brother.

c. padre, Mio si chiama che Piero anni cinquantadue ha.
My father, who is called Piero, is fifty-two.

d. padre mio ed io Nella famiglia mia madre, ci persone: sono tre mia.
In my family there are three people: my mother, my father and I.

e. si Mio che cugino, anni Ivan chiama ha trentasette.
My cousin, who is called Ivan, is thirty-seven.

f. nonno, anni Fernando che Mio si chiama ottantasette ha.
My grandfather, who is called Fernando, is eighty-seven.

g. Vado con madre d'accordo mia. Lei anni cinquant' ha.
I get on well with my mother. She is 50.

2. Complete with the missing letters

a. Mia m__dre h__ quar__nt' ann__.

b. Mio pad__e h__ cin__uantuno a__ni.

c. I miei nonni h__nno ott__nt' an__i.

d. M__a sore__la mino__e ha vent__ __nni.

e. __ia no__na __a sett__ntasei a __ __ __.

f. Mio fr__ tel__o ma__g__ore ha ven__i an__i.

4. Complete

a. in my family: n______ m___ f______________

b. there are: c___ s________

c. who is called: c______ s___ c______________

d. my mother: m___ m__________

e. my father: m____ p__________

f. he is fifty: l____ h____ c______________' a________

g. I am sixty: i__ h___ s______________' a________

h. she is forty: l____ h__ q___________' a________

5. Write a relationship sentence for each person as shown in the example

e.g. Il mio migliore amico si chiama Paolo e ha quindici anni. Vado molto d'accordo con lui.

Name	Relationship to me	Age	How I get on with them
e.g. Paolo	*best friend*	*15*	*very well*
Gianfranco	father	57	well
Lina	mother	45	not well
Rosa	aunt	60	*quite* well
Andrew	uncle	67	not well
Alfonso	grandfather	75	*very* well

Author's note: *quite*=**abbastanza**/ *very*=**molto** ☺
*Vado abbastanza d'accordo con mio zio

TERM 2 - BRINGING IT ALL TOGETHER – 6

1. Mi chiamo Laura e ho otto anni. Il mio compleanno è il tre aprile. Sono di Piacenza, in Italia, ma vivo a Città di San Marino, la capitale di San Marino. Oggi sto abbastanza bene. Sono molto contenta perché dopo vado a casa dei miei nonni. Mi piace molto mia nonna perché è molto simpatica e mi da *(gives me)* sempre le caramelle *(sweets)*.

2. Nella mia famiglia ci sono cinque persone: mio fratello maggiore Giulio, mia sorella minore Martina, mio padre Giovanni, mia madre Angela ed io. Ho anche un cane bianco che si chiama Lilly. Mio nonno si chiama Giacomo e ha ottant'anni e mia nonna si chiama Elena e ha settantanove anni. I miei nonni sono molto pazienti e simpatici.

3. Mio fratello maggiore si chiama Giulio. Giulio ama cantare e suonare la chitarra. Ha tredici anni ed è molto divertente. Il suo compleanno è il tre luglio. Non gli piace fare sport perché non è sportivo *(sporty)*.

4. Io e la mia famiglia viviamo in una casa carina nella periferia di San Marino. Non mi piace la mia casa perché non è molto moderna e non ci sono negozi e ristoranti vicino. È molto noioso. Però, ho un giardino con molti fiori, è la zona preferita della mia casa. Nel tempo libero, mi piace pattinare nel parco. La mia migliore amica si chiama Luisa e anche a lei piace pattinare con me nel parco. È molto divertente.

5. La mia scuola è molto grande ed è nel mio quartiere *(neighbourhood)*. Mi piace la mia scuola perché i professori sono simpatici e divertenti. Però, non vado d'accordo con la professoressa di musica perché è un po' impaziente. La mia materia preferita è la matematica perché mi piace risolvere i problemi e ho i miei amici in classe.

1. Find the Italian equivalent in paragraph 1

a. I am from: s

b. but: m

c. I live: v

d. today: o

e. I feel: s

f. happy: c

g. afterwards: d

h. I am going: v

i. friendly: s

j. gives me: m

2. Complete the statements below about Laura's family based on paragraphs 2 and 3

a. In Laura's family there are _____ people.

b. Her younger sister is called _________.

c. Lilly is their _______ and she is _______ (colour).

d. Her grandparents are very patient and _________.

e. Giulio loves to _________ and __________________.

f. He is _______ years old and is very __________.

g. He does not like doing _______ because he is not __________.

3. Answer the following questions (in English) about paragraph 4

a. Where in San Marino do they live?

b. Why does she not like her house? (3)

c. What is there in her garden?

d. What part of her house does she like the most?

e. What sport does she enjoy doing in the park?

f. What does she have in common with Luisa?

4. Answer the following questions on paragraph 5 (in Italian) as if you were Laura

a. Com'è la tua scuola?

b. Dov'è la tua scuola?

c. Perché ti piace la tua scuola?

d. Con quale professore non vai d'accordo? Perché?

e. Qual è la tua materia preferita? Perché?

Mi chiamo Serena e ho sedici anni. Il mio compleanno è il tre aprile. Sono di Roma, in Italia ma vivo a Dublino, la capitale dell'Irlanda. Oggi sto così così. Sono più o meno *(more or less)* contenta ma sono molto stanca. Dopo vado al ristorante con i miei genitori. Vado molto d'accordo con mia madre perché è molto simpatica e mi ascolta *(listens to me)*.

Nella mia famiglia ci sono cinque persone: mio fratello maggiore, Angelo, mia sorella minore, Anna, mio padre, Alessandro, mia madre Marina, ed io. Abbiamo anche un cane bianco che si chiama Neve. Mio nonno si chiama Michele e ha ottantacinque anni, mia nonna si chiama Carla e ha settantacinque anni. I miei nonni sono molto simpatici e affettuosi.

Mio fratello maggiore si chiama Angelo. Angelo è appassionato di pittura e suona il pianoforte. Ha quattordici anni ed è molto intelligente. Il suo compleanno è il ventidue agosto. Mio fratello è sempre molto bravo e mi aiuta. È davvero un angelo!

Io e la mia famiglia viviamo in una casa nella periferia di Dublino. Non mi piace la mia casa perché è troppo grande. Non ci sono molti negozi e ristoranti nel mio quartiere, è un peccato *(a shame)*. Però, c'è un parco con molti alberi vicino a casa mia. È il posto *(place)* perfetto per leggere libri. Nel tempo libero, mi piace pattinare nel parco. La mia migliore amica si chiama Aoife e anche a lei piace leggere libri nel parco.

La mia scuola è piccola ed è nel mio quartiere. Mi piace la mia scuola perché i professori sono divertenti ed ho molti amici. Però non vado d'accordo con la professoressa d' inglese. Mi sgrida sempre! La mia materia preferita è l'arte perché sono una persona abbastanza creativa. Mi piace dipingere e disegnare animali.

5. Arrange the following information in the same order as it occurs in the text

Serena's birthday is on 3rd April.	
Her grandparents are very kind.	
Her name is Serena and she is 16.	**1**
Her brother always helps her.	
There aren't many restaurants in her area.	
Serena lives in Ireland.	
There is a park near her house.	
Her school is small.	
Serena gets on well with her mother.	
In her free time she goes skating.	
They live in a big house.	
They have a white dog.	
Her older brother loves painting.	

6. Identify the false statements about her school (last paragraph) and correct them

a. Serena's school is big.

b. Serena doesn't like her teachers.

c. Serena has friends in the school.

d. Serena doesn't get on well with her French teacher.

e. Her English teacher always mocks her.

f. Serena likes art.

g. Serena is quite a creative person.

h. She loves to take photos of animals.

7. Circle and translate into English the 5 words on the list below which are found in Serena text

a. troppo   d. per   g. davanti

b. vicino   e. gennaio   h. mai

c. lontano   f. affettuosi   i. sempre

8. The following phrases have been copied incorrectly from Serena's text. Can you fix them?

a. nel tempo libro   e. con molti arbeli

b. non piace la mia casa   f. ho molti amico

c. la mia migliora amica   g. mio fratello majore

d. la mia preferita materia   h. è molto sinpatica

UNIT 7
Describing hair and eyes

In this unit you will learn:

- To describe what a person's hair and eyes are like
- To describe details about their faces (e.g. beard and glasses)
- Colours
- I wear
- He/she wears

You will also revisit:
- Common Italian names
- The verb "Avere" in the first and third person singular
- Numbers from 1 to 16

UNIT 7
Describing hair and eyes

Come ti chiami? *What is your name?*			**Quanti anni hai?** *How old are you?*
Come hai i capelli? *What is your hair like?*			**Di che colore hai gli occhi?** *What colour are your eyes?*

Come si chiama? *What is his/her name?*			**Quanti anni ha?** *How old is he/she?*
Come ha i capelli? *What is his/her hair like?*			**Di che colore ha gli occhi?** *What colour are his/her eyes?*

| **(Io) Mi chiamo** *My name is / I am called / I call myself...*

 (Lui/Lei) Si chiama *He/she is called* | Antonio
 Carlo
 Diego
 Emilia
 Francesca
 Gianfranco
 Giulia
 Isabella
 Marta
 Roberto | **e** *and* | **ho** *I have*

 ha *he/she has* | sei anni — *6 years*
 sette anni — *7 years*
 otto anni — *8 years*
 nove anni — *9 years*
 dieci anni — *10 years*
 undici anni — *11 years*
 dodici anni — *12 years*
 tredici anni — *13 years*
 quattordici anni — *14 years*
 quindici anni — *15 years* |

| **Ho *i capelli** *I have...hair*

 Ha i capelli *He/she has...hair* | **bianchi** *white*
 biondi *blond*
 castani *brown*
 colorati *coloured*
 grigi *grey*
 neri *black*
 rossi *red*
 scuri *dark* | **e** | **a spazzola** — *spiky*
 corti — *short*
 di media lunghezza — *medium length*
 lisci — *straight*
 lunghi — *long*
 ondulati — *wavy*
 rasati — *very short/crew-cut*
 ricci — *curly* |

| **Ho gli occhi** *I have... eyes*

 Ha gli occhi *He/she has... eyes* | **azzurri** *blue*

 marroni *brown*

 neri *black*

 verdi *green* | **e** | **(non) porto** *I (don't) wear*
 (non) porta *he/she (doesn't) wear* → **gli occhiali** *glasses*

 (non) ho *I (don't) have*
 (non) ha *he/she (doesn't) have* → **i baffi** *a moustache* / **la barba** *a beard* |

Author's note: *the word for 'hair'-* **i capelli** *in Italian is a masculine* <u>plural</u> *noun. When describing hair you should follow this order: colour/length/style:* **Ho i capelli castani, lunghi e lisci** ☺. *As a result, all adjectives referring to capelli have to be plural and masculine.*

1. Fill in the blanks

a. Ho i capelli r_ _ _ _ .

b. Mio fratello _ _ i capelli _ _ _ _ _ _ _.

c. Ho _ _ _ occhi _ _ _ _ _ _ _.

d. Antonio _ _ i _ _ _ _ _ _ _ biondi e gli occhi

   _ _ _ _ _ .

e. _ _ _ sorella _ _ _ _ gli occhiali.

f. Ho _ _ _ _ _ _ _ _ corti e a _ _ _ _ _ _ _ _.

g. Luca ha gli _ _ _ _ _ marroni e _ _ _ _ _ la barba.

2. Break the flow

a. Hoicapellicastanielisci.

b. Hagliocchiazzurriegrandi.

c. Haicapellicastaniedimedialunghezza.

d. Haicapellicastanilunghiericci.

e. Nonhacapelli.

f. Hagliocchinerieportagliocchiali.

g. Hagliocchimarroniehaibaffi.

3. Arrange in the correct order

My name is Marcello	1
I am twelve years old.	
My birthday is on the 30th of March.	
I have dark brown, straight, short, hair.	
I am from Foggia, in Italy.	
He is blond and has green eyes.	
He is fifteen years old.	
His birthday is on the 14th of March.	
I have a brother.	

4. Spot the intruders: identify the word in each sentence the speaker is NOT saying

a. Ho i capelli molto lunghi.

b. Ho i capelli di media lunghezza.

c. Mio padre ha i capelli abbastanza corti.

d. Mia madre non ha i capelli lunghi.

e. Mio fratello minore ha i capelli biondi.

f. Mia sorella ha i capelli castani ricci.

5. Listen, spot and correct the errors

a. Ti chiamo Silvia.

b. Ho sedici anni.

c. Sono di Agrigento.

d. ...ma vivo a Cuneo.

e. Ho i capelli biondi e gli occhi marroni.

f. Ho i capelli lunghi e ondulati.

g. La mia migliore amica, Katia, ha diciotto anni.

h. È bella. Ha i capelli biondi, molto lunghi e lisci.

i. Ha gli occhi verdi e porta gli occhiali.

6. Fill in the blanks

a. Ho i capelli a spaz_ _ _ _.

b. Ho i capelli casta_ _ _ _.

c. Ho gli occhi ne_ _ _ _.

d. Ho i capelli lun_ _ _ _.

e. Ho gli occhi azz_ _ _ _.

f. Non porto gli occhi_ _ _ _.

g. Non ho i ba_ _ _ _.

h. Non porto la ba_ _ _ _.

i. Mio padre _ _ _ _ i baffi.

j. Mio fratello ha gli occhi ver_ _ _ _.

7. Narrow listening: gapped translation

My name is Gabriella, I am ____________ years old. My birthday is on the____________ of ____________. In my

family there are ____________ people: my father, my mother, my two ________________ and me. My mother

has _________, _________ and curly hair. She has _________ eyes. My father has grey, _________ and straight

hair. He has _________ eyes. My two sisters have _________, long and straight hair. They both have

_________ eyes. I have brown, ________________ hair. However, before, I used to have it _________.

8. Fill in the grid in English

Name	Age	Birthday	Siblings	Hair (3 details)	Eyes
a. Luigi	12		one brother one sister		brown
b. Andrea		20th June		brown, long, wavy	
c. Lucia	16		two brothers		blue
d. Eugenio		8th March		red, short, spiky	
e. Alice		19th May			

9. Translate the ten sentences you hear into English

a.   f.

b.   g.

c.   h.

d.   i.

e.   j.

Unit 7. Describing hair and eyes: VOCABULARY BUILDING

1. Complete with the missing word

a. Ho i capelli c__________.   *I have brown hair.*

b. Ho i capelli b________.   *I have blond hair.*

c. Porto gli o______________.   *I wear glasses.*

d. Ho gli occhi a__________.   *I have blue eyes.*

e. Non porto gli o____________. *I don't wear glasses.*

f. Ho i capelli n________.   *I have black hair.*

g. Ho i capelli r________.   *I have red hair.*

h. Ho i capelli di me______ lunghe________.
I have mid-length hair.

2. Match up

1. i capelli castani	a. *brown hair*
2. i capelli neri	b. *black eyes*
3. i capelli biondi	c. *moustache*
4. gli occhi neri	d. *green eyes*
5. gli occhiali	e. *black hair*
6. i baffi	f. *short hair*
7. gli occhi azzurri	g. *long hair*
8. gli occhi verdi	h. *red hair*
9. i capelli corti	i. *blond hair*
10. i capelli lunghi	j. *glasses*
11. i capelli rossi	k. *blue eyes*

3. Translate into English

a. i capelli ricci =   e. gli occhi verdi =

b. gli occhi azzurri =   f. i capelli rossi =

c. porto gli occhiali =   g. gli occhi neri =

d. i capelli biondi =   h. i capelli scuri =

4. Add the missing letter

a. lu__ghi   c. ca__elli   e. azzur__i   g. ric__i   i. s__uri   k. o__chi

b. occ__iali   d. baf__i   f. v__rdih. __isci   j. di media lun__hezza   l. por__o

5. Broken words

a. H__ i c__________ r________.   *I have curly hair.*

b. P______ g___ o____________.   *I wear glasses.*

c. __o i c__________ c______.   *I have short hair.*

d. N___ h__ i b________.   *I don't have a moustache.*

e. __o g___ o______ m____________. *I have brown eyes.*

f. __o __a b________.   *I have a beard.*

g. H__ o______ a______.   *I am eight years old.*

h. M__ c________ M______.   *My name is Maria.*

i. __o n______ a______.   *I am nine years old.*

6. Complete with a suitable word

a. Ho dieci __________ .

b. ________ la barba.

c. Mi __________ Antonio Bianchi.

d. Porto gli __________________.

e. Ho i __________ lisci e corti.

f. Ho __ baffi.

g. Ho ____ occhi marroni.

h. Ho ____ capelli neri.

i. Non ____ i baffi.

j. ____ i capelli lunghi e ondulati.

k. ______ chiamo Luca Ferrari.

l. Ho ____________ anni.

Unit 7. Describing hair and eyes: READING

Mi chiamo Marta. Ho dodici anni e vivo a Napoli, il capoluogo della Campania. Ho i capelli neri, lisci e corti e gli occhi azzurri. Porto gli occhiali. Il mio compleanno è il dieci settembre. Mia sorella ha i capelli lisci. Lei ha dieci anni e parla un po' tedesco.

Mi chiamo Alice. Ho quindici anni e vivo a Bellinzona, in Svizzera. Parlo italiano e francese. Ho i capelli rossi, ondulati e lunghi e gli occhi azzurri. Non porto gli occhiali. Il mio compleanno è il sedici dicembre.

Mi chiamo Naima. Ho nove anni e sono indiana. Vivo a Torino, il capoluogo del Piemonte. Ho i capelli castani, ondulati e di media lunghezza e gli occhi marroni. Non porto gli occhiali. Il mio compleanno è il cinque dicembre. Mio fratello si chiama Yamir. Ha quindici anni. Ha i capelli scuri, lunghi e lisci e gli occhi neri. Lui porta gli occhiali. Il suo compleanno è il tredici novembre. È molto muscoloso.

Mi chiamo Federico. Ho otto anni e vivo a Perugia, il capoluogo dell'Umbria. Ho i capelli castani, corti e ricci e gli occhi verdi. Porto gli occhiali. Il mio compleanno è il nove maggio. A casa ho tre animali: un cavallo, un cane e un gatto. Mio fratello si chiama Sergio. Ha quattordici anni. Ha i capelli biondi, lunghi e lisci e gli occhi verdi come me. Porta anche gli occhiali come mio padre. Il suo compleanno è il due giugno. È molto intelligente e parla il cinese.

Mi chiamo Giuseppe. Ho dieci anni e vivo a Bari, il capoluogo della Puglia. Ho i capelli biondi, lisci e corti e gli occhi verdi. Porto gli occhiali. Il mio compleanno è l'otto aprile. Parlo molto bene spagnolo ma non parlo inglese.

1. Find the Italian for the following items in Marta's text

a. my name is:

b. in naples:

c. i wear glasses:

d. my birthday is:

e. the tenth of:

f. i have:

g. straight:

h. speaks german:

i. the eyes:

2. Answer the following questions about Alice's text

a. How old is she?

_______________________.

b. Where is Bellinzona?

_______________________.

c. What colour is her hair?

_______________________.

d. What is her hair like?

_______________________.

e. What languages does she speak?

_______________________.

f. What colour are her eyes?

_______________________.

g. When is her birthday?

_______________________.

3. Complete with the missing words

Mi chiamo Roxana. _______ dieci anni e sono rumena. Vivo _____ Palermo, il capoluogo _______ Sicilia. Ho i _________ biondi, lisci e scalati e gli _______ verdi. _________ gli occhiali. Il mio compleanno ___ il ventisette maggio.

4. Find someone who: answer the questions below about all 5 texts

a. Who has a brother called Sergio?

_______________________.

b. Who is eight years old?

_______________________.

c. Who celebrates their birthday on 9 May?

_______________________.

d. How many people wear glasses?

_______________________.

e. Who has dark brown hair and black-coloured eyes?

_______________________.

f. Who can speak a bit of Chinese?

_______________________.

g. Whose birthday is in April?

_______________________.

h. Who has brown, wavy hair and brown eyes?

_______________________.

Unit 7. Describing hair and eyes: TRANSLATION

1. Faulty translation: spot and correct (in the English) any translation mistakes you find below

a. Ho i capelli biondi: *I have black eyes*

b. Ho gli occhi azzurri: *He has brown eyes*

c. Ho la barba: *He has a beard*

d. Si chiama Pedro: *I am called Pedro*

e. Ha i capelli a spazzola: *I have long hair*

f. Ho i capelli rasati: *I have coloured hair*

g. Vivo a Roma: *He is from Rome*

3. Phrase-level translation

a. 'the' blond hair _______________________

b. i am called_______________________

c. i have_______________________

d. 'the' blue eyes_______________________

e. 'the' straight hair_______________________

f. he has_______________________

g. ten years_______________________

h. i have black eyes_______________________

i. i have nine years_______________________

j. 'the' brown eyes_______________________

k. 'the' black hair_______________________

2. From Italian to English

a. Ho i capelli biondi.

b. Ho gli occhi azzurri.

c. Ho i capelli lisci.

d. Porta gli occhiali.

e. Ho i baffi e la barba.

f. Porto gli occhiali da sole.

g. Non ho la barba.

h. Ho i capelli a spazzola.

i. Ho i capelli ondulati.

4. Sentence-level translation

a. My name is Mark. I am ten years old. I have black and curly hair and blue eyes.

b. I am twelve years old. I have green eyes and blond, straight hair.

c. I am called Jessica. I live in Milan. I have long blond hair and brown eyes.

d. My name is Pietro. I live in Rome. I have black hair, short and spiky.

e. I am fifteen-years-old. I have black, curly long hair and green eyes.

f. I am thirteen years old. I have red, straight long hair and brown eyes.

Unit 7. Describing hair and eyes: WRITING

1. Split sentences

ho i capelli	occhi verdi.
ho la	barba.
ho gli	biondi.
ho i	e ricci.
ho i capelli biondi	capelli neri.
mi chiamo	anni.
ho dieci	Marta.

2. Rewrite the sentences in the correct order

a. capelli i Ho ricci.

b. ho la Non barba.

c. chiamo Mi Riccardo.

d. capelli Ho rossi i.

e. si fratello chiama Paolo Mio.

f. verdi occhi Ho gli.

3. Spot and correct the grammar and spelling errors

a. ho i capelli nero

b. mio fratello mi chiamo Antonio

c. ho capelli ricci

d. si chiamo Nadia

e. o cuatordici anni

f. ho il capello lisci

g. ho l'occhi verde

h. o la barba

i. porto li ochiali

j. ho no baffi

4. Anagrams

a. pellica = capelli

b. rbaba=

c. ohicc=

d. nina=

e. zuzarri=

f. dinbio=

g. rine=

h. cicri=

i. siros=

5. Guided writing – write 3 short paragraphs in the first person singular ['I'] describing the people below

Name	Age	Hair	Eyes	Glasses	Beard	Moustache
Peter	12	brown curly long	green	wears	does not have	has
Carla	11	blond straight short	blue	does not wear	does not have	does not have
Igor	10	red wavy medium length	black	wears	has	does not have

6. Describe this person in the third person:

Name: Cristian

Age: 15

Hair: black, curly, very short

Eyes: brown

Glasses: no

Beard: yes

1. Mi chiamo Angela e ho diciotto anni. Il mio compleanno è il venticinque luglio. Sono di Ischia. Vivo qui con la mia famiglia e il mio gatto, Messer Baffo. Oggi sono molto felice perché è il compleanno del mio gatto. Più tardi vado in spiaggia con i miei genitori e mio fratello Carlo. Amo nuotare nel mare con lui.

2. Nella mia famiglia siamo cinque persone: mio fratello maggiore, Carlo, mia sorella minore, Rosa, mio padre, Luca, mia madre, Isabella, ed io. Abbiamo anche un gatto che si chiama Messer Baffo. Mio padre è biondo e ha i capelli lunghi e lisci. Non porta la barba. Mia madre ha i capelli rossi e di media lunghezza. È molto bella e simpatica.

3. Il mio gatto, Messer Baffo, è piccolo e bianco. È molto divertente però a volte è un po' cattivo. Ha otto anni ed è molto tranquillo. Il suo compleanno è l'undici ottobre. Il suo cibo preferito è il pollo *(chicken)* ed il pesce *(fish)*. È intelligente però molto timido.

4. Mia sorella minore Rosa è molto carina e abbastanza intelligente. Ha gli occhi verdi e i capelli corti e ondulati. È molto divertente e mi fa sempre ridere *(always makes me laugh)*. A scuola la sua materia preferita è la chimica perché va molto d'accordo con la professoressa. Entrambe hanno una chimica perfetta. Non le piace l'arte perche crede che non sia molto utile..

5. Vivo con la mia famiglia e Messer Baffo (il gatto è parte della famiglia) in un appartamento piccolo in un edificio abbastanza moderno sulla costa. Adoro il mio appartamento perché è pulito e ho molti libri nella mia camera. Ci sono molte spiagge carine a Ischia. Vado sempre in spiaggia in bicicletta con la mia migliore amica Simona. La mia spiaggia preferita si chiama Citara.

6. Nel tempo libero mi piace rilassarmi e guardare qualche serie su Netflix. Quando fa bel tempo *(nice weather)* mi piace uscire *(go out)* con i miei amici e andare in centro a comprare vestiti *(clothes)* in qualche negozio. Mi piace anche fare attività all'aria aperta come fare footing nel parco o giocare a tennis. Adoro il cibo locale, il mio piatto preferito è la Parmigiana.

1. Complete the following translation of the first paragraph

My name is Angela and I am __________ years old. My birthday is on the _______ ____ July. I am _______ Ischia. I live here with my _______ and my _______, Lord Whiskers. Today I am very _______ because it is my ________ ___________. Later I am going to go to ____________ with my _________ and my _________ Carlo. I love __________ in the ________ with him.

2. Answer (in English) the questions below on paragraphs 2, 3 and 4

a. Who is Isabella?

b. What is her cat's name?

c. Who has long straight blond hair?

d. Who likes chicken and is sometimes a bit bad?

e. Who makes Angela laugh?

f. Who does Rosa have good chemistry with?

g. What does Rosa think about art?

3. Find the 9 mistakes in the following translation of paragraph 5

I live with my family and Mrs. Whiskers (the dog is really part of the family) in a small flat in a quite old building in the outskirts. I adore my flat because it's pretty and I have a lot of freedom in my bedroom. There are many beautiful trees in Ischia. I never go to the beach by bike with my best friend, Simona. My favourite mountain is called *Citara*.

4. Find the Italian equivalent for the items below in paragraphs 5 & 6

a. a small flat

b. I have many books

c. there are many…

d. beautiful beaches

e. my favourite beach

f. I like to relax

g. I like to go out

h. to the city centre

i. I love local food

j. my favourite dish

UNIT 8
Describing myself and another family member: physical and personality

In this unit you will learn:

- What your immediate family members are like
- Useful adjectives to describe them
- The third person of the verb 'Essere' (to be): 'è' (he is)
- All the persons of the verb 'Avere' in the present indicative

You will also revisit
- Numbers from 1 to 31
- Hair and eyes description

UNIT 8
Describing myself and another family member

Quante persone ci sono nelle tua famiglia?		*How many people are there in your family?*	
Com'è tuo padre/tua madre?		*What is your father/mother like?*	
Vai d'accordo con tuo fratello/tua sorella?		*Do you get on well with your brother/sister?*	

Nella mia famiglia ci sono quattro persone		*In my family there are four people*	
Ci sono cinque persone nella mia famiglia		*There are five people in my family*	

Mi piace *I like* **Non mi piace** *I don't like*	**il mio cane/gatto** *my dog/cat* **mio cugino Ian** *my cousin Ian* **mio fratello maggiore** *my older brother* **mio fratello minore** *my younger brother* **mio nonno Giacomo** *my grandfather Giacomo* **mio padre Gianni** *my father Gianni* **mio zio Ivan** *my uncle Ivan*		**è** *he is* **è abbastanza** *he is quite*	**alto** *tall* **basso** *short* **bello** *handsome* **bravo** *good* **cattivo** mean **chiacchierone** chatty **divertente** *funny* **forte** *strong* **generoso** *generous* **gentile** *kind* **grasso** *fat* **intelligente** *clever* **magro** *slim* **muscoloso** *muscly* **simpatico** *nice* **testardo** *stubborn* **tranquillo** *calm*
Vado d'accordo con *I get on well with* **Non vado d'accordo con** *I get on badly with*	**mia cugina Clara** *my cousin Clara* **mia madre Angela** *my mother Angela* **mia nonna Adele** *my grandmother Adele* **mia sorella maggiore** *my older sister* **mia sorella minore** *my younger sister* **la mia tartaruga** *my turtle* **mia zia Gina** *my aunt Gina*	**perché** *because*	**è molto** *she is very* **è un po'** *she is a bit*	**alta** **bassa** **bella** **brava** **cattiva** **chiacchierona** **divertente** **forte** **generosa** **gentile** **grassa** **intelligente** **magra** **muscolosa** **simpatica** **testarda** **tranquilla**

1. Multiple choice quiz: select which adjective you hear

		a	b	c
a.	My father is…	generous	mean	patient
b.	My older sister is…	silly	funny	muscly
c.	My mother is…	fat	clever	thin
d.	My younger sister is…	tall	short	pretty
e.	My cousin Paolo is…	big	strong	small
f.	My brother is not…	ugly	mean	friendly
g.	My cousin Marta is…	lazy	bad	boring
h.	My grandad is a bit…	mean	stubborn	annoying
i.	My grandma is…	generous	good	funny
j.	My boyfriend is…	patient	fat	muscly

2. Split sentences: listen and match

a. Giacomo		1. funny
b. Silvia		2. boring
c. Gianni		3. short
d. Pietro		4. tall
e. Marina		5. handsome
f. Corinna		**6. bad**
g. Enrico		7. muscly
h. Paolo		8. ugly
i. Paola		9. stubborn
j. Manuele		10. strong

3. Spot the intruders: identify the word in each sentence the speaker is NOT saying

a. Mio fratello è molto bello.

b. Mio zio Pietro ha quarantun anni. È abbastanza divertente.

c. Vado molto d'accordo con mio padre perché è paziente e generoso.

d. Mio cugino Ian non è molto alto.

e. Mio padre non è alto.

f. Mia cugina è troppo chiacchierona.

g. Io sono alto, muscoloso e forte.

4. Spot the differences and correct the text

a. Mia nonna è molto paziente.

b. Mia madre è molto intelligente.

c. Nella mia famiglia ci sono cinque persone: mia madre, mio padre, i miei due fratelli ed io.

d. Come stai?

e. Mio zio ha sessant'anni ma è molto noioso.

f. Non vado d'accordo con i miei genitori, specialmente con mia madre perché è molto antipatica.

g. Nella mia famiglia siamo tutti bassi.

5. Categories: listen to the words below and classify them in positive and negative

AGGETTIVI POSITIVI	AGGETTIVI NEGATIVI

6. Faulty translation: spot and correct the translation errors

a. My name is Luciana. I am 16 years old. I have dark brown hair and green eyes. I am tall, muscly and quite good-looking. I am nice, chatty and quite generous.

b. My mother is called Paola. She is 55 years old. She is short, slim and very funny. She is generous but a bit mean.

c. My father is called Roberto. He is 63 years old. He is neither tall nor short. He is very generous, mean and impatient.

d. My sister is called Carmela. She is 17. She is quite tall and slim, but sometimes a bit mean and boring. She is also quite funny and lazy.

e. I also have a cat. It is very beautiful, but it is funny.

7. Listen and complete with the correct masculine/feminine ending

a. È molto simpatic_ .

b. Sono molto testard _ .

c. Mia madre e mio padre sono molto alt_ .

d. Sono bass_ e pazient_ .

e. Come sei simpatic_!

f. Come sono cattiv_!

g. Le mi_ sorell_ sono molto diligent_ .

h. Come siete divertent_!

8. Listening slalom: follow the speaker from top to bottom and number the boxes accordingly

a. Nina	b. Manuela	c. Giovanni	d. Anna
My name is Nina	My name is Manuela	My name is Giovanni	My name is Anna
I am 15 years old	I am 17 years old and	I am 13 years old	I am 12 years old
I am tall and slim	I am neither tall nor short	I am not very tall	I am short and slim
My older sister is short and slim	My older sister is short and very pretty	My younger brother is short and slim	My younger brother is tall and strong
I like her	I get on very well with him	I get on well with him	I like her a lot
because he is nice and positive	because she is generous	because she is funny	because he is patient and calm. Also,
and kind.	Also, he is very funny.	he is very generous and kind.	and funny.

9. Narrow listening: fill in the grid

Name	Name of sibling or pets	Age of sibling or pets	Birthday of sibling or pets	Character of sibling or pets	Appearance of sibling or pets
a. Felice					
b. Andrea					
c. Eugenio					
d. Melania					

Unit 8. Describing my family: VOCABULARY BUILDING

1. complete with the missing word

a. nella mia famiglia _________ in...   *we are... in my family.*

b. ci sono__________ persone.   *there are five people.*

c. mia _________ giulia _...   *my mother giulia is...*

d. vado d' __________con mio...   *I get on well with my...*

e. non ______d'accordo...   *I don't get on well...*

f. ...con ______ nonno.   *...with my grandfather.*

g. mio zio___ molto educato.   *my uncle is very polite.*

h. mia _____ è molto simpatica.   *my aunt is very nice.*

2. Match up

1. forte	*a. intelligent*
2. simpatica	*b. kind*
3. intelligente	*c. good*
4. bravo	*d. funny*
5. chiacchierone	*e. boring*
6. divertente	*f. generous*
7. generoso	*g. nice*
8. gentile	*h. polite*
9. educato	*i. chatty*
10. noioso	*j. pretty*
11. bella	*k. strong*

3. Translate into English

a. mi piace mio zio.

b. ...perché è generoso.

c. è molto sportivo.

d. vado d'accordo con...

e. non mi piace mia zia...

f. ...perché è cattiva e severa.

g. sono gentile.

h. mio nonno è chiacchierone.

4. Add the missing letter

a. gent_le.   c. _impatico.   e. _ugino.   g. d'ac_ordo.   i. ci s_no.   k. mi pi_ce.

b. pers_ne.   d. n_ioso.   f. di_ertente.   h. ant_patico.   j. m_lto.   l. per_hé.

5. Broken words

a. N______ m__ fam_________c_ s____...
In my family there are.

b. ...q_________ p____________.
Four people.

c. M___ m_________ è m _______s_________________.
My mother is very nice.

d. V______ d'__________c____ ...
I get on well with.

e. M___ z_____ è m________ g________________ .
My uncle is very generous.

f. L_ m_____ f_________ è c___________ da...
My family consists of...

g. M__ s_________ h___ i c__________ l__________ .
My sister has long hair.

h. M___ p_______ è a_____________i________________.
My father is quite clever.

6. Complete with a suitable word

a. ci sono quattro________________

b. ________ simpatica

c. ________ d'accordo

d. è molto _________________

e. ha i ____________ biondi

f. _____ piace mia madre

g. vado ___________ con mia nonna

h. ...perché è _________ e buona

i. ha gli ________blu e grandi

j. mio cugino è _______ divertente

k. mia _________ è intelligente

l. mio nonno ha settant' __________

Unit 8. Describing my family: READING

Mi chiamo Alice. Ho nove anni e vivo a Glasgow, in Scozia. Siamo in cinque nelle mia famiglia: mio padre Mariusz, mia madre Giulia e le mie due sorelle, Olivia e Luna. Vado d'accordo con mia madre perché è paziente e gentile. Invece *[instead]* non vado d'accordo con Olivia perché è antipatica.

Mi chiamo Malika. Sono africana e vivo a Reggio Calabria, nel sud dell'Italia. Mi piace molto mio nonno perché è molto divertente. È intelligente ma timido.

Mio padre è abbastanza alto e grasso. Ha gli occhi marroni e i capelli rasati.

Mi chiamo Manolo. Ho quindici anni, sono argentino e vivo in Sicilia. Ho i capelli biondi a spazzola. Nella mia famiglia siamo in sei. Non vado d'accordo con mia sorella perché è testarda e antipatica. Vado d'accordo con i miei cugini perché sono molto simpatici.

Il mio cugino preferito si chiama Ian, è muscoloso e forte. È anche divertente ed educato. Ha i capelli scuri e corti e porta gli occhiali.

Sono Carlo Rossetti. Ho dieci anni e vivo a Milano, il capoluogo della Lombardia. Sono bello e intelligente. Nelle mia famiglia ci sono otto persone in totale. Mi piace mio zio Cesare e vado d'accordo con lui *[with him]* perché è simpatico e allegro. Invece, non mi piace mia zia perché è antipatica e severa!

Mia zia Maria ha i capelli biondi e ricci e gli occhi azzurri, come me *[like me]*. Il suo compleanno è il cinque maggio.

Mi chiamo Vasile. Ho dieci anni e vivo a Garda, in Italia. La mia famiglia è composta da cinque persone. Non vado d'accordo con mio padre perché è molto noioso e severo. Mi piace molto mia nonna perché è brava e generosa.

1. Find the Italian for the following items in Malika's text

a. I am called:

b. in the south:

c. my grandfather:

d. but:

e. very:

f. my father:

g. brown eyes:

h. very short hair:

2. Answer the following questions about Carlo's text

a. How old is he?

__________________________.

b. Where is he from?

__________________________.

c. Who does he get on well with?

__________________________.

d. Why does he like Cesare?

__________________________.

e. Who does he not like?

__________________________.

f. What does Maria look like?

__________________________.

3. Complete with the missing words

Mi chiamo Francesca e _____ otto anni. Sono indiana ma vivo _____ Verona. Nella mia famiglia ci _______sei persone. Vado d'accordo _______mio nonno perché ___ molto simpatico ___ buono. Mio padre _____ i capelli corti e ______ occhi verdi.

4. Find someone who? – answer the questions below about all 5 texts

a. Who has a granny who is very good?

____

b. Who is 15 years old?

____

c. Who celebrates their birthday on the 5th May?

____

d. Who is African?

____

e. Who gets on well with her mother?

____

f. Who has brown eyes and very short hair?

____

g. Who is muscly and strong?

____

Unit 8. Describing my family: TRANSLATION

1. Faulty translation: spot and correct any translation mistakes (in the English) you find below

a. Nella mia famiglia siamo in quattro:
In my family I have fourteen people

b. Mia madre Lina e mia sorella Katia:
My mother Lina is my cousin Katia

c. Non vado d'accordo con mio padre:
I get on very well with my father

d. Mio zio ha la barba:
My uncle has a moustache

e. Ivan è molto simpatico e gentile:
Ivan is very unfriendly and fun

3. Phrase-level translation

a. he is nice

b. she is generous

c. I get on well with…

d. I do not get along well with…

e. my uncle is fun

f. my little brother

g. I like my cousin Daniela

h. she has short and black hair

i. he has blue eyes

j. I don't like my granddad

k. he is very stubborn

l. …because she is generous

2. From Italian to English

a. Mi piace mio nonno.

b. Mia nonna è molto brava.

c. Mio cugino ha i capelli rasati.

d. Vado d'accordo con mio fratello maggiore.

e. Non vado d'accordo con mia cugina perché è noiosa e chiacchierona.

f. Mi piace mio zio perché è generoso.

g. Mio padre è simpatico e divertente.

h. Mio fratello minore è sportivo e gentile.

i. Non vado d'accordo con mio cugino Luca perché è stupido e cattivo.

4. Sentence-level translation

a. My name is Federico Bellini. I am nine years old. In my family there are four people.

b. My name is Carla. I have blue eyes. I get on well with my brother.

c. I do not like Bowser because he is stubborn and stupid.

d. My name is Peter. I live in Scotland. I like my uncle David because he is kind.

e. I do not get on well with my aunt because she is boring and talkative.

f. In my family we are five. I like my father because he is nice and polite.

Unit 8. Describing my family: WRITING

1. Split sentences

mio padre è	capelli neri
mia madre è	d'accordo con
ha gli	mio zio
ha i	simpatico
non mi piace	occhi neri
mi piace molto	mia zia
vado	generosa

2. Rewrite the sentences in the correct order

a. Nella sei famiglia sono ci mia persone.

_______________________________________.

b. Vado con fratello d'accordo mio.

_______________________________________.

c. È alto zio mio e magro.

_______________________________________.

d. Mia occhi gli madre ha azzurri.

_______________________________________.

e. Mia simpatica e zia è chiacchierona.

_______________________________________.

3. Spot and correct the grammar and spelling errors

a. nella mia famiglia ce sono

b. vado dacordo con

c. no mi piace mi zia

d. mia sorella e bello

e. non andare d'accordo con

f. mio padre e generosa

g. ho i occhi azurri

h. mio fratella sono gentile

i. ha il capello corti e ricci

j. io essere simpatica

4. Anagrams

a. fagliami =

b. patiantica =

c. ducateo =

d. blela =

e. inligtelente =

f. mispatica =

g. votispor =

h. vertendite =

5. Guided writing – write 3 short paragraphs describing the people below in the first person:

Name	Age	Family	Description	Likes	Dislikes
Piero	12	4 people	mother: brown eyes, long blond hair	older brother: because fun	cousin Gemma: because unfriendly
Leo	11	5 people	father: green eyes, short black hair	grandma: because very generous	uncle Emilio: because stubborn
Mike	10	3 people	grandpa: blue eyes, very short grey hair	younger sister: because polite and kind	aunt Carolina: very strong but talkative

6. Describe this person in the third person (*lui*/he):

Name: Uncle Antonio

Hair: blond, crew-cut

Eyes: blue

Opinion: get on well

Physical: tall and strong

Personality: nice, fun, generous.

TERM 2 - BRINGING IT ALL TOGETHER – 8

1. Mi chiamo Liliana. Ho quindici anni. Il mio compleanno è il diciotto marzo. Sono di Berlino, la capitale della Germania. Vivo qui con la mia famiglia. Oggi sono molto felice. Sono emozionata *(excited)* perché più tardi vado al parco con il mio miglior amico Dylan. Il mio amico Dylan è molto alto e divertente. Adoro fare footing con lui.

2. Nella mia famiglia siamo cinque persone: mio fratello maggiore Marco, mia sorella minore,Sofia, mio padre Luigi, mia madre Anna, ed io. Abbiamo anche un topo *(mouse)* grigio che si chiama Splinter. I miei nonni si chiamano Hans e Petra. Hans ha settantacinque anni e Petra ha settantadue anni. Sono molto gentili e simpatici.

3. Mio fratello maggiore si chiama Marco. A Marco piace la pittura (painting) e giocare a pallacanestro. Ha undici anni ed è molto creativo. Il suo compleanno è il venti novembre. Marco ha gli occhi marroni e i capelli rasati. È intelligente ma molto timido.

4. Mia sorella minore è simpatica e generosa. Ha gli occhi azzurri e i capelli lunghi e lisci. È molto bella ed elegante. A scuola la sua materia preferita è l'italiano perché ha i suoi amici in classe e il professore è molto bravo. Non gli piacciono le scienze perché sono un po' noiose.

5. Io e la mia famiglia viviamo in un appartamento in un edificio moderno nella periferia di Berlino. Adoro il mio appartamento perché è luminoso e tranquillo. C'è un parco vicino dove mi piace andare in bici. La mia migliore amica si chiama Lisa e anche a lei piace andare in bici con me *(with me)*. Ci divertiamo *(we have fun)* molto assieme.

6. Frequento *(I attend)* una scuola piccola nel mio quartiere. Non mi piace molto la mia scuola perché i professori sono abbastanza severi. Però, mi piacciono molto le lezioni di geografia perché imparo molto ed ho molti amici in classe. La mia materia preferita è l'inglese perché adoro leggere e scrivere storie.

7. Nel tempo libero mi piace esplorare nuovi posti *(places)* e andare al centro commerciale con la mia famiglia. Mi piace anche fare attività all'aria aperta come andare a passeggio nel parco e giocare a calcio. Non mi piace molto il cibo piccante *(spicy food)*, ma adoro il gelato alla fragola.

1. Complete the following translation of the first paragraph

My name is Lilana and I am ___________ years old. My birthday is on _________ March. I am from Berlin, the _________ of Germany. I live here with my family. Today I am very _______. I am ________ because later I am ______________ with my ______ _______, Dylan. My friend Dylan is very tall and _________. I adore going _________ with him.

2. Answer (in English) the questions below on paragraphs 2, 3 and 4

a. How many people are there in Lily's family?

b. What is her younger sister's name?

c. How old is her grandfather?

d. What two hobbies does her older brother do?

e. Who has a shaved head?

f. Who has long and straight hair?

g. What subject does her younger sister dislike? Why?

3. Find the 8 mistakes in the following translation of paragraph 5

My family and I live in a flat in a modern building in the centre of Berlin. I like my flat because it is spacious and beautiful. There is parking lot nearby where I like to go jogging. My best friend is called Lisa and she, too, likes to go jogging with me. We have a lot of fun at her house.

4. Find the Italian equivalent for the items below in paragraphs 6 and 7

a. A small school.

b. Quite strict.

c. I learn a lot.

d. I have many friends.

e. I adore reading.

f. In my free time.

g. New places.

h. Outdoors.

i. I love ice cream.

j. Strawberry.

1. Mi chiamo Sofia ed ho quattordici anni. Il mio compleanno è il ventitre giugno. Sono di Roma, la capitale italiana. Vivo qui con la mia famiglia. Oggi sono molto contenta. Sono molto felice perché dopo vado al museo con la mia migliore amica, Laura. La mia amica Laura è molto estroversa e divertente. Adoro fare sport con lei.

2. Nella mia famiglia siamo cinque persone: mio fratello maggiore Alessandro, mia sorella minore Valentina, mio padre Andrea, mia madre Elena, ed io. Abbiamo anche un gatto nero che si chiama Aramis. Si chiama così perché è un gatto coraggioso (*brave*). I miei nonni si chiamano Paolo e Martina. Paolo ha ottant'anni e Martina ha settantotto anni. Sono molto affettuosi (*affectionate*) e tranquilli.

3. Mio fratello maggiore si chiama Filippo. A Filippo piace suonare la chitarra e giocare a calcio. Ha dodici anni. Il suo compleanno è il dieci aprile. Filippo ha gli occhi azzurri e i capelli corti. È molto forte, divertente e socievole (*sociable*).

4. Mia cugina Alba è molto sportiva. Ha gli occhi verdi e i capelli lunghi e ricci. È molto intelligente e diligente. A scuola la sua materia preferita è la geografia perché dice che *(she says that)* la professoressa è molto brava e impara molto a lezione. Non le piace l'arte perché dice che non è molto utile.

5. Io e la mia famiglia viviamo in un appartamento piccolo nel centro di Roma, mi piace molto perché è antico e carino. C'è un parco vicino dove mi piace fare footing *(jogging)*. Nel fine settimana mi piace fare footing con la mia amica Carla.

6. Vado in una scuola piccola nel mio quartiere. Mi piace molto la mia scuola perché i professori sono molto intelligenti e mi aiutano sempre. Mi piace molto la storia perché imparo molto e il professore di storia è il mio professore preferito. Mi piace anche la biologia perché adoro imparare nuove cose (*new things*) sugli animali e sul corpo (*body*) umano .

7. Nel tempo libero, mi piace andare in piscina con con la mia famiglia. Mi piace anche andare al cinema a vedere film con i miei amici. Mi piace molto il cibo italiano. Adoro la pizza e il gelato. Il mio gusto (*flavour*) preferito è la stracciatella.

---

5. Spot and circle the 8 differences between the text below and the text in paragraph 1

Mi chiamo Sofia ed ho tredici anni. Il mio compleanno è il ventidue luglio. Sono di Roma, la capitale spagnola. Vivo qui con mia nonna. Oggi sono molto arrabbiata. Sono felice perché dopo vado al centro con la mia migliore amica, Laura. La mia amica Laura è molto estroversa e divertente. Mi piace uscire con lei.

---

6. Answer the following questions about paragraphs 1, 2 and 3

a. How is Sofia feeling today? Why?

b. What does she enjoy doing with Laura?

c. Who is Aramis?

d. Who is 78 years old?

e. What two hobbies does Filippo enjoy?

f. What five details does Sofia provide about Filippo's personality and appearance?

---

7. Complete the following translation of paragraph 4

My _____ Alba is very _______. She has _________ eyes and long ________ hair. She is very intelligent and ___________. At school, her favourite ___________ is geography because she says that the teacher is _____ _____ and that she _______ a lot in lessons. She _____ _____ art because she says it ___ _____ _________.

---

8. Identify and correct any inaccurate statement: paragraphs 5 to 7)

a. They live in a big flat outside Rome.

b. Her flat is modern.

c. She goes jogging every day of the week.

d. Her teachers are nice but not very helpful.

d. She learns a lot in her history lessons.

e. She enjoys going to the swimming pool with her friends.

UNIT 9
Comparing people's appearance and personality

UNIT 9
Comparing people

<table>
<tr><td colspan="5">Com'è il tuo migliore amico/la tua migliore amica? What is your best friend like?</td></tr>
<tr>
<td>Io</td>
<td>sono
am</td>
<td rowspan="2">più..
more

meno...
less</td>
<td>
affettuoso/a affectionate
bello/a good-looking
chiacchierone/a chatty
diligente hard-working
divertente funny
gentile kind
giovane young
grasso/a fat
intelligente intelligent
noioso/a boring
pigro/a lazy
rumoroso/a noisy
serio/a serious
sportivo/a sporty
sciocco/a silly
tranquillo/a relaxed
vecchio/a old
</td>
<td rowspan="2">di...
than</td>
<td>
Christian
Dylan
Gianfranco
Simona
Stefano
me me
te you
noi
voi
loro
mia madre
mia sorella
mio fratello
mio padre
mia zia
mio zio
</td>
</tr>
<tr>
<td>
Lei
Lui
Mia cugina
Mio nonno
La mia amica Sara
Il mio amico Ben
Il mio cane dog
Il mio cavallo horse
Il mio gatto cat
Il mio ragazzo bf
La mia ragazza gf
Francesca
Mario
</td>
<td>è
is</td>
</tr>
<tr>
<td>
I miei amici
I miei fratelli
I miei genitori
I miei zii
Le mie sorelle
Le mie amiche
Le mie zie
</td>
<td>sono
are</td>
<td></td>
<td>
affettuosi/e
gentili
giovani
sportivi/e
tranquilli/e
</td>
<td colspan="2">
del mio gatto
than my cat
del mio pappagallo
than my parrot

della mia tartaruga
than my turtle
</td>
</tr>
</table>

Mio fratello è serio quanto me	*My brother is as serious as me*
I miei amici sono gentili quanto me	*My friends are as kind as me*

Author's note: 1 The adjectives above ending in '**o**' change to '**a**' with feminine nouns. Ex. *Io sono bello/ Mia sorella è bella* 2 Feminine adjective ending in '**a**' change into '**e**' in the plural. *Ex. Le mie sorelle sono belle*
3 Adjectives ending in '**e**' do not change in the feminine. However, they change to '**i**' in the plural.
Ex: Mio fratello è intelligente / I miei fratelli sono intelligenti
* Comparison of equality in Italian uses '*tanto*' (as) … and '*quanto*' (as). However, '*tanto*' is only used in highly formal language and is frequently omitted in informal language. Ex: *Sono alto* **quanto** *mio fratello /Lei è bella* **come** me.

1. Multiple choice quiz: select the correct adjective

	1	2	3
a. Alex	boring	tall	friendly
b. Rosa	short	mean	young
c. Paolo	hard-working	noisy	calm
d. Franco	fat	slim	good-looking
e. Ada	strong	lazy	silly
f. Peppe	short	mean	young
g. Marta	strong	fat	silly
h. Samuele	slim	lazy	friendly
i. Teo	strong	sporty	serious
j. Lea	hard-working	noisy	lazy

2. Listening for detail: masculine or feminine?

	MASCULINE	FEMININE
a.	noioso	noiosa
b.	simpatico	simpatica
c.	pigro	pigra
d.	rumoroso	rumorosa
e.	tranquillo	tranquilla
f.	alto	alta
g.	simpatico	simpatica
h.	serio	seria
i.	magro	magra

3. Complete with 'più…di, 'meno…di or 'tanto…quanto as shown in the example

*e.g. Mia madre è **più** alta **di** mio padre.*

a. Mio fratello è _____ sportivo _____ me.

b. Il mio gatto è tranquillo _____ il mio cane.

c. Io sono _____ forte _____ mio cugino.

d. Mio nonno è _____ vecchio _____ mia nonna.

e. Il mio migliore amico è basso _____ me.

f. Mio zio è _____ grasso _____mio padre.

g. Mio cugino Ian è bello _____mio cugino Max.

4. Listen and fill in the middle column with the missing information in English.
e.g. Angela is taller than Filippo.

a. Silvia		**Alfonso**
b. Alfio		**Diego**
c. Michele		**Giacomo**
d. Matilde		**Gabriele**
e. Cornelia		**Paola**
f. Giulio		**Iolanda**
g. Filippo		**Giorgio**
h. Dylan		**Samuele**
i. Veronica		**Sergio**

5. Spot the differences and correct the text

a. Io sono più alto di mia madre.

b. Mio cugino è pigro quanto me.

c. Il mio migliore amico è più diligente di me.

d. Mia sorella è bella di mia madre.

e. Il mio cane è più rumoroso della mia tartaruga.

f. Mio nonno è meno serio di mia sorella.

g. Mia madre è tanto sportiva quanto mio fratello.

6. Listen, spot and correct the errors

a. Mia madre è più alta quanto me.

b. Mio fratello maggiore sono più forte di mio fratello minore.

c. Mio padre è più diligente di io.

d. Mio nonno è più vecchia di mia nonna.

e. I miei zii sono molti più vecchi dei miei genitori.

f. I miei nonni materni sono vecchio quanto i miei paterni nonni.

g. Io sono più magra di miei genitori.

h. I miei cugini è più ricchi di nostri.

8. Answer the questions below about Enzo

a. How old is he?

b. Where does he live?

c. How many people are there in the family?

d. Paolo is_____________ and ___________ than Giulio.

e. Giulio is ____________ and ____________than Paolo.

f. Why does he prefer his father?

g. He is as _____________ as his mother.

h. Which of his pets is the most talkative?

7. Listen and complete the translation

Person	Description
a. My father is...	
b. My mother is...	
c. My older brother is...	
d. My younger brother is...	
e. My sister is...	
f. My uncle is...	
g. My grandma is...	
h. My best friend is...	
i. My girlfriend is...	
j. My dog is...	

9. Listening slalom: follow the speaker from top to bottom and number the boxes accordingly

a	b	c	d
My father is more	My aunt is as	My mother is as	My friend is
affectionate as my father,	**talkative than my mother,**	less hard–working than my brother,	hard–working as my uncle,
as sporty as	as lazy as	**as tall as**	less generous than
my sister	me	my older sister	**my younger brother**
and a bit more	and more	**and nicer**	and as
boring	**than**	funny	intelligent than
as my cousin.	her sister.	than my goldfish.	**my older brother.**

Unit 9. Comparing people : VOCABULARY BUILDING

1. Complete with the missing word

a. Mio padre è più alto _______ mio fratello maggiore.   *My father is taller than my older brother.*

b. Mia madre è ________ chiacchierona di mia ________.   *My mother is less chatty than my aunt.*

c. Mio ________ è più basso di _____ padre.   *My grandfather is shorter than my father.*

d. I miei cugini sono più ___________ di _________.   *My cousins are lazier than us.*

e. Il mio cane _____ più ___________ del mio ________ .   *My dog is more noisy than my cat.*

f. Mia zia è ________ bella di ______ madre.   *My aunt is less pretty than my mother.*

g. Mio ___________ è più ________________ di me.   *My brother is more hard-working than me.*

h. Il mio maestro ___ più ______________ del mio pesce.   *My teacher is more chatty than my fish.*

i. Mio fratello minore è alto ________ me.   *My brother is as tall as me.*

2. Translate into English

a. i miei cugini sono

b. più affettuosi

c. meno simpatici

d. più diligente

e. di mia sorella

f. forte quanto

g. è più bello

h. della mia migliore amica

i. sono meno alto

j. è più vecchio

k. siamo più intelligenti

l. quanto mio zio

3. Spot and correct any English translation mistakes

a. Lui è più alto di me.   *He is taller than you.*

b. Lui è serio quanto me.   *He is as good-looking as me.*

c. Lui è meno tranquillo delle sue sorelle.   *He is less quiet than me.*

d. Io sono meno grasso di mio zio.   *I am stronger than my uncle.*

e. Siamo meno giovani di voi.   *We are shorter than us.*

f. Tu sei vecchia quanto lei.   *She is as old as him.*

g. Lara è sportiva quanto Mara.   *Lara is as sporty as Mara.*

4. Complete with a suitable word

a. Mia madre è ________ alta ________ me.

b. ____ padre _____ più giovane di mio zio.

c. I miei genitori sono alti quanto i _______ cugini.

d. I _____ fratelli ________ più sportivi delle mie sorelle.

e. Il mio _________ è meno affettuoso _______ mio cane.

f. I miei nonni _______ tranquilli ________ il mio gatto.

g. La mia amica è _______ bella della ____ tartaruga.

h. Mio zio non _____ forte ________ mia ___________.

5. Match the opposites

1. bello	a. basso
2. diligente	b. noioso
3. giovane	c. brutto
4. alto	d. sciocco
5. divertente	e. meno
6. simpatico	f. pigro
7. più	g. vecchio
8. intelligente	h. antipatico

Unit 9. Comparing people : READING

Mi chiamo Fausto. Ho ventitré anni e vivo in Svizzera. Nella mia famiglia siamo in cinque: mamma, papà, i miei fratelli Ale e Stefano ed io. Stefano è più alto, bello e forte di Ale, però Ale è più intelligente e diligente di Stefano. I miei genitori si chiamano Antonio e Nina. **Entrambi [both]** sono molto carini, ma mio padre è più severo di mia madre. Inoltre, mia madre è più paziente e meno testarda di mio padre. Io sono testardo quanto mio padre! In casa abbiamo due animali: un'anatra e un gatto. Sono entrambi molto simpatici, ma l'anatra è più rumorosa. Rumorosa quanto me...

Mi chiamo Mauro Ferrari. Ho quindici anni e vivo a Montalcino, in Toscana. La mia famiglia è composta da cinque persone: mamma, papà, mio fratello Marco e mia sorella Barbara. Marco è più sportivo di Barbara, ma Barbara è più alta e forte. I miei genitori si chiamano Fabio e Gabriella. Mi piace mio padre perché è meno severo di mia madre. Inoltre, mia madre è più antipatica di mio padre. In casa abbiamo due animali: un pappagallo e un criceto. Entrambi sono molto simpatici, ma il mio pappagallo è più chiacchierone. Chiacchierone quanto me...

Mi chiamo Victoria. Ho venti anni e vivo a Siena con i miei genitori e le mie due sorelle Ava e Grace. Ava è più bella di Grace, ma Grace è più simpatica.

I miei genitori sono affettuosi e gentili, ma mia madre è più divertente di mio padre. Inoltre, mia mamma è più buffa del mio papà . Io sono buffa quanto mio madre!

In casa abbiamo due animali: un cane e un coniglio. Entrambi sono molto grassi, ma il mio cane è più pigro. Pigro quanto me...

1. Find the Italian for the following in Fausto's text

a. I live in:

b. mum, dad:

c. good-looking:

d. hard-working:

e. less stubborn:

f. more patient:

g. but:

h. duck:

i. two pets:

j. very kind:

k. as stubborn as:

2. Complete the statements below based on Victoria's text

a. I am _______ years old.

b. Ava is more _________ than Grace.

c. Grace is more_______.

d. My parents are very _________ and ________.

e. My mum is __________ than my dad.

f. I am as ____________ as my mother.

g. We have _______ pets.

h. My dog is ________lazy.

3. Correct any of the statements below [about Mauro Ferrari's text] which are incorrect

a. Mauro Ferrari ha tre animali.

b. Marco è meno sportivo di Barbara.

c. Marco è più alto di Barbara.

d. Mauro è chiacchierone quanto il criceto.

e. Suo [his] padre è più severo di sua madre

4. Answer the questions on the three texts above

a. Where does Mauro Ferrari live?

b. Who is stricter, his mother or his father?

c. Who is as talkative as their parrot?

d. Who is as noisy as their duck?

e. Who has a stubborn father?

f. Who has a rabbit?

g. Who has a hamster?

h. Which one of Mauro's siblings is sportier?

i. Who is as funny as their mum?

Unit 9. Comparing people: TRANSLATION/WRITING

1. Translate into English

a. è pigro quanto…

b. è più giovane di….

c. meno gentile di…

d. sportivo quanto…

e. sono meno chiacchierone di…

f. è più testardo del mio amico…

g. sciocco quanto te…

h. sono più bello di lui…

i. è più brutto di me…

j. più… di…

k. meno…di…

l. sono forte quanto lei…

m. è più debole di loro…

n. …quanto

2. Gapped sentences

a. Mia mamma è _______ alta ______ mia zia.
My mum is taller than my aunt.

b. _____ padre _____ più _________ di mio fratello Maggiore.
My father is stronger than my older brother.

c. I miei cugini ________ meno_____________ di noi.
My cousins are less sporty than us.

d. _______ fratello è _______sciocco del suo ____________.
My brother is more stupid than his friend.

e. Mia nonna _____ gentile _________ mio nonno.
My granmother is as kind as my grandfather.

f. Alberta è _________ diligente di __________.
Alberta is more hard-working than us.

g. Il mio gatto è meno _____________ del_____ cane.
My cat is less friendly than my dog.

h. Andrew _____ _________ testardo ______ sua moglie.
Andrew is more stubborn than his wife.

3. Phrase-level feminine translation [En to It]

a. my mother is…

b. taller than…

c. as slim as…

d. less stubborn than…

e. I am shorter than…

f. my parents are…

g. my cousins are…

h. as fat as…

i. they are as strong as…

j. my grandparents are…

k. I am as lazy as…

4. Sentence-level translation [En to It]

a. My older sister is taller than my younger sister.

b. My father is as stubborn as my mother.

c. My teacher is more hard-working than me.

d. I am less intelligent than my brother.

e. My best friend is stronger and sportier than me.

f. My tortoise is less fast than my hamster.

g. My cousins are as friendly as my friends.

h. My duck is noisier than my dog.

i. Pedro is younger than Leonardo.

j. Ronaldo is faster than Giorgio.

k. We are as kind as my parents.

TERM 2 - BRINGING IT ALL TOGETHER – 9

1. Mi chiamo Nora ed ho quindici anni. Il mio compleanno è il venticinque agosto. Sono di un piccolo paese del Ticino in Svizzera che si chiama Airolo ma ora vivo a Milano, in Italia, con la mia famiglia. Oggi sono felice perché dopo vado in piscina per nuotare *(swim)* con il mio migliore amico Luca. Luca è molto divertente ed ha sempre buone idee. Adoro giocare a tennis con lui.

2. Nella mia famiglia siamo cinque persone: mio fratello maggiore Daniele, mia sorella minore, Sofia, mio padre Andrea, mia madre Maria, ed io. Preferisco mio padre perché è meno severo di mia madre. Però, mia madre è molto più paziente di mio padre. I miei nonni si chiamano Carlo e Anna. Carlo ha ottant'anni e Anna ha settant'anni. Sono molto affettuosi e giocano *(play)* sempre con noi *(with us)*. Mia madre è affettuosa quanto mia nonna ma mio nonno è più paziente di mio padre.

3. Mio fratello maggiore si chiama Daniele. A Daniele piace suonare la chitarra e giocare a pallacanestro. Ha diciassette anni ed è molto talentuoso *(talented)*. Il suo compleanno è il sette novembre. Daniele ha i capelli ricci e gli occhi verdi. Daniele è più alto di me, ma io sono un po' più divertente di lui.

4. Mia sorella minore, Sofia, è più creativa di mio fratello. Ha gli occhi azzurri e i capelli lisci. Le piace disegnare e fare danza classica. A scuola, la sua materia preferita è la storia perché le piace imparare cose interessanti (interesting things) sul passato *(about the past).* Non le piace la matematica perché è un po' complicata.

5. Io e la mia famglia viviamo in un appartamento accogliente nella periferia di Milano. Adoro il mio appartamento perché è luminoso. È sempre pulito. C'è un centro sportivo vicino casa mia dove mi piace fare sport. La mia migliore amica si chiama Emma e le piace andare in bici. Ci divertiamo molto insieme.

6. Vado in un liceo artistico nel mio quartiere. Mi piace la mia scuola perché i professori sono creativi e diligenti e ci aiutano sempre *(they always help us)*. Adoro anche le lezioni di danza contemporanea perché posso ballare liberamente con le mie amiche. La mia materia preferita è la pittura a olio *(oil painting)* perché adoro mescolare *(mix)* i colori e creare opere d'arte *(works of art)* mozzafiato *(impressive)*.

1. Complete the translation of paragraph 1

My name is Nora and I am _____ years old. My birthday is on ___ ______. I am from a ______ town in Ticino, Switzerland which is called Airolo, but now I live in Milan, in ______with my family. Today I am _____ because later I am going to go to the _______ to ______ with my _____ _____, Luca. Luca is very _____ and always has _____ _____. I ______ playing tennis with him.

2. Answer the following questions about paragraphs 2 to 4

a. Why does Nora prefer her father?

b. Who is very affectionate?

c. What hobbies does Daniele like?

d. What is Daniele's hair like?

e. Who is taller between Nora and Daniele?

f. Who is Sofia?

g. Why does Sofia dislike maths?

3. Find the Italian equivalent for the following in paragraphs 4 and 5

a. my younger sister.

b. straight hair.

c. her favourite subject.

d. we live in.

e. our flat.

f. it is always clean.

g. she likes to ride the bike.

4. Find the ten mistakes in the following translation of paragraph 6

I go to a science school in my town. I like my school because the teachers are creative and kind and always shout at us. Also, I like the classic dance class because I can chat freely with my male friends. My favourite hobby is oil painting because I adoro to choose colours and create beautiful works of art.

Mi chiamo Lucia e ho dodici anni. Il mio compleanno è il tre dicembre. Sono di Mantova, in Lombardia, ma ora vivo a Londra, la capitale dell'Inghilterra, con la mia famiglia. Oggi sono felice perché dopo vado a fare compere (*go shopping*) per comprare un regalo per mio fratello Luca. Vado con mia madre. Domenica è il suo compleanno! Luca è molto divertente e intelligente. Adoro giocare a pallacanestro con lui.

Nella mia famiglia siamo sei persone: mio fratello maggiore, Luca, mia sorella minore, Laura, mio padre Leo, mia madre Alice, mia nonna, Gloria, ed io. Preferisco mia nonna perché è più simpatica di mio padre. Mio padre è molto forte. Secondo me (*in my opinion*) si chiama Leo perché è forte come un leone. Mia nonna è molto buona con noi e ci ascolta *(listens to us)* sempre. Mia madre è divertente quanto mia nonna ed è molto più paziente di mio padre.

Mio fratello maggiore si chiama Luca. A Luca piace suonare il sassofono e giocare a scacchi. Ha quattordici anni ed è molto intelligente. Il suo compleanno è il sedici giugno. Luca ha i capelli neri, molto lunghi e lisci ed ha gli occhi marroni. Luca è più alto di me, ma io sono più bella.

Mia sorella maggiore Laura è più sportiva di me. Ha gli occhi marroni ed i capelli ricci. Le piace fare pesi (*to do weights*) e giocare a pallacanestro . A scuola, la sua materia preferita è l'educazione fisica perché, in questo modo, può fare ancora più sport *(even more sport)*. Non le piace l'arte perché lei non è molto artistica.

Io e la mia famiglia viviamo in una casa vecchia ma accogliente a Barking, nell'est di Londra. Mi piace la nostra casa perché è comoda. A volte non è pulita. Ho un cane grande che si chiama Rufus. Vicino a casa mia ci sono un parco e un lago dove mi piace fare footing e nuotare. La mia migliore amica si chiama Katie e anche a lei piace nuotare nel lago. Ci facciamo un sacco di risate *(we laugh)* assieme.

Vado in una scuola piccola nel mio quartiere. Mi piace la mia scuola perché i professori sono molto bravi e pazienti. Adoro le lezioni di storia perché il professore spiega le cose *(explains things)* molto bene ed ho molte amiche in classe. La mia materia preferita è il francese perché adoro parlare in francese e cantiamo *(we sing songs)* in classe.

5. Find someone who…

a. …is happy today.

b. …is intelligent.

c. …is as strong as a lion.

d. …always listens to Lucia.

e. …plays chess.

f. …has brown hair and curly hair.

g. …enjoys swimming in the lake.

h. …likes French.

6. Complete the sentences below

a. Today Lucia is going to go __________.

b. She and her mum are going to buy _______.

c. Her mum is as _______ as her grandmother.

d. Luca is _________ than Lucia.

e. Laura enjoys doing weights and __________.

f. Lucia's house is old but _________.

g. Lucia's house is not too clean at times because ___________.

h. Katie also enjoys__________________.

i. Lucia enjoys her history lessons because her teacher _______________.

j. Lucia enjoys speaking ___________.

7. Answer the following questions as if you were Lucia

a. Di dove sei?

b. Come stai oggi?

c. Quante persone ci sono nella tua famiglia?

d. Come sono i tuoi genitori?

e. Che cosa fa Luca nel tempo libero?

f. Quale sport piace a Laura?

g. Qual è la sua materia preferita?

h. Com'è la tua casa?

i. Chi è Rufus?

j. Com'è la tua scuola?

k. Come sono i professori?

l. Che ne pensi delle lezioni di storia?

m. Perché ti piace il francese?

TERM 2 – MIDPOINT – RETRIEVAL PRACTICE

1. Answer the following questions in Italian

Come ti chiami?	
Come stai oggi?	
Quante persone ci sono nella tua famiglia?	
Con chi vai d'accordo nella tua famiglia? Perché?	
Con chi non vai d'accordo nella tua famiglia? Perché?	
Quanti anni ha tuo fratello/tua sorella?	
Com'è tuo fratello/tua sorella?	
Quanti anni ha?	
Quando è il suo compleanno?	
Qual è il tuo professore preferito/la tua professoressa preferita? Perché?	
C'è un professore/una professoressa che non ti piace? Chi è? Perché?	

2. Write a paragraph in the first person singular (I) providing the following details

a. Your name is Sandra. You are 11 and are from England.

b. Today you are feeling good.

c. In your family there are four people: your father, mother and your younger sister.

d. You get on well with your mother but not with your father because he is very strict.

e. Your father is 40. He is quite tall and blond. He is intelligent and friendly .

f. Your mother is 38. She is short and has dark-hair. She is very kind and hard–working.

g. Your sister is called Deborah. She is 9. Her birthday is on 20th May. She is more hard-working and sporty than you but you are funnier.

h. Your school is big and you like it a lot because the teachers are kind and always listen to you.

i. You love Italian because the teacher is good, fun and always helps you. Also, you have friends in the class.

3. Write a paragraph in the third person singular (he/she) providing the following details about a friend

a. Name, age, birthday and where he/she lives.

b. How many people there are in their family and who they are.

c. Describe him/her in detail both in terms of appearance and personality.

d. Compare him/her with you in terms of height and personality.

e. Say if he/she gets on with their siblings or parents and why/why not.

f. Say how he/she feels about school.

g. Say which subjects they like/dislike and why.

h. Say who his/her favourite teacher is and why.

UNIT 10 – Describing my teachers and saying why I like them

In this unit will learn:
- How to say which teachers you like/dislike
- To give reasons for liking a teacher
- The good/bad qualities of a teacher
- More adjectives for describing people

You will revisit the following:
- School subjects
- Adjectival agreements – masculine/feminine

Unit 10
Describing my teachers and saying why I like them

Che professore/essa (non) ti piace? Perché?				Which teacher do you (not) like? Why?	
Ti piace il tuo professore di italiano ? Perché?				*Do you like your Italian teacher? Why?*	

Adoro *I adore* **Mi piace** *I like* **Non mi piace** *I don't like*	**il professore**	**di**	arte **educazione fisica** **francese** **informatica** **inglese** **italiano** **matematica** **musica** **scienze** **spagnolo** **storia** **teatro** **tedesco** **tecnologia**	**perché (non) è** *because he/she is (not)*	**antipatico** *mean* **diligente** *hard-working* **divertente** *funny* **noioso** *boring* **simpatico** *nice* **severo** *strict* **gentile** *kind* **impaziente** *impatient* **intelligente** *intelligent* **interessante** *interesting* **paziente** *patient* **antipatica** **diligente** **divertente** **noiosa** **simpatica** **severa**
	la professoressa				

Inoltre, *Furthermore*	**mi piace** *I like him/her* **non mi piace** *I don't like him/her*	**perché** **perché non**	**ci dà pochi compiti** *gives us little homework* **ci dà molti compiti** *gives us lots of homework* **mi aiuta** *helps me* **mi ascolta** *listens to me* **mi capisce** *understands me* **mi sgrida** *tells me off* **si arrabbia** *gets angry*	**raramente** *rarely* **sempre** *always* **mai** *ever*

1. Tick or cross? Tick the words you hear in each sentence and cross the ones you don't

a. arte

b. scienze

c. storia

d. teatro

e. matematica

f. geografia

g. italiano

h. tedesco

2. Fill in the gaps

a. Mi piace il professore di _________.

b. Mi _________ la professoressa di matematica.

c. Non mi piace ___ professore di tecnologia.

d. Non mi piace il professore di _________.

e. Mi piace la professoressa di _________.

f. Mi piace molto il professore di _________.

g. Mi piace la professoressa di _________.

h. Mi piace _________ la professoressa di italiano.

3. Spot the intruder

a. Mi piace molto il la professore di storia perché è paciente.

b. Mi piace la professoressa di inglese perché è raramente gentile.

c. Non mi piace il professore di tedesco perché è divertente.

d. Mi piace molto il professore di arte perché è molto diligente.

e. Non mi piace la professoressa di italiano perché non è noiosa.

f. Non mi piace la professoressa di scienze perché raramente ci dà molti compliti.

4. Faulty translation: correct the wrong translations

a. I like the Italian teacher a lot.

b. He does not get angry.

c. She gives us a lot of homework.

d. He never listens to me.

e. The art teacher helps me a lot.

f. She always tells me off.

5. Listen and write the Italian translation next to each sentence

a. I like my Italian teacher

b. she does not get angry

c. he understands me

d. he helps me

e. I like my science teacher

f. he is nice

g. he is mean

h. she is hardworking

6. Subjects & teachers: listen and tick the appropriate box

	Masculine	Feminine
a.		
b.		
c.		
d.		
e.		
f.		
g.		
h.		

7. Gapped translation

I like my school __ _______. My favourite subject is _______ because the teacher is very _______ and gives us _______ homework. Furthermore, he is very _______ and _______ __ a lot. I also like my _______ teacher because she is very kind and ___________and _____________me. She never _______ __________ and never _________ at me. However, I don't like my __________ teacher because he is very strict and _______. He always _______ ___ ___ and gives us __ _______ of homework.

<table>
<tr><td>

8. Complete with the missing letters

a. La professoress_ d_ stori_ è diligent_.

b. Il professor_ di geograf_a è antipatic_.

c. Mi piac_ la profe_soressa di sc_enze perché è gentil_.

d. Non m_ piac_ la professoressa di _rte perch_ è sever_.

e. Il mio profess_re di ing_ese è molto dili_ente e br_vo.

f. Il mio _rofessore di edu_azion_ fisica è m_lto noios_.

g. Ado_o la professore_sa di fra_cese perc_è è divertent_.

h. _on mi piac_ il p_ofessore di tede_co perché è sever_ .

</td><td>

9. Guess the next word, then listen to the track to see if you guessed right

a. La professoressa di scienze è...

b. Il professore di storia è...

c. Il professore di inglese è...

d. La professoressa di arte mi...

e. La professoressa di geografia è...

f. Il professore di tecnologia è...

g. La professoressa di musica è...

</td></tr>
</table>

10. Listen and fill in the grid

	Which subject?	Opinion	Why? (2 details)
e.g.	*French*	*Y*	*Teacher is funny and helps me a lot*
a.			
b.			
c.			
d.			
e.			
f.			
g.			

11. Listening slalom: follow the speaker from top to bottom and number the boxes accordingly

a	b	c	d
Mi piace	Non mi piace	Adoro	Mi piace molto
Il professore di inglese	**la professoressa di storia**	la professoressa di scienze	la professoressa di italiano
perché è divertente	perché è antipatica	**perché è simpatica**	perché è molto divertente
e interessante.	e diligente.	e pigra	**e paziente.**
È molto paziente	Non ci dà	**Lei mi capisce**	e non
molti compiti.	e non mi sgrida.	mi aiuta	**e mi aiuta sempre.**

Unit 10. Describing my teachers: VOCAB BUILDING

1. Match

è interessante	he is nice
è paziente	he is mean
è intelligente	he is interesting
è diligente	he is intelligent
è simpatico	he is patient
è antipatico	he is hard–working
è divertente	he is good
è bravo	he is boring
è noioso	he is fun

2. Translate into English

a. Mi piace:

b. La professoressa di storia:

c. Adoro:

d. È antipatica:

e. È simpatico:

f. Mi sgrida:

g. Ci dà molti compiti:

h. È divertente:

i. Mi aiuta:

j. Sempre:

3. Break the flow

a. Mipiacelaprofessoressadiscienzeperchéèmoltodiligente.

b. Nonmipiacelaprofessoressadiingleseperchéèmoltosevera.

c. Nonmipiaceilprofessoredimatematicaperchécidàmolticompiti.

d. Adoroilprofessoredimusicaperchénonsiarrabbiamai.

e. Mipiaceilprofessoredieducazionefisicaperchéèsimpatico.

f. Nonmipiaceilprofessoredifranceseperchéènoioso.

g. Adorolaprofessoressaditecnologiaperchéèdivertente.

h. Mipiacemoltoilprofessorediitalianoperchéègentileemicapisce.

4. Faulty translation

a. Il professore di tedesco: *The science teacher*

b. Mi piace molto: *I like him/her a bit*

c. Adoro: *I hate him*

d. Il professore di arte: *The history teacher*

e. Ci dà molti compiti: *He gives us little homework*

f. Mi aiuta sempre: *She always tells me off*

g. Non mi capisce: *He understands me*

h. Non si arrabbia mai: *He always gets angry*

i. È noiosa: *She is angry*

j. Lei è divertente: *He is funny*

5. Complete the table

Italiano	English
noioso	
divertente	
	kind
interessante	
simpatico	
	mean
paziente	
	hard–working

Unit 10. Describing my teachers: VOCAB BUILDING

6. Gapped Italian to English translation

a. Mi piace la professoressa di scienze.   *I like the _________ teacher.*

b. È molto severa.   *She is very _________.*

c. Ci dà molti compiti.   *He gives us __ _____ __homework.*

d. Adoro la professoressa di musica.   *I _________ the music teacher.*

e. Non si arrabbia mai.   *He _______ gets angry.*

f. Non mi piace il professore perché è noioso.   *I don't like the teacher because he is _________.*

g. Adoro la professoressa perché è divertente.   *I adore the teacher because she is _______.*

h. Mi piace molto perché è divertente.   *I like him a lot because he is _________.*

7. Complete with the correct option

a. Mi piace la professoressa di _________ perché è molto diligente.

b. Non mi piace la professoressa di inglese perché è molto _________.

c. Non mi piace la professoressa di matematica perché ci _________ molti compiti.

d. _________ la professoressa di musica perche non si arrabbia mai.

e. Mi piace il _________ di educazione física perché è gentile.

f. Non mi piace il professore di francese perché è _________.

g. Mi piace molto il professore di italiano _________ è divertente.

severa
professore
dà
adoro
noioso
perché
scienze

8. Sentence puzzle

a. professoressa la simpatica è   *The teacher is nice*

b. è il antipatico professore.   *The teacher is mean*

c. mi professoressa la piace.   *I like the teacher*

d. di inglese il professore.   *The English teacher*

e. professoressa la spagnolo di.   *The Spanish teacher*

f. la divertente professoressa è.   *The teacher is funny*

g. è professore il gentile.   *The teacher is kind*

9. Anagrams

e.g. coimspati: simpatico

a. rpfoereross

b. paticotian

c. verdidtente

d. im sgidra

e. ileentg

f. timol tipicom

10. Choose the correct word

a. La professoressa di *scienze/chienze.*

b. Il professore è *noiosa/noioso.*

c. *Si arrabbia/se arrabbia* sempre.

d. È *gentili/gentile.*

e. Il professore è *molto/molti* divertente.

f. Mi piace la professoressa perché è *simpatico/simpatica.*

g. Adoro la professoressa perché è *paziente/pazienta.*

h. Mi piace *molte/molto* il professore di spagnolo.

Unit 10. Describing my teachers: READING

Mi chiamo Marta. Ho undici anni e vivo a Bologna. La mia scuola si chiama 'Liceo Classico Virgilio' ed è molto buona. Studio molte materie. La mia materia preferita è lo spagnolo perché il professore è molto divertente, gentile e paziente e non ci dà molti compiti. Mi piace anche la professoressa di inglese perché è molto divertente, interessante e mi aiuta quando ho problemi. Non mi piace la professoressa di arte, perché è molto noiosa e antipatica. Mi sgrida sempre. Non mi piace neanche la professoressa di scienze perché ci dà molti compiti e si arrabbia sempre. Inoltre non mi aiuta mai.

Mi chiamo Giuseppe. Ho quindici anni e vivo a Cagliari. La mia scuola si chiama 'Liceo Scientifico Volta'. Studio molte materie, però mi piacciono solo la storia e la geografia perché i professori sono simpatici e molto bravi. Il professore di storia mi aiuta sempre quando non capisco qualcosa e il professore di geografia è gentile. Non mi piacciono le scienze perché la professoressa è noiosa e ci sgrida sempre. Non mi piace nemmeno la matematica perché la professoressa è molto severa e si arrabbia sempre. Odio (*I hate*) anche l'inglese perché il professore è molto antipatico e non mi aiuta mai quando ho problemi.

Mi chiamo Roberto. Ho tredici anni e vivo a Napoli. La mia scuola si chiama 'Liceo Linguistico Cervantes' ed è molto grande e buona. Studio molte materie e mi piacciono tutte. Adoro l'inglese perché la professoressa è molto gentile, diligente e molto divertente. Mi piacciono molto anche le scienze perché il professore è molto divertente e paziente, e mi aiuta sempre quando ho problemi. Inoltre, adoro la storia perché il professore è molto simpatico, divertente e imparo molte cose in classe. Non ci sgrida mai.

1. Find the Italian for the following in Marta's text

a. good

b. subjects

c. funny

d. homework

e. also

f. helps me

g. patient

h. very

i. mean

j. shouts at me

k. gets angry

2. Complete the statements below based on Giuseppe's text

a. I study _______ subjects.

b. I _____ like history and geography.

c. The history teacher always _________ ____ when I _____________.

d. The science teacher is _________ and __________.

e. Neither do I like maths because the teacher is very ___________ and ________ _________ easily.

3. Correct the incorrect statements about Roberto's text

a. Roberto only likes English, science and history.

b. The history teacher is boring.

c. The science teacher is funny.

d. The English teacher is a bit lazy.

e. The history teacher tells him off often.

4. Find someone who...

a. ...doesn't like science because the teacher is boring.

b. ...has a hard-working English teacher.

c. ...has a boring and mean art teacher.

d. ...has a helpful history teacher.

e. ...has a funny Spanish teacher.

f. ...learns a lot in the history lessons.

g. ...goes to a school which is big and good.

h. ...has an art teacher who always tells them off.

i. ...hates English.

j. ...has a geography teacher who's kind.

k. ...has a very fun history teacher.

Unit 10. Describing my teachers: WRITING

1. Translate into Italian
Please note: f = feminine, m = masculine

a. nice [f]

b. funny [m]

c. mean [f]

d. boring [m]

e. interesting

f. patient

g. fun [f]

2. Complete with a suitable word

a. Adoro la _ _ _ _ _ _ _ _ _ _ _ _ di scienze.

b. La professoressa di matematica _ gentile.

c. Mi _ _ _ _ _ perché è simpatico.

d. _ _ _ mi piace perché è impaziente.

e. Mi piace molto il professore di _ _ _ _ _ _ _ _.

f. Non mi piace _ _ _ _ _ _ è molto antipatico.

g. La professoressa di inglese è _ _ _ _ _ divertente.

h. _ _ professore di arte è molto noioso.

3. Broken words

a. la professo_ _ _ _ _ di scien_ _

b. è diver_ _ _ _ _

c. m_ sgr_ _ _

d. si arrab_ _ _

e. è no_ _ _a

f. è noi_ _ _

g. la _ _ _fessoressa di itali_ _ _

h. è molto inte_ _ _ _ _ _ _

i. ci d_ pochi comp_ _ _

j. ci _a mol_ _ com_ _ _ _

k. i_ professore è pazi_ _ _ _

l. mi aiu_ _ semp_ _

4. Complete the table

Masculine	Feminine
noioso	
divertente	
	brava
paziente	
	interessante
buono	
antipatico	

5. Spot and add in the missing word

a. La professoressa scienze.

b. Mi piace la professoressa di arte perché divertente.

c. Non piace il professore di educazione física.

d. Professore di matematica è molto noioso.

e. Il professore di spagnolo arrabbia sempre.

f. Adoro la professoressa di tedesco perché simpatica.

g. Il professore di storia ci molti compiti.

6. Tangled translation: into Italian

a. Non mi **like** la professoressa **of French.**

b. **I Adore the teacher** di **English.**

c. **She gives us a lot of** compiti.

d. Il professore di scienze **is patient.**

e. ci **gives few** compiti.

f. Il **teacher of maths** è molto **funny.**

g. La professoressa di **Spanish** mi **tells off.**

h. **The teacher** (m) **gets angry** sempre.

7. Translate into Italian

a. I don't like the science teacher because she is boring.

b. The French teacher gives a lot of homework.

c. The German teacher always helps me.

d. The maths teacher rarely gets angry.

e. The art teacher is funny and understands me.

f. The PE teacher is funny and gives us little homework.

g. The music teacher is mean and impatient.

h. The English teacher is interesting and hard-working.

TERM 2 - BRINGING IT ALL TOGETHER – 10

1. Mi chiamo Ornella ed ho quattordici anni. Il mio compleanno è il sedici giugno. Sono inglese ma vivo a Oslo, in Norvegia.

2. Nella mia famiglia siamo cinque persone: mio fratello maggiore, Luca, mia sorella minore, Marta, mio padre, William, mia madre, Claudia, ed io. Preferisco mia madre perché è più rilassata di mio padre. Mio padre è più severo.

3. I miei nonni si chiamano David e Mary. David ha sessantotto anni e Mary ha sessantanove anni. Sono molto affettuosi e a loro piace passare del tempo con noi. Mia madre è affettuosa quanto mia nonna, però mio nonno è più divertente di mio padre.

4. Mio fratello maggiore si chiama Luca. A Luca piace suonare il pianoforte e giocare a rugby. Ha sedici anni, è molto veloce e forte. Il suo compleanno è il nove ottobre. Luca ha i capelli castani e gli occhi azzurri. Luca è più organizzato di me ma io sono più creativa di lui.

5. Mia sorella minore è più artistica di mio fratello. Ha gli occhi verdi e i capelli ricci. A lei piace dipingere e ballare hip-hop. A scuola la sua materia preferita è l'informatica perché è utile per il futuro. Non le piace la matematica perché è complicata e noiosa.

6. Vado in una scuola abbastanza grande nel mio quartiere. Adoro la mia scuola perché i professori sono molto bravi. Sono comprensivi e ci aiutano quando abbiamo un problema. Inoltre, adoro le lezioni di musica perché posso esplorare diverse melodie con il pianoforte e scrivere canzoni. La mia materia preferita è la storia perché imparo molto in classe. La professoressa è abbastanza severa e a volte mi sgrida, ma è anche divertente e spiega le cose molto bene. Non so *(I don't know)* se mi piace o no.

7. Il mio professore preferito è il professore di geografia. Mi aiuta sempre quando non capisco ed è gentile. Però, non vado d'accordo con la mia professoressa di cinese perché si arrabbia sempre. Non imparo molto in classe.

1. Find the Italian equivalent for the following in paragraphs 1 to 4

a. I am from England

b. we are

c. my older brother

d. stricter

e. are called

f. they are affectionate

g. to spend time

h. he likes to play

i. strong

2. Complete the translation of paragraph 5

My _______ sister is more artistic than my brother. She has _____ eyes and _____ hair. She enjoys _______ and dancing hip hop. At school, her favourite subject is _______ because it is _______ for the future. She doesn't like maths because it is a bit complicated and _________.

3. Answer the following questions about paragraph 6

a. Where is Ornella's school located?

b. Why does she like her school?

c. What are her teachers like? (2)

d. Why does she like the music lesssons? (2)

e. What is her favourite subject? Why?

4. Translate the following phrases taken from paragraphs 6 and 7

a. sono comprensivi

b. ci aiutano

c. scrivere canzoni

d. imparo molto

e. mi sgrida

f. mi aiuta

g. gentile

h. però

i. non vado d'accordo

j. si arrabbia sempre

1. Mi chiamo Finn e ho tredici anni. Il mio compleanno è il diciotto luglio. Sono irlandese e ora vivo a Dublino la capitale d'Irlanda, con la mia famiglia. Sono tranquillo perché è domenica e non ho scuola.

2. Nella mia famiglia siamo cinque persone: mio fratello maggiore, Darragh, mia sorella minore, Aoife, mio padre, James, mia madre, Liz, ed io. Preferisco mio padre perché è più divertente di mia madre e mi aiuta sempre. I miei nonni si chiamano Eoin e Angela. Eoin ha sessantatré anni e Angela ha sessantaquattro anni. Sono molto divertenti e a loro piace andare al parco con noi. Mia madre è chiacchierona quanto mia nonna, ma mio nonno è più pigro di mio padre.

3. A Darragh, mio fratello maggiore, piace suonare la batteria (drums). Suona in un gruppo *(he plays in a band)* con i suoi amici. Ha quindici anni ed è molto gentile e tranquillo. Il suo compleanno è l'undici aprile. Darragh ha i capelli biondi e gli occhi verdi. Lui è più diligente di me, ma io sono più forte di lui.

4. Mia sorella minore Aoife è più bassa di mio fratello. Ha gli occhi marroni e i capelli lisci. Le piace andare al centro commerciale con le amiche a comprare vestiti. A scuola, la sua materia preferita è la chimica *(chemistry)* perché la professoressa è molto brava e impara molto in classe. Non le piace il teatro perché dice che è noioso.

5. Vado in una scuola molto grande nella mia città. La mia scuola è molto buona perché i professori sono molto intelligenti, divertenti e diligenti. Mi aiutano sempre se non capisco qualcosa. Adoro l'inglese perché mi piace leggere e scrivere storie *(write stories)*. La mia materia preferita è la musica perché la professoressa è molto divertente e mi aiuta sempre. È la mia professoressa preferita.

6. Il professore preferito di mia sorella è la professoressa di scienze. La aiuta sempre quando non capisce qualcosa ed è molto divertente. Però, non va d'accordo con la professoressa di storia perché dà molti compiti e la sgrida sempre (perché Aoife non fa i compiti). Aoife dice che non impara molto in classe.

5. Find someone who…

a. …is feeling calm today.

b. …always helps Finn.

c. …is 64 years old.

d. …enjoys playing the drums.

e. …has brown eyes and straight hair.

f. …has fun and hard–working teachers.

g. …is very kind and calm.

h. …always helps Finn when he doesn't understand something.

i. …likes buying clothes with friends.

6. Find the Italian in paragraph 4

a. shorter

b. straight hair

c. to buy clothes

d. very good

e. she says that

f. it is boring

7. Correct the errors in the following translation of paragraph 5

I go to a very small school in my city. The school is very good because the teachers are very intelligent, understanding and helpful. They always listen to me if I don't understand something. I like the English class because I love to speak and to write stories. My favourite game is music because the teacher is very talented and always praises me. She is my favourite teacher.

8. Find out the 4 words on the list below, which are not included in paragraph 6

a. is	e. also	i. a lot
b. but	f. always	j. my
c. however	g. never	k. in
d. with	h. that	l. for

UNIT 11
Saying what I and others do
in our free time

In this unit you will learn how to say:

- What activities you do using the verbs
  'giocare' (play), 'fare' (do) and 'andare' (go)
- How to use these verbs in the present
  indicative
- Other free time activities

You will revisit:
- Time and frequency markers
- Weather
- Expressing likes/dislikes
- Adjectives

THE LANGUAGE GYM
ITALIAN TRILOGY I

UNIT 11
Saying what I and others do in our free time

Che cosa fai nel tuo tempo libero?	*What do you do in your free time?*
Che cosa fa il tuo amico nel tempo libero?	*What does your friend do in their free time?*
Quale sport fai?	*What sports do you do?*
Fai un'altra attività?	*Do you do another activity?*
Ogni quanto fai sport?	*How often do you do sport?*

A volte *Sometimes* **Nel mio tempo libero** *In my free time* **Tutti i giorni** *Every day* **Il venerdì** *Friday* **Il sabato** *Saturday* **La domenica** *Sunday* *** Una volta alla settimana** *Once a week* ***Due volte alla settimana** *Twice a week* **Quando fa bel tempo** *When the weather is good* **Quando fa brutto tempo** *When the weather is bad*	**gioco** *I play* **il mio amico gioca** *my friend plays*	**a**	**pallacanestro**	*basketball*
			pallone/calcio	*football*
			pallavolo	*volleyball*
			scacchi	*chess*
			tennis	*tennis*
		alla	**playstation**	*PlayStation*
	faccio *I do* **il mio amico fa** *my friend does*		**atletica**	*athletics*
			arrampicata	*rock climbing*
			ciclismo	*cycling*
			equitazione	*horse riding*
			ginnastica	*exercise*
			i compiti	*homework*
			jogging	*jogging*
			nuoto	*swimming*
			pesi	*weights*
			trekking	*hiking*
			sci	*skiing*
	vado *I go* **il mio amico va** *my friend goes*		**a casa del mio amico**	*to my friend's house*
			al centro sportivo	*to the sports centre*
			al cinema	*to the cinema*
			al parco	*to the park*
			a pesca	*fishing*
			a sciare	*skiing*
			in bicicletta	*on a bike ride*
			in discoteca	*clubbing*
			in montagna	*to the mountains*
			in palestra	*to the gym*
			in piscina	*to the pool*
			in spiaggia	*to the beach*

***Note:** *Most adverbs or expressions of frequency (sometimes/ every day etc) can go either at the start or end of the sentence.*
E.g. ***Tutti i giorni faccio pesi/Faccio i pesi tutti i giorni.*** *However, some expressions, such as **due volte alla settimana** (twice a week) work better at the end of the sentence.*

1. Complete with GIOCO, FACCIO or VADO

a. ______________ a scacchi.

b. ____________ pesi.

c. ______________ a carte.

d. ______________ arrampicata.

e. ______________ in piscina.

f. ______________ in discoteca.

g. ______________ a casa del mio amico.

h. ______________ in palestra.

2. Complete with the missing syllables

a. Gioco ai videogio_ _ _.

b. Faccio ginnasti _ _.

c. Vado in pisci_ _.

d. Vado in disco_ _ _ _.

e. Faccio cicli_ _ _.

f. Vado in monta _ _ _.

g. _ _ _ co a tennis.

h. Vado in spiag _ _ _.

i. Vado al par_ _.

j. Faccio nuo_ _.

3. Listening for detail: what activities does Alice do each day? Tick the correct one

a.	**Monday**	▪ Cycling ▪ Chess ▪ Rock climbing
b.	**Tuesday**	▪ Going to the mountain ▪ Swimming ▪ Going clubbing
c.	**Wednesday**	▪ Going to the gym ▪ Playing basketball ▪ Playing tennis
d.	**Thursday**	▪ Jogging ▪ Homework ▪ Horse riding
e.	**Friday**	▪ Skiing ▪ Weights ▪ Chess
f.	**Saturday**	▪ Hiking ▪ Weights ▪ Bike riding
g.	**Sunday**	▪ Swimming ▪ Weights ▪ Fishing

4. Spot the intruder

Mi chiamo Daniel. Sono un tedesco. Sono molto sportivo. Nel mio tempo libero faccio molto sport. Il mio sport preferito è l'arrampicata libera. Faccio arrampicata quasi tutti i giorni. Quando c'è brutto tempo in generale rimango a casa e gioco a scacchi o gioco a carte con mio fratello minore. Mi piace anche molto fare nuoto. Faccio il nuoto quasi tutti i fine settimana nella piscina vicino a la casa mia.

5. Faulty translation: correct the translation

a. My name is Laura. I am red-haired and am very friendly and talkative.

b. I am not very sporty. I prefer to read books, to play chess, play cards and go shopping.

c. When the weather is nice I like to go hiking and from time to time…

d. … I go to the park with my boyfriend. I rarely go to the gym.

e. It is very boring in my opinion. I prefer to go jogging.

6. Listen to Dylan talk about his friends and fill in the grid below - in English

Name	Age	Description	Favourite subject	Favourite teacher	Favourite sport	How often they practise sport
a. Chris						
b. Aaron						
c. Mirella						
d. Stella						

7. Narrow listening - Gapped translation

My name is ___________ and I am ___________ years old. I am ___________ and I am a Sardinian. I am a

person from the the beautiful island of _______________. I live there with my ___________, two ___________

and one ___________. My parents are very ___________ and ___________. My brothers are very ___________

and my sister is _______ __ ______ helpful. My favourite subjects are ___________ and ___________. In my

free time I do a lot of ___________. I play ___________ at school ___________. I often do ___________ at

the gym near my house. Three times a week I ___ ___________ and from time to time I go to ______

___________ with my brothers. Besides sport, I also play ___________ and go to ___________ ` once a

week. I love _______________. Goodbye.

__Author's note:__ Please note that Sardinia is not named after sardines. The fish is actually named after the island due to its large presence in the waters surrounding the island. Sardinians are renowned for their healthy lifestyle, culinary expertise and unique cultural heritage and traditions.

Unit 11. Free time: VOCABULARY BUILDING

1. Match up

1. gioco a pallavolo	*a. I do horse-riding*
2. gioco a golf	*b. I play volleyball*
3. faccio equitazione	*c. I play basketball*
4. gioco a carte	*d. I play golf*
5. faccio ciclismo	*e. I go swimming*
6. faccio nuoto	*f. I play football*
7. gioco a calcio	*g. I go cycling*
8. gioco a pallacanestro	*h. I play cards*

2. Complete with the missing word

a. Gioco a ___________. *I play chess.*

b. ___________ equitazione. *I go horse riding.*

c. ___________ a carte. *I play cards.*

d. Mi piace fare _____________. *I like doing exercise.*

e. Gioco a ________________. *I play basketball.*

f. Faccio _______________. *I do athletics.*

g. Mi piace fare _____________. *I like going swimming.*

h. Faccio __________________. *I go rock climbing*

i. Faccio _______________. *I do weights.*

j. Non faccio i _____________ . *I don't do my homework.*

gioco	pesi	atletica	arrampicata	faccio
compiti	ginnastica	scacchi	pallacanestro	nuoto

3. Translate into English

a. Nel mio tempo libero gioco a calcio.

b. Spesso gioco a pallacanestro.

c. A volte faccio arrampicata.

d. Faccio raramente equitazione.

e. Quando fa bel tempo vado a pesca.

f. Tutti i giorni mi piace fare ciclismo.

g. Vado raramente in discoteca.

h. La domenica vado al cinema.

i. Quando fa bel tempo, vado in spiaggia

j. Faccio i compiti tutti i giorni.

k. A volte, vado a casa del mio amico.

4. Broken words

a. Faccio e_______________ *I go horse-riding*

b. Faccio n_______________ *I go swimming*

c. Vado a p_______________ *I go fishing*

d. Vado in b_______________ *I go on a bike ride*

e. Gioco a s_______________ *I play chess*

f. Vado in d_______________ *I go clubbing*

g. Gioco a c_______________ *I play cards*

h. Faccio a_______________ *I do rock climbing*

5. 'Vado', 'Gioco' or 'Faccio'?

a. __________ a pallacanestro

b. __________ in bicicletta

c. __________ a carte

d. __________ nuoto

e. __________ in montagna

f. __________ a tennis

g. __________ pesi

h. __________ equitazione

6. Bad translation – spot any translation errors and fix them

a. non vado mai in discoteca *I often go clubbing*

b. gioco a carte una volta alla settimana *I play chess often*

c. raramente faccio trekking *I go swimming rarely.*

d. quando fa bel tempo *when the weather is bad*

e. gioco a pallacanestro *I play football*

f. vado in bici due volte a settimana. *I go biking every day*

g. spesso gioco a scacchi *I never play chess*

h. faccio sempre arrampicata *I never go hiking*

i. spesso vado in piscina *I go swimming from time to time*

Mi chiamo Thomas. Sono tedesco. Nel mio tempo libero faccio molto sport. Il mio sport preferito è l'arrampicata. Faccio arrampicata tutti i giorni. Quando fa brutto tempo **sto a casa** *[I stay at home]* e gioco a scacchi o a carte. Mi piace giocare ai videogiochi, alla Playstation o alla Xbox. Gioco sempre alla Playstation.

Mi chiamo Veronica. Sono spagnola, di Barbastro. Ho i capelli rossi. Sono molto simpatica e divertente, ma non sono molto sportiva. Preferisco leggere libri *[reading books]*, giocare ai videogiochi o a scacchi e ascoltare musica. Quando fa bel tempo, tuttavia, corro nel parco del **mio quartiere** *[my area]* o gioco a tennis con mio fratello. Non mi piace andare in palestra, né in piscina. Odio il nuoto perché non mi piace l'acqua.

Mi chiamo Nicola. Sono inglese. Nel mio tempo libero mi piace molto leggere libri e giornali. Mi piace anche giocare a carte e a scacchi. Non sono molto sportiva ma vado in palestra una volta alla settimana e faccio pesi. Inoltre, quando fa bel tempo faccio trekking in campagna con il mio cane. Il mio cane si chiama Doug ed è grande e bianco.

Mi chiamo Annie. Sono francese. Adoro andare in bicicletta. Vado in bici tutti i giorni con i miei amici. È il mio sport preferito. A volte faccio arrampicata, nuoto o trekking. Non mi piace né il tennis né il calcio. Odio anche il nuoto. Mi piace giocare sul telefonino e **inviare** *[to send]* WhatsApp ai miei amici. Due volte alla settimana vado in discoteca col mio ragazzo. Amo ballare.

1. Find the Italian for the following in Thomas' text

a. I do a lot of sport

b. My favourite sport

c. Climbing

d. Every day

e. When the weather's bad

f. I play chess

g. Always

h. I play on the Playstation

2. Find the Italian in Annie's text for

a. I adore biking

b. With my friends

c. Sometimes

d. I do swimming

e. I go clubbing

f. I go rock climbing

g. With my boyfriend

h. Playing on the phone

3. Complete the following statements about Veronica

a. She is _____________ from _____________________.

b. She is very ______________ and _________________.

c. She plays videogames or _____________________.

d. When the weather is nice she _________________.

e. She also plays tennis with her_________________.

f. She doesn't enjoy the gym nor the _______________.

4. List 8 details about Nicola

1. _______________________.

2. _______________________.

3. _______________________.

4. _______________________.

5. _______________________.

6. _______________________.

7. _______________________.

8. _______________________.

5. Find someone who…

a. …enjoys reading newspapers.

b. …hates swimming.

c. …does a lot of sport.

d. …does weight lifting.

e. …goes clubbing twice a week.

Unit 11. Free time: TRANSLATION

1. Gapped translation

a. non vado mai in discoteca: *I ___________ go clubbing*

b. spesso gioco a pallacanestro: *I often play ______________*

c. gioco a tennis: *_ ______________ tennis*

d. due volte alla settimana: *____________ a week*

e. gioco a pallavolo: *I play ________________*

f. tutti i giorni gioco a carte: *every day I ________ ________*

g. a volte, vado al parco: *____________, I go to the park*

h. non faccio mai pesi: *I never do ______________*

i. quando fa bel tempo: *when the ________ __ ____*

j. faccio corsa: *I go _______________*

2. Translate to English

a. due volte a settimana

b. a volte

c. quando fa brutto tempo

d. a casa del mio amico

e. al centro sportivo

f. tutti i giorni

g. faccio arrampicata

h. vado in spiaggia

i. vado a pesca

3. Translate into English

a. Non vado mai a pesca con mio padre.

b. Gioco a carte con mio fratello.

c. Faccio trekking con mia madre.

d. Gioco a pallone con la mia migliore amica.

e. Raramente gioco alla playstation con mio cugino.

f. Spesso vado al cinema con la mia ragazza *[girlfriend]*.

4. Translate into Italian

a. bike: b________________________

b. rock climbing: a________________

c. basketball: p__________________

d. fishing: p____________________

e. weights: p___________________

f. videogames: v_________________

g. chess: s_____________________

h. cards: c_____________________

i. hiking: t____________________

j. jogging: c___________________

5. Translate into Italian

a. I do jogging

b. I play chess

c. I do rock climbing

d. I do swimming

e. I do horse riding

f. I do weights

g. I do my homework

h. I play videogames

i. I do cycling

j. I do exercise

Unit 11. Free time: WRITING

1. Split sentences

vado al centro	parco
spesso gioco	volte a settimana
vado a casa	sportivo tutti i giorni
faccio corsa nel	a pallavolo
gioco a	bicicletta
faccio sport due	della mia amica
a volte vado in	in palestra
faccio pesi	carte

2. Complete the sentences with a suitable word

a. Non _________ ginnastica.

b. A volte ____________ a pallavolo.

c. Raramente _________ arrampicata.

d. Spesso _________ equitazione.

e. Gioco a tennis _________ _____ giorni.

f. Vado a _________ del mio amico John.

g. Nel mio _________ libero mi piace nuotare.

h. Mi _________ giocare a rugby.

i. Gioco _____ golf una volta a settimana.

3. Spot and correct mistakes
[note: in some cases a word is missing]

a. Facio ecquitazione:

b. Giooco a palavolo:

c. Vado a casa mio amico:

d. Tutti giorni vado bicicletta:

e. Faccio gli compiti:

f. Vado a piscina:

g. Gioco a calicio:

h. Mi piace gioco a tennis:

4. Complete the words

a. Sca________________

b. Pallac________________

c. Ginn______________

d. Video______________

e. Equi______________

f. Atle______________

g. Pall________________

h. Pisc______________

5. Write a paragraph for each of the people below in the first person singular (I):

Name	Sport I do	How often	Who with	Where	Why I like it
Giovanni	hiking	every day	with my friend	in the countryside	it's fun
Dylan	weight-lifting	often	with my friend James	at home	it's healthy
Simona	jogging	when the weather is nice	alone	in the park	it's relaxing

1. Mi chiamo Liam e ho quindici anni. Il mio compleanno è il ventitré settembre. Sono irlandese ma ora vivo a Manchester, nel nordovest dell'Inghilterra, con la mia famiglia.

2. Nella mia famiglia siamo quattro persone: mio fratello maggiore, Noel, mio padre, Tommy, mia madre Margaret, ed io. Preferisco mia madre perché è più tranquilla di mio padre. Mio padre è molto diligente. I miei nonni si chiamano Thomas e Mary. Thomas ha settandadue anni e Mary ha sessantanove anni. Sono molto affettuosi e buoni con noi.

3. Mio fratello maggiore si chiama Noel. A Noel piace suonare la chitarra e cantare. Ha diciassette anni ed è molto talentuoso. Il suo compleanno è il quattordici novembre. Noel ha i capelli neri e gli occhi verdi. Noel è più organizzato di me, ma io canto meglio *(I sing better)* di lui.

4. A scuola, la mia materia preferita è la musica. Adoro scrivere canzoni *(writing songs)* e cantare *(singing)*. Non mi piace l'arte perché è un po' noiosa e non so se è utile per il futuro.

5. Adoro la mia scuola perché i professori sono bravi. Sono diligenti e sono sempre disposti *(willing)* ad aiutare quando abbiamo un problema. Inoltre, adoro la musica perché posso esplorare diversi ritmi con il pianoforte e comporre *(compose)* le mie canzoni. La mia materia preferita è la chimica perché mi piace capire *(understand)* le reazioni e fare esperimenti. La mia professoressa di chimica è esigente *(demanding)* ma anche divertente, e mi aiuta sempre in classe.

6. Nel mio tempo libero faccio molto sport. Il mio sport preferito è l'arrampicata. Faccio arrampicata tutti i giorni. Quando c'è brutto tempo rimango a casa e gioco ai videogiochi o a carte. Mi piace anche molto giocare alla Playstation con i miei amici. Quando c'è bel tempo, a volte, faccio jogging nel parco della mia zona o gioco a tennis con mio fratello Noel. Inoltre *(furthermore)*, mi piace andare in palestra e in piscina due volte alla settimana. Il nuoto è stancante ma molto divertente.

1. Answer the following questions in English

a. Where is Liam from?

b. Why does he prefer his mother to his father?

c. How old are his grandparents?

d. What is Noel's hair like?

e. Why does he not enjoy art at school?

f. Why does he like his school?

g. What's his favourite subject? Why? (2)

h. What is his favourite sport? How often does he play it?

i. What does he say about swimming? (2)

2. Find the Italian equivalent for the following in Liam's text

a. but now I live (par. 1)

b. we are (par. 2)

c. they are very affectionate (par. 2)

d. he is very talented (par. 3)

e. he has black hair (par. 3)

f. I don't know (par. 4)

g. the teachers are very good (par. 5)

h. I like to understand (par. 5)

i. she always helps me in lessons (par. 5)

j. in my free time (par. 6)

k. when the weather is bad (par. 6)

l. sometimes I go jogging (par. 6)

m. swimming is tiring (par. 6)

3. Complete the translation of paragraph 6 below

In my free time I do a lot of _______. My favourite sport is ________. I go ________ every day. When ____ ________ __ ____ I stay at home and I play videogames or _______. I also _______ _______ to play PlayStation with my friends. When the ________ is ________, sometimes I go ________ in the park in my ___________ or I play tennis with my ________ Noel. ________, I enjoy going to the _________ and to the ___________ twice a week. Swimming is ________ but very ________.

1. Mi chiamo Dora ed ho dodici anni. Il mio compleanno è il ventotto marzo. Sono inglese ma ora vivo a Valencia, nel sudest della Spagna, con la mia famiglia. Oggi sto così così perché sono stressata.

2. Nella mia famiglia ci sono tre persone: mio padre Alan, mia madre Becky ed io. Vado molto d'accordo con mia madre perché è più paziente di mio padre. Mio padre è molto pigro. I miei nonni si chiamano John e Louise. John ha settantasette anni e Louise ha sessantotto anni. Sono molto simpatici con me *(with me)* ma a volte mio nonno mi sgrida. Mio nonno è la persona più impaziente della mia famiglia, molto di più di mio padre e di mia madre.

3. Il mio migliore amico si chiama Chris. A Chris piace andare in spiaggia e fare surf con suo padre. Gli piace anche giocare ai videogiochi nel suo tempo libero. Ha dodici anni, come me. Il suo compleanno è il diciannove settembre. Chris ha i capelli biondi e gli occhi azzurri. Chris è più bello di me, ma è anche un po' più sciocco!

4. A scuola, la mia materia preferita è l'arte. Mi piace disegnare e dipingere. Però non mi piace molto la geografia perché è un po' noiosa. La verità *(the truth)* è che non mi interessa.

5. La mia scuola si chiama St. Mary's e i professori sono eccellenti. Sono molto intelligenti e mi ascoltano sempre quando ho un problema. Inoltre *(furthermore)*, mi piace l'inglese perché posso esplorare diversi stili e scrivere le mie storie. La mia materia preferita è la storia perché mi piace imparare cose sul *(about)* passato o sui personaggi storici famosi. La mia professoressa è molto divertente, mi aiuta sempre e non ci dà molti compiti.

6. Nel mio tempo libero leggo libri e ascolto la musica. Il mio gruppo preferito è 'Måneskin'. Mi piace anche cantare e suonare la chitarra. Lo faccio tutti i giorni. Quando c'è brutto tempo rimango a casa e guardo un film o leggo fumetti *(comics)*. Mi piace anche giocare ai videogiochi con i miei amici. Quando c'è bel tempo mi piace giocare a calcio nel centro sportivo *(sports centre)* vicino a casa mia. Inoltre, mi piace andare allo stadio a guardare le partite di calcio. La squadra dell'Inter è molto brava!

4. Answer the following questions about paragraphs 1 and 2 in Italian as if you were Dora

a. Come ti chiami?

b. Quanti anni hai?

c. Di dove sei?

d. Dove vivi ora?

e. Con chi vivi?

f. Come stai oggi?

g. Quante persone ci sono nella tua famiglia?

h. Chi è più paziente di tuo padre?

i. Quanti anni hanno i tuoi nonni?

j. Chi ti sgrida ogni tanto?

5. Translate the following words from paragraphs 3 and 4

a. migliore	h. più
b. andare	i. materia
c. fare	j. dipingere
d. il suo	k. però
e. anche	l. noiosa
f. ha	m. verità
g. come	n. che

6. Correct the following statements about Dora, based on paragraph 5

a. I professori di Dora non sono bravi.

b. I professori di Dora non l'ascoltano.

c. A Dora non piace l'inglese.

d. La sua materia preferita è la geografía.

e. La sua professoressa di storia è molto noiosa.

f. La sua professoressa di storia dà molti compiti.

7. Find the Italian equivalents in paragraph 5 and 6

a. I read: l	f. to sing: c
b. group: g	g. good: b
c. also: a	h. team: s
d. weather: t	i. films: f
e. comics: f	j. I watch: g

TERM 2 - BRINGING IT ALL TOGETHER – QUESTION SKILLS

1. Fill in the missing question words ((•

a. Q _____ persone ci sono nella tua famiglia?

b. C __ _____ vai d'accordo nella tua famiglia?

c. ___ ___ _ '_______ con qualcuno?______?

d. V__ _'_______ con tuo padre?

e. Q______ anni ha tuo fratello?

f. C_______ è tuo fratello?

g. Q______ è il suo compleanno?

h. T_ _____ il tuo professore di inglese?

i. C_______ è il tuo professore preferito?

j. _______ professore che non ti piace?

k. _______ professore ti aiuta sempre?

l. _______ è la tua materia preferita?

m. ___ _______ _____ nel tuo tempo libero?

n. _______ sport pratichi?

o. ___ _______ ___quando c'è brutto tempo?

2. Listen and choose the option that you hear ((•

a. Nella mia famiglia ci sono **quattro / tre** persone.

b. Vado d'accordo con mia **sorella / madre**.

c. Non vado d'accordo con mio **padre / fratello**.

d. A volte non vado d'accordo con mia **madre /sorella**.

e. Mio fratello ha **otto / nove** anni.

f. È abbastanza **alto / basso**, ha i capelli biondi.

g. Il suo compleanno è il diciannove **maggio / marzo**.

h. Sì, mi piace **abbastanza / molto**.

i. La mia materia preferita è l'**informatica / arte**.

j. Non mi piace molto la professoressa di **arte / storia**.

k. Il mio professore di **inglese / tecnologia**.

l. Adoro **le scienze / la matematica**.

m. Faccio **pesi/ciclismo**.

n. Vado in **palestra / piscina**.

o. **Rimango a casa / vado a casa dei miei amici**.

3. Listen and write in the missing information to the questions for exercise 1 ((•

a. Nella mia _______ ci sono _______ persone, i miei _______, mio _______ minore ed io.

b. Vado ___________con mia _______ perché è molto ___________.

c. A volte non _______ d'accordo con mio _______ perché è un po' _______.

d. Vado ______ _________ con mio _______ perché è molto ___________.

e. Mio _______ ha _______ anni.

f. È abbastanza _______, ha i capelli _______ e gli occhi _______.

g. Il suo ___________ è il ___________ di _______.

h. _______, mi piace _______ perché _______ le _______ molto _______.

i. Il mio professore ___________ è il professore di _________ perché è molto ___________.

j. Non mi _______ molto la mia professoressa di _________ perché è troppo _______.

k. Il mio professore di ___________ mi _______ sempre.

l. _______ le _______ perché _______ molto utili per il _______.

m. Nel mio tempo _______, vado a _______ del mio migliore _______ e giochiamo ai _________.

n. Faccio _______ e gioco a _________, e a volte gioco a _______.

o. Quando c'è _______ tempo, _______ a casa e_______ una serie o _______ un libro.

126

4. Fill in the grid with your personal information

Question	
1. Quante persone ci sono nella tua famiglia?	
2. Con chi vai d'accordo?	
3. Vai d'accordo con tuo padre/tua madre?	
4. Quanti anni ha tuo fratello/tua sorella?	
5. Com'è tuo fratello?	
6. Quando è il suo compleanno?	
7. Qual è il tuo professore preferito?	
8. C'è un professore che non ti piace?	
9. Qual è la tua materia preferita?	
10. Che cosa fai nel tuo tempo libero?	
11. Quale sport pratichi?	
12. Che cosa fai quando c'è bel tempo?	

5. Survey two of your classmates using the same questions as above– write down the main information you hear in Italian

Q.	Person 1	Person 2
1.		
2.		
3.		
4.		
5.		
6.		
7.		
8.		
9.		
10.		
11.		
12.		

No Snakes No Ladders

START

1 — There are four people in my family

2 — I get on well with my father

3 — I get on badly with my uncle

4 — He/she is twenty years old

5 — I like my mum because she is kind

6 — I don't like my cousin because he is stubborn

7 — My grandma is very good and fun

8 — My brother is quite clever and nice

9 — My cat is fatter than my dog

10 — My sister is more sporty than my brother

11 — My turtle is lazier than me

12 — I adore my German teacher (f)

13 — I don't like my science teacher (m)

14 — He is nice and interesting

15 — She is kind and hardworking

16 — He/she always helps me

17 — He/she always listens to me

18 — He/she never tells me off

19 — He/she always gives us lots of homework

20 — I like him/her because he/she never shouts at me

21 — He/she is always kind

22 — I always play cards

23 — I play football in the park

24 — I do horseriding with my friend

25 — I play with my friends

26 — When the weather is bad...

27 — When the weather is good...

28 — I go to the beach every day

29 — I go to the sports centre twice a week

30 — I go fishing with my father

FINISH

TERM 2

No Snakes No Ladders

PARTENZA	1 Ci sono quattro persone nella mia famiglia	2 Non vado d'accordo con mio padre	3 Non vado d'accordo con mio zio	4 Ha Vent'anni	5 Mi piace mia madre perché è gentile	6 Non mi piace mio cugino perché è testardo	7 Mia nonna è molto buona e divertente
15 (lei) è gentile e diligente	14 (lui) è simpatico ed interesante	13 Non mi piace la professoressa di scienze	12 Adoro la professoressa di tedesco	11 La mia tartaruga è più pigra di me	10 Mia sorella è più sportiva di mio fratello	9 Il mio gatto è più grasso del mio cane	8 Mio fratello è abbastanza intelligente e simpatico
16 Mi aiuta sempre	17 Mi ascolta sempre	18 Non mi sgrida mai	19 Ci dà sempre molti compiti	20 Mi piace perché non mi sgrida	21 È sempre gentile	22 Gioco sempre a carte	23 Gioco a calcio nel parco
ARRIVO	30 Vado a pesca con mio padre	29 Vado al centro sportivo due volte alla settimana	28 Vado in spiaggia tutti i giorni	27 Quando c'è brutto tempo…	26 Quando c'è bel tempo…	25 Gioco con i miei amici	24 Faccio equitazione con il mio amico

PYRAMID TRANSLATION

Term 2 - Recap - Free Time

Translate each part of the pyramid out loud with your partner, then write it into the spaces provided below.

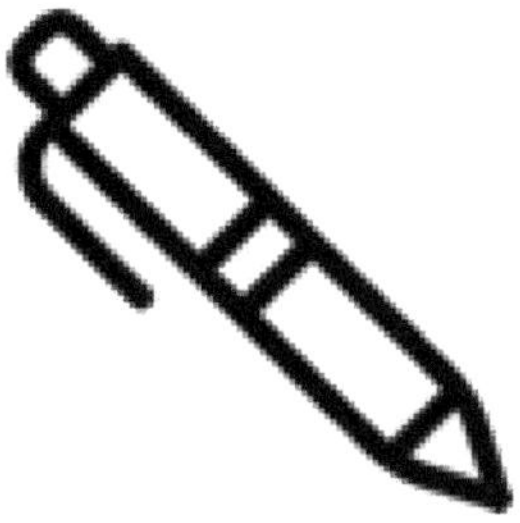

a. When...

b. When the weather is nice, I sometimes go jogging.

c. When the weather is nice, I sometimes go jogging in the park or play tennis...

d. When the weather is nice, I sometimes go jogging in the park or play tennis with my brother.

e. When the weather is nice, I sometimes go jogging in the park or play tennis with my brother. I do not go to the gym because it is very tiring.

f. When the weather is nice, I sometimes go jogging in the park or play tennis with my brother. I do not go to the gym because it is very tiring. However, I go to the pool every day. I adore it!

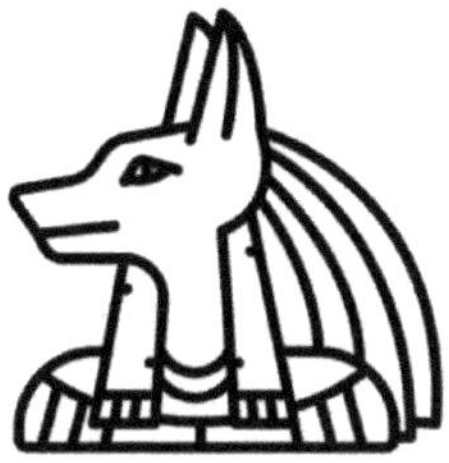

Write your translation here

SOLUTION: *Quando c'è bel tempo, a volte faccio trekking nel parco o gioco a tennis con mio fratello. Non vado in palestra perché è molto stancante. Però, vado in piscina tutti i giorni. Lo adoro!*

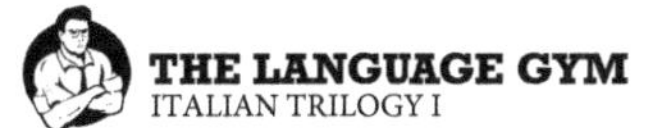

One pen One dice

Play in pairs. You only have 1 pen and 1 dice.
One person has the pen and starts translating the sentence into **English.** The other person rolls the dice until they roll a 6, they swap the pen and translate. The winner is the person who finishes translating all the sentences first.

1. Ci sono cinque persone nella mia famiglia.	
2. Vado d'accordo con mia madre.	
3. Ha quarant'anni.	
4. Mi piace mia nonna perché è gentile.	
5. Il mio cane è più divertente del mio gatto.	
6. Mia nonna è timida, ma è simpatica.	
7. Il mio professore mi aiuta sempre.	
8. Non mi sgrida.	
9. Quando c'è bel tempo...	
10. Vado sempre in spiaggia.	

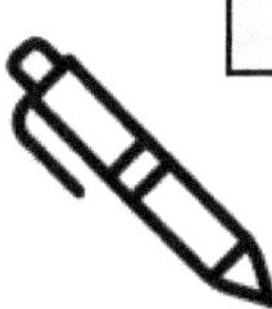

One pen One dice

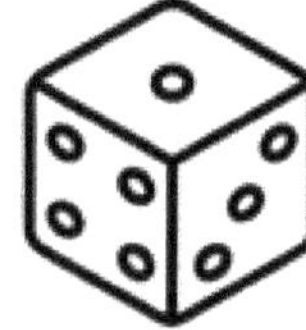

Play in pairs. You only have 1 pen and 1 dice.
One person has the pen and starts translating the sentence into **Italian.** The other person rolls the dice until they roll a 6, they swap the pen and translate. The winner is the person who finishes translating all the sentences first.

1. There are five people in my family.	
2. I get on well with my mother.	
3. She is forty years old.	
4. I like my grandma because she is caring.	
5. My dog is funnier than my cat.	
6. My grandmother is shy, but nice.	
7. My teacher (m) always helps me.	
8. He/she does not tells me off.	
9. When the weather is good...	
10. I always go to the beach.	

TERM 3 – OVERVIEW

This term you will learn:

Unit 12 - How to talk about daily routine/school day
- What you do every day
- What time you do it
- Linking sentences using 'poi, & 'dopo'

Unit 13 - How to talk about weekend plans
- To talk about your plans for the weekend
- To say where you are going using the present tense
- How to use "al", "allo" & "in" for places
- To say what you are going to do using "per + infinitive"

Unit 14 – How to talk about food – likes/dislikes
- How to say what food you like/dislike
- Why you like/dislike food
- Grammar: ARE verbs – amare/adorare/odiare

Unit 15 -How to talk about holiday plans
- Where you are going to go/stay
- How you will travel & who with
- What you will do there

KEY QUESTIONS

- A che ora ti svegli?	*What time do you wake up?*
- Che cosa fai la mattina?	*What do you do in the morning?*
- Che cosa mangi generalmente per colazione?	*What do you have for breakfast, normally?*
- A che ora esci di casa?	*What time do you leave the house?*
- Come vai a scuola?	*How do you get to school?*
- Quali programmi hai per la settimana prossima?	*What plans do you have for next weekend?*
- Dove vorresti andare?	*Where would you like to go?*
- Con chi vai?	*Who are you going to go with?*
- Che altro vorresti fare?	*What else would you like to do?*
- Cosa (non) ti piace mangiare? Perché?	*What do you (not) like to eat? Why?*
- Ti piace il pesce?	*Do you like fish?*
- Qual è il tuo cibo preferito?	*What is your favourite food?*
- Cosa odi mangiare?	*What do you hate to eat?*
- Dove andrai in vacanza quest'estate?	*Where are you going to go on holiday this summer?*
- Come viaggerai?	*How are you going to travel?*
- Quanto tempo passerai lì?	*How long are you going to spend there?*
- Dove starai?	*Where are you going to stay?*
- Che cosa ti piacerebbe fare lì?	*What would you like to do there?*

UNIT 12
Talking about my
daily routine/school day

UNIT 12
Talking about my daily routine/school day

Parlami della tua routine quotidiana				*Talk to me about your daily routine*		
A che ora ti alzi?				*What time do you get up?*		
Come vai a scuola?				*How do you get to school?*		
Che cosa fai dopo la scuola?				*What do you do after school?*		

	ceno *I have dinner*	* **all'una** *1*			**cinque** *5*
Di solito *Usually*	**esco di casa** *I leave my house*	**alle** *at*	**due** *2*	**e** *past* **meno** *to*	**dieci** *10*
Normalmente *Normally*	**faccio colazione** *I have breakfast*	**verso le** *at around*	**cinque** *5*		**un quarto** *quarter*
La mattina *In the morning*	**faccio i compiti** *I do my homework*		**sei** *6*		**venti** *20*
Il pomeriggio *In the afternoon*	**faccio la doccia** *I shower*	**dalle...alle** *from...to*	**sette** *7*		**venticinque** *25*
La sera *In the evening*	**mi alzo** *I get up*	**presto** *early*	**otto** *8*		
Lunedì *On Monday*	**mi lavo i denti** *I brush my teeth*	**tardi** *late*	**nove** *9*	**e mezza** *half past*	
Martedì *On Tuesday*	**mi pettino** *I comb my hair*	**poi** *then*	**dieci** *10*		
Mercoledì *On Wednesday*	**mi rilasso** *I relax*		**undici** *11*		
Giovedì *On Thursday*	**mi riposo** *I have a rest*	**dopo** *after*	**dodici** *12*	**in punto** *o' clock / on the dot*	
Venerdì *On Friday*	**mi sveglio** *I wake up*	**a** *at*	**mezzogiorno** *12pm / noon / midday*		
	mi vesto *I get dressed*		**mezzanotte** *12 am / midnight*		
Sabato *On Saturday*	**pranzo** *I have lunch*	**alle sette di mattina / del mattino** *at 7 in the morning*			
Domenica *On Sunday*	**vado a letto** *I go to bed*	**alle otto di sera / del pomeriggio** *at 8 in the evening*			
Tutti i giorni *Everyday*	**vado a scuola** *I go to school* **torno a casa** *I return home*	**a piedi** *on foot*	**in autobus** *by bus*	**in bici** *by bike*	

Author's note: * before *una* (1 o'clock) *la* shortens to *l'* before vowel. This means that in Italian you would say: *all'una (at 1) / verso l'una (at about 1) / dalle dodici all'una... (from 12 until 1 p.m.)*

1. Listen and fill in the gaps

a. Sono le sei e __ __ __ __ __ __ __ __.

b. È l' __ __ __.

c. Sono le sette e __ __ __ __ __ __.

d. Mi alzo verso le __ __ __ .

e. Esco di casa alle __ __ __ e mezza.

f. Vado a scuola alle sette __ __ __ __ un quarto.

g. Pranzo a __ __ __ __ __ __ __ __ __ __ __ __.

h. Faccio i compiti __ __ __ __ __ le cinque.

i. Vado a letto __ __ __ __ __ le nove.

2. Multiple choice quiz: daily routine times

	1	2	3
a.	6:00 pm	7:00 am	9:00 pm
b.	10:00 am	10:05 pm	10:10 am
c.	2:45 pm	3:45 pm	2:15 am
d.	6:15 pm	5:45 pm	6:05 am
e.	11:05 pm	10:55 am	10:25 am
f.	2:30 pm	2:15 am	2:20 pm
g.	3:15 pm	2:45 pm	2:35 pm
h.	12 pm	12 am	1 pm
i.	7:20 pm	7:10 am	7:45 am
j.	8:15 am	7:45 am	2:35 pm

3. Spot the differences and correct your text

a. Mi chiamo Federico. Sono francese. Mi sveglio sempre verso le sei e mezza.

b. Dopo mi faccio la doccia e mi lavo i denti .

c. La mattina non faccio colazione, ma mio fratello Valerio fa colazione in garage.

d. Vado a scuola in bici verso le sette e un quarto.

e. Torno a casa verso le quattro e dopo mi rilasso un po'.

f. Generalmente guardo la televisione in salotto.

g. Dopo navigo in internet, guardo una serie su Netflix o guardo i video di TikTok nella mia cucina.

h. Dopo, alle otto, preparo la cena con mia madre in cucina.

i. Adoro preparare l'insalata perché è deliziosa.

j. Vado a letto tardi, verso le undici.

4. Listen and write in English what Carmen does at each time

Time	Activity
6:30	
7:15	
8:00	
9:15	
3:30	
4:00	
6:30	
10:00	
11.00	

5. Listening slalom: follow the speaker and number the boxes accordingly

a. Miriam	b. Lucio	c. Paola	d. Sofia
Mi sveglio.	Mi alzo,	Mi faccio la doccia,	Mi vesto,
dopo vado in palestra.	Dopo mi alzo.	dopo faccio colazione.	esco di casa
e vado a scuola.	Dopo mi vesto	Più tardi preparo lo zaino	Dopo faccio la doccia
e poi esco di casa.	e poi esco di casa.	e poi mi pettino.	Torno a casa alle quattro
Dopo faccio i compiti.	e mi rilasso un po'.	Dopo, vado a scuola in macchina con mio padre.	Dopo vado a scuola.

6. Narrow listening: gapped translation

My name is Valentina. I am __________. I am from __________. My daily routine is very __________. Generally, I get up __________, at around five thirty. Then I shower and I get __________. __________, I have breakfast with my brothers. Then I ______ __ ________ and prepare my __________. At around __________ past seven I leave home and go to school. I __________ home at around four. Then I relax ___ ________. Generally I read my __________comics. From six to __________I do my homework. Then, at eight, I have __________. Afterwards, I read a __________or go on the __________. Then I __ ___ ____at 10:35.

7. Fill in the grid: What do the different people do?

	a. Me	b. My mother	c. My father	d. My sister
At 7:30				
At 8:15				
At 12:00				
From 3:00 to 4:00				
From 6:00 to 8:00				
From 8:30 to 11:00				

Unit 12. Talking about my daily routine: VOCAB BUILDING (Part 1)

1. Match up

1. mi alzo	*a. I have lunch*
2. vado a scuola	*b. I have dinner*
3. vado a letto	*c. I get up*
4. pranzo	*d. I have breakfast*
5. ceno	*e. I do my homework*
6. faccio colazione	*f. I go to school*
7. faccio i compiti	*g. I go back home*
8. torno a casa	*h. I go to bed*

2. Translate into English

a. Mi alzo alle sei del mattino.

b. Vado a letto alle undici di sera.

c. Mi lavo i denti.

d. Faccio colazione alle sette.

e. Torno a casa alle tre e mezza del pomeriggio.

f. Ceno verso le nove e poi mi riposo.

g. Guardo la televisione verso le quattro.

h. Vado a scuola alle otto.

i. Vado in palestra verso le otto e un quarto.

3. Complete with the missing words

a. _____________ a scuola. *I go to school.*

b. _____________ di casa. *I leave the house.*

c. _____________ a casa. *I come back home.*

d. _____________ la televisione. *I watch television.*

e. _____________ i compiti. *I do my homework.*

f. _______ _____ lavoro. *I go to work.*

g. _____________ sul telefonino. *I play on the phone.*

h. _____________ all'una. *I have lunch at one.*

4. Complete with the missing letters

a. _____ccio la doccia. *I have a shower.*

b. _____rno a ___asa. *I go back home.*

c. _____ lavo i de______. *I brush my teeth.*

d. _____nzo. *I have lunch.*

e. ___eno. *I have dinner.*

f. ___do a scuola. *I go to school.*

g. Mi _____zo. *I get up.*

h. Va___ a le_____. *I go to bed.*

i. ______rdo la televisione. *I watch tv.*

5. Faulty translation – spot and correct any translation mistakes. Not all translations are wrong.

a. Mi alzo sempre alle sei *I always shower at 6am*

b. Vado a letto a mezzanotte *I go to bed at noon*

c. Lunedì faccio i compiti *I do my homework on Tuesday*

d. Pranzo *I have lunch*

e. Vado a scuola *I come back from school*

f. Torno a casa *I leave the house*

g. Guardo la televisione *I watch television*

h. Esco di casa *I leave school*

i. Sabato suono il pianoforte *On Friday I play music*

6. Translate the following days and times into Italian

a. Monday at 6.30am

b. Thursday at 7.30am

c. Sunday at 8.20pm

d. Wednesday at midday

e. Friday at 9.20am

f. Tuesday at 11.00pm

g. Saturday at midnight

h. Today at 5.15pm

Unit 12. Talking about my daily routine: VOCAB BUILDING (Part 2)

1. Complete the table

vado a letto	
	I relax
mi alzo	
	I go back home
alle otto e un quarto	
pranzo	
	I have dinner
gioco sul telefonino	
	I leave the house
faccio colazione	
vado a scuola	
	I do my homework
mi vesto	

2. Complete the sentences using the words in the table below

a. alle sette e ____________   *at seven thirty*

b. ________ le cinque   *at around five o'clock*

c. alle________ del mattino   *at 8am*

d. a ________________   *at noon*

e. alle __________ e un quarto *at 11.15*

f. verso le tre ________ venti   *at around 2.40*

g. a ________________   *at midnight*

h. verso ________ quattro   *at around four o'clock*

i. _____ sette e venti   *at 7.20*

j. alle otto meno ________   *at 7.55*

cinque	mezza	alle	otto	mezzogiorno
undici	le	meno	verso	mezzanotte

3. Translate into English (numerical)

a. alle otto e mezza.   *at 8:30*

b. alle nove e un quarto.   ____________

c. alle dieci meno cinque.   ____________

d. a mezzogiorno.   ____________

e. a mezzanotte.   ____________

f. alle undici meno cinque.   ____________

g. alle dodici e venti.   ____________

h. alle sei e mezza.   ____________

4. Complete

a. Al____ c________ e m__________
At 5:30

b. Ve______ l__ o______ e u__ q________
At around 8:15

c. A m__________________
At noon

d. Verso l__ o______ m______ un q________
At around 7:45

e. A m__________________
At midnight

f. A____ u________ e m__________
At 11:30

g. Dal________ t______ alle qu____________
From 3 to 4

5. Translate the following into Italian

a. I go to school at around 8 ____

b. I come back home at around 4 ____

c. I have dinner at 7:30 ____

d. I do my homework at around 5:30 ____

e. I have breakfast at 6:45 ____

f. I go to bed at midnight ____

g. I have lunch at midday ____

Unit 12. Talking about my daily routine: READING (Part 1)

Mi chiamo Hiroto. Sono giapponese. Di solito durante il giorno faccio questo: mi alzo verso le sei, faccio la doccia e mi vesto. Dopo, faccio colazione con mio padre e mio fratello minore. Poi, mi lavo i denti e mi pettino. Verso le sette e mezza esco di casa e vado a scuola in bici. Torno a casa verso le quattro e guardo la televisione. Poi, vado al parco con i miei amici fino alle sei. Mi piace perché è divertente! La sera, dalle sei alle sette e mezza faccio i compiti e verso le otto, ceno con la mia famiglia. Non mangio molto. Solo un hamburger. Poi, guardo un film in tv e verso le undici, vado a letto.

Mi chiamo Andreas. Sono tedesco. Questa è la mia giornata tipica. Di solito, mi alzo **presto** *[early]*, verso le cinque. Faccio una corsa e poi faccio la doccia e mi vesto. Dopo, verso le sei e mezza, faccio colazione con mia madre e mia sorella. Mangio frutta. Poi mi lavo i denti e preparo lo zaino. Verso le sette e un quarto vado a scuola. Torno a casa verso le tre e mezza. Nel pomeriggio di solito guardo la tele o chatto con i miei amici su internet. Dalle sei alle otto faccio i compiti. Poi, alle otto e un quarto, ceno con la mia famiglia. Dopo cena, gioco alla playstation fino a mezzanotte. A mio parere, è appassionante. Ma a mia madre non piace! Infine, vado a **dormire** *[sleep]*.

Mi chiamo Raúl. Sono messicano. Di solito, mi alzo alle sei e un quarto. Poi faccio la doccia e faccio colazione con i miei fratelli. Dopo mi lavo i denti e preparo lo zaino. Verso le sette vado a scuola a piedi. Torno a casa verso le tre e mezza. Dopo mi riposo un po'. Normalmente navigo su internet, guardo una serie su Netflix o chatto con i miei amici su WhatsApp o Snapchat. Dalle cinque alle sei faccio i compiti. Secondo me è noioso. Ceno alle sette e mezza. Mangio riso o insalata. Poi guardo la tele e verso le undici e mezza vado a letto.

1. Answer the following questions about Hiroto

a. Where is he from?

b. At what time does he get up?

c. With whom does he have breakfast?

d. At what time does he leave the house?

e. Until what time does he stay at the park?

f. Why does he like it?

2. Find the Italian for the phrases below in Hiroto's text

a. at around eleven

b. with my friends

c. I go by bike

d. I go to the park

e. I shower and get dressed

f. I don't eat much

g. from six to seven thirty

h. I do my homework

3. Complete the statements below about Andreas' text

a. He gets up ____________ at around____________________.

b. He comes back from school at ____________________.

c. For breakfast he eats ________________________________.

d. He has breakfast with ______________ and ________________.

e. After getting up he ________________ and then showers.

f. Then he brushes his teeth and prepares ____________
____________. Around 7.15 he ____________________ .

g. Usually he ________________________________ until midnight, but
his mum ____________________________________.

4. Find the Italian for the following chunks in Raúl's text

a. I am Mexican

b. I shower

c. with my brothers

d. I relax a bit

e. I eat rice or salad

f. I surf the internet

g. I have dinner at half past seven

Unit 12. Talking about my daily routine: READING (Part 2)

Mi chiamo Yang. Ho dodici anni. Sono cinese. Questa è la mia giornata tipica. Di solito, mi alzo verso le sei e mezza. Poi faccio la doccia e mi vesto. Poi, faccio colazione con mia madre e mio fratello, Li Wei. Dopo mi lavo i denti e preparo lo zaino. Verso le sette e mezza esco di casa e vado a scuola. Torno a casa verso le quattro e mi riposo un po'. Nel pomeriggio guardo la televisione, ascolto la musica o gioco sul telefonino perché penso che è rilassante. Dalle sei alle sette e mezza faccio i compiti. Dopo, alle otto, ceno con la mia famiglia. Non mangio molto. Infine guardo un film e verso le undici vado a letto.

Mi chiamo Kim, sono inglese. Ho quindici anni. La mia routine quotidiana è molto semplice. Normalmente, mi sveglio presto, verso le cinque e mezza. Faccio una corsa e poi mi lavo e mi vesto. Dopo, verso le sette, faccio colazione con mia madre e la mia sorellastra. Poi, mi lavo i denti e preparo lo zaino. Verso le sette e mezza esco di casa e vado a scuola. Torno a casa dopo le tre. Poi, mi riposo un po'. Di solito, ascolto la musica o chatto con i miei amici su WhatsApp. Dalle sei alle otto faccio i compiti. Alle otto e un quarto, ceno con la mia famiglia. Dopo, guardo un film in tv **fino a** *[until]* mezzanotte. Infine, vado a letto.

Mi chiamo Anna. Sono italiana. La mia routine quotidiana è molto semplice. Di solito, mi alzo alle sei e un quarto. Poi faccio colazione con la mia sorella maggiore. Dopo mi lavo i denti e preparo lo zaino. Verso le sette vado a scuola in autobus. Torno a casa verso le due e mezza. Nel pomeriggio navigo su internet, guardo la televisione o leggo riviste di moda. A mio parere è fantastico! Verso le otto ceno con la mia famiglia. Mangio frutta o un'insalata. Poi leggo un libro o gioco sul tablet e verso le undici e mezza, vado a letto.

1. Find the Italian for the following in Yang's text

a. I am Chinese

b. my typical day

c. I shower

d. I prepare my bag

e. at around 7.30

f. I don't eat much

g. I watch television

h. I go to school

i. I do my homework

j. from six to seven thirty

k. I watch a movie

2. Translate these items from Kim's text

a. I am English

b. normally

c. around 5.30

d. with my mum and stepsister

e. I go back home

f. after three

g. I have dinner with my family

h. I rest a bit

i. I brush my teeth

j. I go for a run

3. Answer the following questions on Anna's text

a. What nationality is Anna?

b. At what time does she get up?

c. What three things does she do after school?

d. How does she go to school?

e. With whom does she have breakfast?

f. At what time does she go to bed?

g. What does she eat for dinner?

h. What does she do before going to bed?

4. Find someone who...

a. has breakfast with their older sister.

b. doesn't watch television at night.

c. reads fashion magazines.

d. gets up at 5.30am.

e. has breakfast with their brother and mother.

f. chats with their friends online after school.

g. does exercise in the morning.

Unit 12. Talking about my daily routine: WRITING

1. Split sentences

vado a scuola	casa
torno a	compiti
faccio i	in autobus
guardo	sul telefonino
gioco	alle dieci e mezza
mi alzo	di casa
vado a letto	verso le sei
esco	la televisione

2. Complete with the correct option

a. Mi alzo _______ sette del mattino.

b. Faccio _____ compiti.

c. Guardo _______ televisione.

d. _________ sul telefonino.

e. Vado a ____________ alle undici.

f. Torno _______ casa.

g. Esco di _________.

h. Vado a scuola _________ autobus.

a	letto	alle	in
la	i	casa	gioco

3. Spot and correct the grammar and spelling mistakes [in several cases a word is missing]

a. Vado a squola in bici.

b. Mi alzo a sette e mezza.

c. Esco casa alle otto.

d. Torno al casa.

e. Vado scuola in autobus.

f. Vado di letto verso le dieci.

g. Ceno alle oto meno quarto.

h. Faccio mio compiti alle cinque mezza.

4. Complete the words

a. qu_______.   *quarter*

b. me_______   *half*

c. al_____ di_____   *at 10*

d. v_______ l__ s_____   *at around six*

e. al_____ o_______   *at 8*

f. ve________   *twenty*

g. p___   *then*

h. p__________   *I have lunch*

i. e________ di casa   *I leave home*

j. g__________   *I play*

5. Guided writing – write 3 short paragraphs in the first person [I] using the details below

Person	Gets up	Showers	Goes to school	Comes back home	Watches television	Has dinner	Goes to bed
June	6.30	7.00	8.05	3.30	6.00	8.10	11.10
Frank	6.40	7.10	7.40	4.00	6.30	8.15	12.00
Anita	7.15	7.30	8.00	3.15	6.40	8.20	11.30

1. Mi chiamo Aoife e ho quindici anni. Il mio compleanno è il sette maggio. Sono irlandese e vivo a Limerick, nell'ovest dell' Irlanda, con la mia famiglia. Oggi sono felice perché è il mio compleanno, e anche il compleanno di mia sorella gemella (twin) Orla. Facciamo una festa di compleanno.

2. Nella mia famiglia siamo cinque persone: mio fratello maggiore, Conor, mia sorella gemella, Órla, mio padre, Patrick, mia madre, Siobhán, ed io. Preferisco mia madre perché è più paziente di mio padre. Mio padre è più interessante. I miei nonni si chiamano Sean e Maureen. Sean ha settantatre anni e Maureen ha sessantanove anni. Sono molto gentili e bravi.

3. Mio fratello maggiore si chiama Conor. A Conor piace suonare la batteria e praticare arti marziali. Ha diciassette anni ed è intelligente e diligente. Il suo compleanno è il ventidue novembre. Conor ha i capelli castani e gli occhi verdi. Conor è più bello di me, però io sono più divertente di lui.

4. La mia routine quotidiana è molto semplice *(simple)*. Generalmente, mi alzo presto, verso le sei e mezza. Faccio esercizio e dopo mi lavo e mi vesto. Dopo, verso le sette e un quarto, faccio colazione con mia madre e mia sorella Órla. Poi mi lavo i denti e preparo lo zaino. Verso le sette e mezza esco di casa e vado a scuola. Vado a scuola a cavallo perché è veloce e divertente.

5. A scuola, la mia materia preferita è l'italiano. Adoro cantare canzoni e parlare in italiano in classe. Ho molti amici in classe e il mio professore è molto divertente. Non mi piace molto la storia perché è un po' noiosa, ma è abbastanza utile per il futuro.

6. Torno a casa verso le tre. Poi, mi rilasso un po'. Generalmente, ascolto la musica o chiacchiero con i miei amici su internet. Dalle sei alle sette faccio i compiti e leggo un libro. Poi, alle otto e un quarto, ceno con la mia famiglia. Mi piace l' insalata. Poi, guardo un film alla televisione con mio fratello e mia sorella fino alle undici. Dopo, vado a dormire alle undici e un quarto.

---

1. Complete the sentences below using paragraphs 1, 2 and 3 as reference

a. My name is Aoife and I am _____________ years old.

b. Today I am feeling _____________.

c. My mother is more _____________ than my father.

d. My grandparents are very kind and _____________.

e. Conor enjoys playing _____________.

f. Conor is very intelligent and _____________.

g. He is more _____________ than Aoife.

---

2. Find the Italian equivalent for the following in paragraph 4

a. simple: s

b. early: p

c. then: p

d. I get dressed: m

e. around: v

f. I have breakfast: f

g. I brush my teeth: m

h. on horseback: a

---

3. Answer (in English) the following questions about paragraphs 5 and 6

a. What is Aoife's favourite subject?

b. Why? (4 details)

c. Why does she not like history?

d. What is good about history, though?

e. What does she do at 3:00 pm?

f. What does she do on the internet? (2 details)

g. What does she do from 6:00 to 7:00 pm?

h. At what time does she have dinner?

i. What kind of food does she like?

j. What does she do until 11:00?

k. Who with?

l. At what time does she go to bed?

1. Mi chiamo Orla ed ho quindici anni, come mia sorella gemella, Aoife! Il mio compleanno è il sette maggio. Sono irlandese e vivo a Limerick, nel over dell'Irlanda, con la mia famiglia.

2. Nella mia famiglia siamo cinque persone: mio fratello maggiore, Conor, mia sorella gemella, Aoife, mio padre Patrick, mia madre, Siobhán, ed io. Preferisco mia sorella gemella perché è più divertente di mio fratello. Mio padre è più severo di mia madre. I miei nonni si chiamano Sean e Maureen e sono molto divertenti ed affettuosi.

3. La mia migliore amica si chiama Ciara. A Ciara piace leggere libri e guardare la televisione. Ha quattordici anni ed è molto chiacchierona. È bassa e forte. Il suo compleanno è l'otto ottobre. Ciara ha i capelli neri, lunghi e lisci e gli occhi verdi.

4. La mia routine quotidiana è abbastanza semplice *(simple)*. Generalmente, mi alzo verso le sette meno un quarto. È abbastanza presto. Dopo faccio la doccia e mi pettino. Poi mi vesto e mi metto l'uniforme. Dopo faccio colazione con mia madre e mia sorella Aoife. Dopo mi lavo i denti e preparo lo zaino. Verso le sette e mezza esco di casa e vado a scuola con Aoife. Andiamo a scuola a cavallo perché è veloce e divertente.

5. A scuola, la mia materia preferita è il tedesco. Adoro parlare in tedesco in classe e la mia professoressa spiega sempre le cose molto bene. Ho molti amici in classe e la mia professoressa è molto divertente. Non mi piace molto la musica perché è un po' difficile e complicata.

6. Torno a casa verso le tre e mezza. Dopo, faccio i miei compiti. Generalmente, dopo i compiti vado in palestra e faccio arrampicata con i miei amici. Dalle sei alle sette mi metto su internet e chiacchiero con i miei amici. Dopo, alle otto e un quarto, ceno con la mia famiglia. Poi, guardo un film con mio fratello Conor e mia sorella Aoife fino alle undici. Dopo vado a letto alle undici e un quarto.

4. Find the Italian equivalent in par. 1 to 3

a. same as: c	h. than: d
b. birthday: c	i. to read: l
c. I live: v	j. books: l
d. older: m	k. to watch: g
e. twin sister: s	l. talkative: c
f. funnier: p	m. hair: c
g. strict: s	n. straight: l

5. Find the 13 mistakes in the following English translation of paragraph 4

My daily routine is very simple. Normally, I wake up at around seven-fifteen. It is quite late. Afterwards, I wash and I brush my teeth. Then, I get dressed and I put on my uniform. Afterwards, I have lunch with my mother and my cousin Aoife. Afterwards, I brush my hair and prepare my lunch. Around eight-thirty I leave the house and go to school with Aoife. We go to school by bike because it is fast and comfortable.

6. Answer the questions below on paragraphs 5 and 6 in Italian, as if you were Órla

a. Qual è la tua materia preferita?

b. Perché ti piace il tedesco?

c. Perché non ti piace la musica?

d. A che ora torni a casa generalmente?

e. Che cosa fai quando torni a casa?

f. Che cosa fai dopo i compiti?

g. Che cosa fai dalle sei alle sette del pomeriggio?

h. Con chi guardi la televisione dopo la cena?

i. A che ora vai a letto?

7. Identify and translate into English the SEVEN items on the list below which are not included in paragraph 6

a. dalle...alle...	e. verso	i. divertente
b. sorella	f. un po'	j. semplice
c. dopo	g. film	k. ceno
d. colazione	h. compiti	l. mi metto

UNIT 13 – Talking about weekend plans

In this unit you will learn:

- To talk about your plans for the weekend
- To say where you are going using the present tense
- How to use "al", "allo" & "in" for places
- To say what you are going to do using "per + infinitive"

You will revisit the following:

- Places
- Activities
- Friends and family members
- Adjectives

UNIT 13
Talking about weekend plans

Che programmi hai per il prossimo fine settimana?	*What plans do you have for next weekend?*
Dove vorresti andare?	*Where would you like to go?*
Che programmi ha tuo fratello/ tua sorella?	*What plans does your brother/sister have?*
Dove va tuo fratello/tua sorella?	*Where is your brother/sister going to go?*

Domani *Tomorrow* **Dopodomani** *The day after tomorrow* **La settimana prossima** *Next week* **Il fine settimana prossimo** *Next weekend* **Venerdì** *On Friday* **Sabato** *On Saturday*	**vado** *I am going to go* **vorrei andare** *I would like to go* **il mio amico/la mia amica va** *my friend is going to go* **mio* fratello va** *my brother is going to go* **mia* sorella va** *my sister is going to go* **vorrebbe andare** *he/she would like to go*	**al**	**centro commerciale** **centro sportivo** **cinema** **parco** **ristorante**	*shopping mall* *sports centre* *cinema* *park* *restaurant*
		allo	**stadio** **zoo**	*stadium* *zoo*
		in	**centro** **discoteca** **palestra** **piscina** **spiaggia** **vacanza**	*city centre* *disco* *gym* *pool* *beach* *holiday*

...con *...with*	**la mia** *my (f)* **la sua** *his/her (f)*	**migliore amica** *best friend (f)* **ragazza** *girlfriend*	**per** *(in order) to*	**andare in bici** **ballare** **comprare delle cose** **comprare vestiti** **fare pesi** **giocare a calcio** **mangiare** **nuotare** **prendere il sole** **guardare un film** **guardare una partita**	*ride a bike* *dance* *buy some things* *buy clothes* *do weights* *play football* *to eat* *swim* *sunbathe* *watch a film* *watch a match*
	il mio *my (m)* **il suo** *his/her (m)*	**migliore amico** *best friend (m)* **ragazzo** *boyfriend*			
	mia* *my (f)* **sua*** *his/her(f)*	**sorella** *sister*			
	mio* *my (m)* **suo*** *his/her (m)*	**fratello** *brother*			

Sarà noioso *It will be boring*	**Sarà stancante** *It will be tiring*	**Sarà divertente** *It will be fun*	**Sarà rilassante** *It will be relaxing*

***Author's note: when talking about singular family members, e.g. "mia sorella"** *my sister* **or "mio fratello"** *my brother* **you should omit the definite article "il/la". The same applies with other close family such as "mamma"** *mum* **"padre"** *dad* **"nonno"** *granddad* **& 'nonna'** *grandma.*

1. Sentence puzzle

a. fine il settimana prossimo

b. cinema al vado

c. amico va il piscina in mio

d. vorrei allo andare i con miei stadio amici

e. centro vado in

f. vado parco andare al bici in per

g. al cinema per guardare vado un film

h. vado centro al commerciale cose per delle comprare

2. Tick or cross

a. piscina

b. discoteca

c. cinema

d. stadio

e. centro

f. sport

g. partita

h. palestra

3. Listen and fill in the gaps

a. Il _______ settimana _________ vado al ________.

b. Vado ___ centro ___________ per comprare_________.

c. Il mio ________ amico va in _________ per _______ il sole.

d. Vado ____ parco_____ fare _______.

e. Vorrei ________ allo _________per guardare una _________.

f. Vado ____ cinema per ________ un ______.

g. Vado al ________ per _________ in bici con ___ miei amici.

h. Vado ____ discoteca _____ mia _______ maggiore.

4. Break the flow

a. Vadoalparco.

b. Vadoalcinema.

c. Vadoinspiaggia.

d. Ilmioamicovainpiscina.

e. Vadoalcentrocommerciale.

f. Vorreiandareallostadio.

g. Vadoalparcoperandareinbici.

h. Vadoallostadio.

5. Spot and cross out the intruder in each sentence

a. Il fine settimana no prossimo vado in discoteca.

b. Vado allo stadio per guardare in una partita di calcio.

c. Il mio amico Pietro va al parco con il mio fratello.

d. Il sabato mia sorella va al centro commerciale.

e. Domani vado in piscina. Sarà molto rilassante!

f. Il fine alla settimana prossimo vado in spiaggia.

6. Faulty translation: spot and fix the translation errors

a. I am going to the beach.

b. I am going to the gym.

c. I am going to the park.

d. I am going to the zoo.

e. I am going to buy clothes.

f. I am going to the beach.

7. Gapped translation: word level

_____ _________I am doing many things. First of all, on _____, after school, I am going to the _______ __________with my mother and _____ to buy clothes and other _____. It will be a bit _____. On Saturday I am going to the park to _______my _______and after that I am playing _____ with my friends. It will be _____. In the evening we are going to the _______ with my parents. On Sunday I am going to the _____ with my _____ to lift weights. It will be _____. After that, I am going ___ ____ _____with my_________Dino.

8. Write which place each person is going to go to

a.	
b.	
c.	
d.	
e.	
f.	
g.	

9. Gapped translation: phrase level

a. On Saturday I am going to the _________________________.

b. On Sunday I am going to the _________________________.

c. Next weekend I am going to the _________________________.

d. On Saturday I am going to the _________________________.

e. On Sunday I am going to the _________________________.

f. On Saturday I am going to the _________________________.

g. Next weekend I am going to the _________________________.

10. Arrange in the correct order

I'm going to the gym with my brother	
to watch an Inter Milan match.	
First, on Saturday	
I'm going to the stadium	
to do weights	
with my friends	
Next weekend	**1**
Then, on Sunday	
I'm doing many things.	
and to the pool to swim.	

11. Broken words

a. V_ _ _ _ al ci_ _ _ _ _ per guard_ _ _ un film.

b. Il fin_ setti_ _na pross_ _ _ vado al par_ _.

c. Saba_ _ vado allo st_ _ _ _ _.

d. Domeni _ _ vado in pa_ _ str_.

e. Sa_ _ stanca_ _ _ ma divert_ _te.

f. V_ _o al ce_tro co_ _erciale.

g. Vado _ _ pisc_ _ _ per nuot_ _ _.

h. Vado _ _ ristor_ _ _ _ per mangiare con la mi_ famig_ _ _.

12. Listening slalom

a.	b.	c.	d.
Next weekend	Next Saturday	Next Sunday	Today
I am going to the swimming pool	I am going to the gym	I am going to the park	I am going to the shopping centre
to do weights	to ride my bike	with my sister	to swim
with my best friend.	to buy clothes and other things.	with my friends.	with my older brother.
It will be relaxing.	It will be fun.	It will be tiring.	It will be a bit boring.

Unit 13. Talking about weekend plans: VOCAB BUILDING

1. Gapped translation

a. Vado al parco — *I am going to go to the _______________*

b. Vado in centro — *I am going to go to the _______________*

c. Vado in piscina — *I am going to go to the _______________*

d. Vado in palestra. — *I am going to go to the _______________*

e. Vado al centro commerciale. *I am going to go to the _______________*

f. Sarà stancante — *It will be _______________*

g. Sarà rilassante — *It will be _______________*

h. Sarà noioso — *It will be _______________*

i. Sarà divertente — *It will be _______________*

2. Match

piscina	bike
stancante	pool
spiaggia	park
bici	centre
ristorante	tiring
centro	restaurant
parco	gym
palestra	beach

3. Faulty translation

a. Vado al centro commerciale per comprare delle cose. — *I am going to the mall to buy clothes.*

b. Vado in piscina per nuotare. — *I am going to the swimming pool to play golf.*

c. Vado al parco per andare in bici. — *I am going to the park to go jogging.*

d. Vado in spiaggia per prendere il sole. — *I am going to the beach to play beach volley.*

e. Vado al centro commerciale per comprare vestiti. — *I am going to the sports centre to swim.*

f. Vado in centro. Sarà rilassante. — *I am going to the centre. It will be tiring.*

g. Mia sorella va in discoteca. Sarà divertente. — *My sister is going to shopping. It will be fun.*

h. Il mio migliore amico va allo stadio. — *My best friend is going to the disco.*

4. Complete with the correct option

a. Vado ____ parco — *I am going to the park*

b. Il fine settimana _______________ — *Next weekend*

c. Vado _____ spiaggia — *I am going the beach*

d. Vado a __________ — *I am going fishing*

e. Mi piacerebbe andare in ______ — *I would like to go to the disco*

f. Vado _____ discoteca — *I am going to the disco*

g. Per _____________ il sole — *To sunbathe*

h. Per andare in ____________ — *To ride a bike*

prendere	al	in	pesca
bici	**in**	**discoteca**	**prossimo**

5. Sentence puzzle

a. vado parco al

b. amico allo stadio mio va il

c. in vado centro

d. vado piscina in

e. al vado commerciale centro

f. va in mia sorella discoteca

g. vado palestra in

h. cose comprare per delle

i. spiaggia andare vorrei in

j. mio ristorante va al fratello

Unit 13. Talking about weekend plans: VOCAB BUILDING

6. Find the Italian for the words/phrases below

a	n	d	a	r	e	i	n	b	i	c	i	l
c	e	n	t	r	o	p	b	y	h	s	t	i
n	t	a	a	i	g	g	a	i	p	s	e	s
d	g	n	i	o	p	r	r	r	a	z	a	l
e	l	d	a	b	i	g	b	q	c	a	c	a
t	o	a	a	s	s	k	i	l	p	o	e	h
v	d	r	z	e	c	l	o	r	i	e	t	o
a	l	e	p	a	r	c	o	p	s	d	o	r
t	i	b	v	o	r	r	e	i	c	a	c	a
s	t	a	n	c	a	n	t	e	i	o	s	d
p	a	l	e	s	t	r	a	í	n	h	i	e
e	s	t	v	i	d	u	x	o	a	e	d	t

1. ride the bike
2. centre
3. gym
4. I would like
5. disco
6. park
7. swimming pool
8. to go
9. beach
10. tiring

7. Break the flow

a. Vadoalcentrocommercialepercomprarecose.

b. Vadoincentropercomprarevestiti.

c. Vadoalparcoperandareinbici.

d. Vadoindiscoteca.Saràdivertente.

e. Vadoinpalestraperfarepesi.Saràstancante.

f. Vadoinpiscinapernuotare.Saràrilassante.

8. Translate into English

a. Vado in centro

b. Vado in piscina

c. Vado in palestra

d. Vado al centro sportivo

e. Vado al parco per andare in bici

f. Vado in vacanza

9. Tick the 3 sentences which are error free and cross & correct the ones which contain errors

a. Vado in parco

b. Vado per comprare delle cose

c. Vado al discoteca

d. Vado in palestra

e. ...per andare allo bici

f. Il fine di settimana prossimo

g. Sarà rilaxante

h. Vorrei a andare a

i. Sarà noioso

10. Split sentences

Vado al	centro
Vado in	parco
Vado in piscina	commerciale
Vado al centro	stancante
Sarà	per nuotare
Vorrei	guardare un film
Vado al cinema per	andare in bici
Vado al parco per	andare in spiaggia

11. Complete with the missing letters

a. Vado in cen____

b. Vado in bi____

c. Sarà stanca____

d. Vorrei andare in discot____

e. Non vado al cin____

f. Sarà rilassa____

g. Vado al par____

h. Sarà diverte____

nte
ci
nte
eca
tro
nte
ema
co

Unit 13. Talking about weekend plans: READING

Mi chiamo Yang. Ho dodici anni. Sono cinese. Generalmente, il fine settimana non faccio molto. Sabato faccio i compiti, vado in internet e vado al centro commerciale con i miei amici. Domenica, ascolto la musica, gioco alla playstation e a volte gioco a scacchi con mio fratello maggiore. È molto divertente!

Il fine settimana prossimo, faccio molto sport. Sabato, vado al parco per andare in bici e al centro sportivo per giocare a pallacanestro con i miei amici. Domenica vado in piscina per fare nuoto con mio fratello maggiore e dopo in palestra per fare pesi. Sarà stancante!

Mi chiamo Kim. Generalmente, Il fine settimana faccio molto sport. La mattina faccio footing nel parco, gioco a calcio con i miei amici nel campo da calcio vicino casa mia e vado in piscina per fare pallanuoto.

Il fine settimana prossimo non faccio sport. Sabato vado al centro commerciale con i miei genitori per comprare delle magliette e un telefono nuovo. Dopo andiamo al ristorante italiano per mangiare una pizza. Il pomeriggio faccio i compiti. Domenica vado al parco per giocare a pallacanestro con con i miei amici e dopo vado al cinema con loro per guardare un film di fantascienza. Dopo vado a casa del mio migliore amico per giocare alla PlayStation.

Mi chiamo Anna. Generalmente, i fine settimana sono abbastanza noiosi. Vado al centro commerciale con mia madre, leggo un libro o guardo la televisione.

Sabato prossimo, vado in centro per comprare vestiti e un computer nuovo. Dopo, vado al cinema con le mie amiche per guardare un film comico. Domenica faccio molto sport. Vado al parco per correre e dopo vado al centro sportivo per fare ginnastica. Dopo vado a fare una passeggiata per il centro città con la mia migliore amica. Sarà divertente!

1. Find the Italian for the following in Yang's text

a. I don't do much

b. on Saturday

c. I play chess

d. next weekend

e. a lot of sport

f. to ride the bike

g. to play basketball

h. on Sunday

i. I am going to

j. older brother

k. afterwards

l. to do weights

2. Complete based on Kim's text

a. On weekends I do a lot of ___________.

b. In the morning I go ___________ in the park.

c. The football pitch is ___________ my house.

d. Next weekend I am ______ doing sport.

e. On Saturday I am going ___________ with my parents and I am going to buy a new ___________.

f. On Sunday I am going to the park to ___________.

g. After the cinema I am going to ___________ ___________ to play PlayStation.

4. Find someone who, next weekend, is going to...

a. ...buy a new computer

b. ...go to the city centre

c. ...do their homework

d. ...do weightlifting

e. ...do a lot of sport

f. ...buy T-shirts

g. ...swim with a sibling

3. Answer the following questions on Anna's text

a. What three things does Anna usually do at the weekend?

b. What is she buying in the city centre?

c. What is she watching at the cinema?

d. What is she doing at the park?

e. What is she doing at the sports centre?

f. What is she doing in the city centre?

Unit 13. Talking about weekend plans: WRITING

1. Broken words

a. vado al ci_ _ ma con i mi_ _ amic_.

b. i_ fin_ settimana pross_ _

c. vorr_ _ anda_ _ al par_ _

d. vad_ al centr_ commerciale con mi_ padre

e. vado _ _ pales_ _ _ p_r fa_ _ pes_

f. mio fratello v_ in c_ntro con mia madre

g. il mi_ migli_re amic_ v_ in spiagg_ _ per pr_ndere il s_le

h. vado allo sta_ _ _ per guard_ _ _ una partit_

2. Anagrams: unscramble the weird word

a. vado in trecno

b. sarà vertedinte

c. vorrei andare a scaep

d. vado in cipisan

e. il mio roeglimi amico va in palestra

f. vado allo stadio rep guardare una partita

g. vado in spiaggia per derepne il sole

h. il fine settimana porssomi vado al parco

3. Tangled translation: into Italian

a. vado in **swimming pool**

b. il mio **best** amico **is going** in **gym**

c. mio fratello **older** va allo stadio **to watch** una partita

d. vado in **beach** per prendere il **sun**

e. **the** fine settimana **next** vado al **park**

f. **I would like** andare **to the centre**

g. vado **to the** centro **commercial** per **to buy** vestiti **and** altre **things**

h. **it will be** divertente ma **tiring**

4. Spot and correct the errors

a. vado al piscina

b. la settimana prossimo vado al parco

c. vorrei andare in spiaggia al prendere il sole

d. vado al cinema per guardare film

e. la mia migliore amica vado in palestra

f. mio fratello va in stadio

g. vado allo centro commerciale per comprare cose

h. vado al spiaggia per nuoto

5. Translate into Italian

a. Next weekend I am going to the park to ride the bike

b. Next Saturday I am going to the cinema to watch a movie..

c. Next Sunday I am going to the beach with my friends.

d. I am going to the gym to do weights. It will be tiring.

e. Next weekend my friend is going to the stadium to watch a match.

f. I am going to the park to ride my bike.

g. My friend is going to the shopping centre to buy clothes .

h. I am going to the city centre to buy some things.

i. I am going to the sports centre to swim.

TERM 3 - BRINGING IT ALL TOGETHER – 13

1. Mi chiamo Jonas ed ho sedici anni. Il mio compleanno è il sette settembre. Sono tedesco e ora vivo ad Amburgo, una città grande, con la mia famiglia. Sono molto felice perché più tardi vado a guardare la partita di calcio della mia squadra preferita, l' Amburgo SV.

2. Nella mia famiglia siamo quattro persone: mia sorella maggiore, Lisa, mio padre, Thomas, mia madre, Andrea, ed io. Vado molto d'accordo con mia madre perché è molto affettuosa, un po' più di mio padre. Mio padre è più severo di mia madre. I miei nonni si chiamano Wolfgang ed Helga. Sono molto simpatici e andiamo sempre al parco o in spiaggia insieme *(together)*.

3. Mia sorella maggiore si chiama Lisa. A Lisa piace la pittura e ballare. Ha diciotto anni ed è bella e talentuosa. Il suo compleanno è il ventidue novembre. Lisa ha i capelli biondi e gli occhi azzurri. Lisa è più artistica di me, ma io sono più sportivo di lei.

4. La mia routine quotidiana è abbastanza semplice. In generale, mi sveglio presto, intorno alle sette del mattino. Dopo mi lavo e mi vesto. Dopo, intorno alle sette e mezza, faccio colazione con mio padre e mia madre. Dopo, preparo il mio zaino ed esco di casa.

5. A scuola, la mia materia preferita è la musica. Adoro suonare la chitarra e comporre le mie canzoni. Tutti i fine settimana suono con il mio gruppo *(my band)*.

6. Adoro la mia scuola perché i professori sono intelligenti e mi aiutano sempre quando ho dei dubbi *(doubts)*. Inoltre, mi piace l'educazione fisica perché posso praticare diversi sport e posso mantenermi in forma *(stay in shape)*. Il mio professore di italiano è esigente *(demanding)* ma anche molto bravo, ci motiva sempre.

7. Il fine settimana prossimo faccio molto sport. Sabato vado al parco per andare in bici e al centro sportivo per giocare a pallacanestro con i miei amici. Domenica vado in piscina per nuotare con mio fratello maggiore e dopo vado in palestra per fare pesi. Sarà stancante!

1. Find the Italian for the following in the paragraphs indicated in brackets

a. a big city (1)

b. happy (1)

c. later (1)

d. affectionate (2)

e. we always go (2)

f. to dance (3)

g. beautiful (3)

h. more…than (3)

i. simple (4)

j. I wake up early (4)

k. I have breakfast (4)

l. I go out of the house (4)

m. I love (5)

n. my own songs (5)

o. (they) help me (6)

p. I am going to do (7)

q. I am going to go (7)

2. Complete the following translation of paragraph 4

My daily routine is quite _______. In general, I wake up _______, at around seven o'clock in the __________. Afterwards I wash and __________. Then at about seven-thirty, I __________ with my father and my mother. After that I _________ my _________ and _____________.

3. Correct the 10 mistakes in the following translation of paragraph 7

Next week I am going to do a lot of things. On Friday, I am going to go to the park to ride my horse and to the stadium to play handball with my friends. On Saturday I am going to go to the lake to swim with my younger brother and then to the gym to do some gymnastics. It will be fun!

1. Mi chiamo Annike e ho quindici anni. Il mio compleanno è il due maggio. Sono austriaca e ora vivo a Vienna, la capitale, con la mia famiglia. Sono molto felice perché dopo vado a guardare una partita di calcio. Gioca la mia squadra preferita, Austria Wien.

2. Nella mia famiglia siamo quattro persone: mia sorella maggiore, Sonja, mio padre, Heinrich, mia madre, Heidi, ed io. Vado molto d'accordo con mia madre perché è molto simpatica. Generalmente è molto simpatica, ma a volte può essere un po' antipatica quando è stressata. I miei nonni si chiamano Christian e Beatrice. Christian ha settantacinque anni e Beatrice ha settantatré anni. Sono molto simpatici e andiamo sempre al parco o in spiaggia insieme *(together)*.

3. Mia sorella maggiore Sonja ha diciotto anni, è molto bella e diligente. Prende sempre buoni voti a scuola. Il suo compleanno è il venticinque dicembre. Sonja ha i capelli castani e gli occhi marroni.

4. Durante la settimana, mi sveglio presto, intorno alle sei e mezza di mattina. Dopo mi faccio la doccia e mi lavo la faccia. Dopo, intorno alle sette, faccio colazione in cucina con la mia famiglia. Esco di casa alle sette e mezza e vado a scuola in macchina.

5. A scuola, la mia materia preferita è l'informatica. Adoro lavorare con il computer. In futuro, vorrei diventare programmatrice, come mio padre.

6. La mia scuola è abbastanza buona. I professori sono molto severi e ci danno sempre molti compiti. Però, mi piace la mia scuola perché imparo molto e ho molti amici. Mi aiutano sempre quando ho un problema. Inoltre, mi piace l'italiano perché posso imparare molte cose sulla cultura italiana. In futuro mi piacerebbe visitare l'Italia.

7. Il fine settimana prossimo faccio molte cose con i miei amici. Sabato vado al centro commerciale per comprare delle cose e vado al mio ristorante italiano preferito. Domenica vado in palestra per fare pesi e dopo vado al cinema per guardare un film. Sarà divertente!

---

4. Answer the following questions about paragraphs 1 to 4 in Italian, as if you were Annike

a. Di dove sei?

b. Come stai oggi? Perché?

c. Quante persone ci sono nella tua famiglia?

d. Com'è tua madre?

e. Come si chiamano i tuoi nonni?

f. Come sono i tuoi nonni?

g. Chi è più bella e diligente nella tua famiglia?

h. A che ora ti svegli?

i. Che cosa fai dopo?

j. Dove fai colazione?

k. Dove vai alle sette e mezza?

---

5. Find the Italian equivalent for the following in paragraphs 5 and 6

a. my favourite subject

b. I love to work

c. in the future

d. same as my father

e. is quite good

f. they always give us

g. I learn a lot

h. they always help me

i. I can learn a lot of things

---

6. Paragraph 7 was copied incorrectly. Spot and correct the 10 mistakes

Il fine settimana prossima faccio molte cosa con i miei amici. Il sabato vado al centro commerciale per comprare al cose e va al mio ristorante italiano preferite. Domenica vai in palestra per faccio pesi e dopo vado al parco per guardare un cinema. Sarà divertente.

---

7. Translate the following phrases from paragraph 7 into English

a. fare molte cose

b. comprare delle cose

c. fare pesi

d. guardare un film

e. sarà divertente

TERM 3 – MIDPOINT – RETRIEVAL PRACTICE

1. Answer the following questions in Italian

A che ora ti svegli generalmente?	
Che cosa fai prima di andare a scuola?	
A che ora esci di casa per andare a scuola?	
Come vai a scuola?	
Qual è la tua materia preferita? Perché?	
Che cosa fai dopo la scuola?	
Che cosa fai prima di andare a letto?	
A che ora fai colazione?	
A che ora ceni?	
Che cosa fai il fine settimana generalmente?	
Che cosa fai il fine settimana che viene?	

2. Write a paragraph in the first person singular (I) providing the following details

a. Your name is Lorenzo. You are 12. You are from Switzerland but live in London.

b. Your daily routine is simple: every day you get up at 6, then you shower, have breakfast with your brother and then go to school by bus at 7:30. You come back home around 4.

c. In the afternoon you do your homework, it is very boring.

d. Later you play PlayStation, go on the internet and watch a film on TV with your family.

e. You don't like school because the teachers are too strict and give too much homework. However, you love art because the teacher is fun and always helps you.

f. Next weekend you will do a lot of sport: you are going to the gym, to the swimming pool and you are also playing tennis. You are also going to the shopping centre to buy clothes with your friends. Finally, you are going to the cinema to watch a movie.

3. Write a paragraph in the third person singular (he/she) providing the following details about a real or fictitious friend

a. Brief introduction (10 words min)

b. Daily routine (20 words min)

c. Description of 2 family members (10 words min)

d. At what time he/she has breakfast, lunch and dinner (20 words min)

d. How he/she feels about school and teachers. Subjects he/she likes and dislikes and why (20 words min)

e. What he/she normally does at the weekend (20 words min)

f. His/her plans for the weekend (20 words min)

UNIT 14
Talking about food:
likes, dislikes, reasons

UNIT 14
Talking about food: likes, dislikes, reasons

Che cosa ti piace mangiare e bere? Perché? *What do you like to eat and drink? Why?*

Singular

Amo/Adoro *I love / I adore*	il caffè	*coffee*		**caldo/a**	*hot*
	il cioccolato	*chocolate*		**delizioso/a**	*delicious*
Mi piace molto *I like a lot*	il formaggio	*cheese*		**disgustoso/a**	*disgusting*
	il latte	*milk*		**dolce**	*sweet*
Mi piace *I like*	il miele	*honey*		**grasso/a**	*fatty*
	il pane	*bread*		**insipido/a**	*bland*
Mi piace un po' *I like a bit*	il pesce	*fish*	**perché è** *because it is*	**malsano/a**	*unhealthy*
	il pollo arrosto	*roast chicken*		**piccante**	*spicy*
Non mi piace *I don't like*	il riso	*rice*		**ricco/a di vitamine** *rich in vitamins*	
	il succo di frutta	*fruit juice*			
Odio *I hate*	l'acqua	*water*		**rinfrescante**	*refreshing*
	la carne	*meat*		**salutare / sano/a**	*healthy*
Preferisco *I prefer*	la frutta	*fruit*		**saporito/a**	*tasty*

Plural

Amo/adoro *I love/ I adore*	i cioccolatini	*chocolates*		**caldi/e**	
	i gamberi	*prawns*		**deliziosi/e**	
Mi piacciono molto *I like a lot*	i pomodori	*tomatoes*		**disgustosi/e**	
	le arance	*oranges*		**dolci**	
Mi piacciono *I like*	le banane	*bananas*	**perché sono** *because they are*	**grassi/e**	
	le mele	*apples*		**insipidi/e**	
Mi piacciono un po' *I like a bit*	le melanzane *aubergines/eggplants*			**malsani/e**	
	le uova	*eggs*		**piccanti**	
Non mi piacciono *I don't like*	le verdure	*vegetables*		**ricchi/ricche di proteine**	
Odio *I hate*	gli hamburger	*burgers*		**rinfrescanti**	
Preferisco *I prefer*				**salutari / sani/e**	

Author's notes:
1 The adjectives above ending in '**o**' change to '**a**' with feminine nouns.
E.g.. *Mi piace **la** frutta perché è deliziosa*
2 Adjectives ending in '**e**' do not change in the feminine. However, they change to 'i' in the plural.
E.g.: *La mela è dolce / Le mele sono dolci.*
3 When used in the plural, the adjectives in 'o' change to 'i' and the adjective in 'a' change to 'e'.
E.g..: *Mi piacciono **i** gamberi perché sono saporiti /Mi piacciono **le** verdure perché sono sane*

1. Listen and fill in the gaps

a. Amo i ________________.

b. Adoro il ________________.

c. Mi piace molto il ________________.

d. Preferisco la ____________ di fragola.

e. Odio le ______________.

f. Mi piacciono un po' le ________________.

g. Mi piace molto il ____________.

h. Odio le ____________.

i. Adoro il ________ ________ piccante.

2. Mystery words: guess the words, then listen and see how many you guessed right

a. l' a_ _ _ a

b. il m _ e _ _

c. le u_ v _

d. la _ a _ n_

e. il p _ _ c_

f. la m _ l _

g. il _ _ n_

h. il r _ _ o

3. Spot the differences and correct your text

a. Amo la frutta, soprattutto le fragole.

b. Odio la verdura, soprattutto i funghi.

c. Non mi piace il pollo fritto.

d. Mi piace molto il pane.

e. Mi piace molto la pasta.

f. Adoro il succo di mela.

g. La carne rossa non è piccante.

h. Il caffè è saporito.

i. Gli hamburger sono sani.

j. La verdura è saporita.

k. Le mele sono dolci.

l. Non mi piace il latte.

4. Listen, spot and correct the spelling and grammar errors

a. Mi piacciono la verdura perché è sana.

b. Adoro le hamburger.

c. Il pesce a la carne sono saporite.

d. Il succo d'arancia mi piacciono un po'.

e. Mangio molto pesce perché sono ricco di proteine.

f. Non mi piace le carne perché è grassa.

g. Amo la pollo arrosto perché è saporito.

h. Mi piace molto i calamari fritti anche se non sono molto sani.

5. Faulty translation: spot the translation errors and correct them

My name is Filippo. What do I enjoy eating? I love fruit, especially bananas. I drink them every day. My favourite vegetables are tomatoes and potatoes because they are healthy. I also like jam because it is delicious and meat because it is tasty. I hate turkey and burgers. They are rich in protein but they are not spicy.

6. Why do they like/dislike these foods?

People and what they like/dislike	Reasons why they like/dislike
a. I like fruit	
b. My brother loves eggs	
c. Silvia hates vegetables	
d. Giacomo likes fish	
e. Corinna loves oranges	
f. Raffaele loves Indian food	
g. Ahmed dislikes pork	
h. Paola dislikes tomatoes	
i. Susanna hates carrots	

7. Listening slalom: follow the speaker from top to bottom and number the boxes

a	b	c	d
I love	I hate	I can't stand	I love
chocolate	meat	spinach	burgers
and cakes	sausages	because it is	and tomatoes
and fries	because they are sweet	because they are	tasty
and delicious	disgusting.	and rich in protein.	because they are
not	I eat it with salad	I prefer	although they are
not very healthy.	healthy.	or fries.	carrots.

8. Answer the questions below about Marta

a. How many people are there in Marta's family?
b. What does her father love?
c. What does her mother hate?
d. What does her brother Raffaele love?
e. What does her brother Giacomo adore?
f. What does Marta love?
g. What does she hate?
h. Why?

Unit 14. Talking about food (Part 1): VOCABULARY BUILDING (Part 1)

1. Match up

1. le banane	a. eggs
2. le fragole	b. apples
3. la carne	c. prawns
4. il pollo	d. milk
5. l'acqua	e. fruit
6. il latte	f. water
7. le uova	g. burgers
8. i gamberi	h. chicken
9. gli hamburger	i. meat
10. la frutta	j. bananas
11. le mele	k. strawberries

2. Complete

a. mi piace molto il __________ — *I like chicken a lot*

b. adoro i ______________ — *I adore prawns*

c. mi piacciono le __________ — *I like strawberries*

d. amo il ____________ — *I love milk*

e. adoro le ______________ — *I adore bananas*

f. preferisco l'________ minerale — *I prefer mineral water*

g. non mi piacciono i __________ — *I don't like tomatoes*

h. odio il ____________ — *I hate fish*

i. amo la ____________ — *I love fruit*

j. non mi piacciono le __________ — *I don't like eggs*

3. Translate into English

a. mi piace la frutta

b. odio le uova

c. amo il pollo arrosto

d. mi piacciono le mele

e. odio la carne

f. preferisco l'insalata verde

g. non mi piacciono i pomodori

h. odio il latte

4. Complete the words

a. le uo__________

b. le ban__________

c. la fr__________

d. le verd____________

e. gli hamb______________

f. i gam__________

g. i pom____________

h. l'ac________

5. Fill the gaps with either *'mi piace'* or *'mi piacciono'* as appropriate

a. Non ________________________ le uova.

b. ________________________ l'acqua.

c. ________________________ il pollo.

d. ________________________ gli hamburger.

e. ________________________ le verdure.

f. ________________________ la carne.

g. ________________________ la frutta.

h. ________________________ i gamberi.

i. ________________________ la pasta.

6. Translate into Italian

a. I like eggs.

b. I love oranges.

c. I hate tomatoes.

d. I don't like prawns.

e. I love fruit juice.

f. I don't like vegetables.

g. I really like milk.

h. I like apples but I prefer oranges.

i. I don't like cheese.

Unit 14. Talking about food (Part 1): VOCABULARY BUILDING (Part 2)

1. Complete with the missing words. The initial letter of each word is given

a. Queste banane sono d________________
These bananas are disgusting

b. Queste mele sono d________________
These apples are delicious

c. Questo pollo è molto p________________
This chicken is very spicy

d. Non mi piace la c________________
I don't like meat

e. Questo caffè è molto d________________
This coffee is very sweet

f. Le salsicce sono m________________
Sausages are unhealthy

g. Le verdure sono s________________
Vegetables are healthy

h. Amo il l________________
I love milk

2. Complete the table

Italiano	English
il latte	
	roast chicken
il pesce	
le uova	
	water
	bread
i cereali	
il pane tostato	
	vegetables

3. Complete with 'mi piace' or 'mi piacciono' as appropriate

a. ________________ le mele

b. ________________ il latte

c. Non ________________ i cereali

d. ________________ il pane tostato

e. ________________ il succo di frutta

f. Non ________________ la pasta

g. ________________ il riso

h. Non ________________ il caffè

4. Broken words

a. N___ m___ p__________ l__ u________ *I don't like eggs.*

b. A__________ l______ m__________ *I love apples.*

c. O______ g____ h__________ *I hate burgers.*

d. M___ p__________ m________ i c________________
I really like chocolates.

e. ___l m___c________ è c________ *My coffee is hot.*

f. ___l p__________ è s________ *Fish is healthy.*

g. I__ curry indiano è p__________ *Indian curry is spicy.*

5. Complete each sentence in a way which is logical and grammatically correct

a. Le ____________ non sono sane.

b. Le banane sono ______________.

c. Non mi __________ il latte.

d. Mi __________ il pollo arrosto.

e. ____________ il pesce perché è saporito.

f. ____________ la carne rossa perché è malsana.

g. ____________ le verdure perché sono ricche di vitamine.

Unit 14. Talking about food (Part 1): READING

Ciao, mi chiamo Manuela. Cosa preferisco mangiare? Amo i frutti di mare, quindi mi piacciono molto i gamberi ed i calamari perché sono deliziosi. Mi piace molto il pesce perché è saporito e ricco di proteine. Soprattutto mangio il salmone, prodotto tipico scozzese, dove vivo. Mi piace abbastanza il pollo arrosto. Inoltre, amo la frutta soprattutto l'uva e le fragole. Non mi piacciono molto le verdure perché non sono saporite, ma fanno bene alla salute!

Salve, mi chiamo Alessandro. Cosa preferisco mangiare? Amo le verdure. Le mangio tutti i giorni. Le mie verdure preferite sono gli spinaci, le carote e le melanzane perché sono ricche di vitamine e minerali. Mi piace anche la frutta perché è sana, rinfrescante e deliziosa. Sono vegetariano. Odio la carne e il pesce. Anche se sono ricchi di proteine, non sono saporiti.

Ciao, mi chiamo Violetta. Cosa preferisco mangiare? Adoro la carne, soprattutto la carne di agnello, perché è molto saporita. Mi piace molto il pollo arrosto piccante, lo trovo saporito ed è ricco di proteine. Mi piacciono abbastanza le uova. Sono sane e ricche di vitamine e proteine. Mi piace abbastanza la frutta, soprattutto le ciliegie. Sono molto deliziose. Però non mi piacciono per niente le mele.

Ciao, mi chiamo James. Cosa mi piace mangiare? Preferisco la carne. La adoro perché è saporita, soprattutto mi piacciono molto gli hamburger. Mi piace anche la frutta perché è dolce. Non mi piacciono le verdure. Odio i pomodori e le carote. Non mi piacciono le uova. Sono ricche di vitamine e proteine ma sono disgustose. Non mi piacciono le patate fritte perché sono malsane.

Salve, mi chiamo Fernando. Cosa mi piace mangiare? Amo la carne rossa perché è saporita e ricca di proteine. Non mangio molto pesce perché è disgustoso. Mi piacciono abbastanza i calamari fritti, però non fanno bene alla salute. Mi piace moltissimo la frutta, preferisco le banane, perché sono deliziose, ricche di vitamine e non sono care. Non mi piacciono le mele e odio le arance. Non mangio verdure.

1. Find the Italian for the following in Manuela's text

a. I love seafood

b. I like prawns a lot

c. They are delicious

d. Because it is tasty

e. I eat salmon

f. I quite like

g. Moreover

h. Above all

i. They are not tasty

2. Fernando or Manuela? Write *F* or *M* next to each statement below

a. I love seafood - *M*

b. I hate oranges

c. I like fruit a lot

d. I don't like vegetables

e. I eat salmon

f. I quite like squid

g. I prefer bananas

h. I don't eat much fish

i. I love red meat

3. Complete the following sentences based on Alessandro's text

a. Alessandro loves________________________

b. He eats them ___________________________

c. His favourite vegetables are _______________,
________________ and _______________

d. He also likes _______________ because it is
____________ ____________ and _______________

e. He hates _______________ and _______________

4. Fill in the table below about James

loves	likes a lot	hates	doesn't like

Unit 14. Talking about food (Part 1): TRANSLATION 1

1. Faulty translation: spot and correct [IN THE ENGLISH] any translation mistakes you find below

a. Adoro i gamberi: *I hate prawns*

b. Odio il pollo e la zuppa: *I like meat and soup*

c. Mi piace il miele: *I don't like honey*

d. Amo le arance e l'uva: *I love apples and grapes*

e. Le uova sono disgustose: *Eggs are tasty*

f. Il pesce è salutare: *Fish is unhealthy*

g. Preferisco la cioccolata calda: *I prefer hot water*

h. Il pane non è salato: *Fish is not salty*

i. Il curry indiano è piccante: *Indian curry is sweet*

j. I cioccolatini fanno male alla salute:
Chocolates are healthy

k. Mi piace il riso perché è senza glutine:
I hate rice because it is gluten-free

l. Le banane sono ricche di vitamine:
Bananas are rich in protein

2. Translate into English

a. I gamberi sono saporiti e sani.

b. Il pesce è delizioso e ricco di vitamine.

c. Il pollo è ricco di proteine.

d. Amo il riso perché è senza glutine.

e. La carne rossa è malsana.

f. La frutta è rinfrescante e dolce.

g. Le uova sono saporite e ricche di proteine.

h. Preferisco l'acqua minerale.

i. La zuppa è buona e salutare.

j. Non mi piacciono le verdure.

k. Mi piacciono le carote.

l. Questo caffè è molto dolce.

m. Una mela disgustosa.

n. Le arance sono disgustose.

3. Phrase-level translation [En to It]

a. Spicy chicken:

b. This coffee:

c. I quite like:

d. Very sweet:

e. A disgusting apple:

f. Some delicious oranges:

g. I don't like:

h. I love pizza because:

i. It is refreshing:

j. Mineral water:

k. It is bland:

4. Sentence-level translation [En to It]

a. I like spicy chicken a lot.

b. I like oranges because they are healthy.

c. Meat is tasty but unhealthy.

d. This coffee is hot.

e. Eggs are disgusting but healthy.

f. I love oranges. They are delicious and rich in vitamins.

g. I love fish. It is tasty and rich in protein.

h. Vegetables are disgusting

i. I prefer fruit because is refreshing.

j. This tea is sweet.

Unit 14. Talking about food (Part 1): TRANSLATION 2

Paragraph 1	Tick a box each time you spot the correct translation in the text				Translate the paragraph into English
Ciao, mi chiamo Albert e sono australiano. Faccio colazione alle sette. Mi piace mangiare la frutta perché è sana. A pranzo mangio un panino al formaggio o una zuppa di verdure. Di solito bevo dell' acqua o una limonata. La sera ceno a casa. Amo le salsicce perché sono saporite.	For lunch I eat	I have breakfast	or a vegetable soup	In the evening	______________ ______________
	because it is healthy	at seven	and Italian fluently	I love sausages	______________ ______________
	Hi, my name is Albert	a cheese sandwich	because they are tasty	I usually drink	______________ ______________
	and I am Australian	water or lemonade	I like eating fruit	I have dinner at home	______________
Paragraph 2					
Salve, io sono Gloria. Normalmente a colazione mangio i cereali e bevo un caffè in cucina. Di solito pranzo verso l'una, mangio un'insalata o una pizza. Mi piace moltissimo. Non mangio mai le patate fritte perché secondo me sono malsane. Odio il pesce perché è insipido.	Hello, I am Gloria	I never eat	I really like it	and I drink	______________ ______________
	I usually have lunch	because in my opinion	Normally for breakfast	they are unhealthy	______________ ______________
	chips	in the kitchen	it is bland	I eat cereal	______________ ______________
	a coffee	a salad or a pizza	I hate fish because	around 1pm, I eat	______________ ______________
Paragraph 3					
Buonasera, mi chiamo Yan. Sono cinese ma parlo italiano. Di solito non faccio colazione perché non ho tempo. A pranzo mangio sempre del riso con verdure e pollo e bevo un té. Mi piacciono i cioccolatini anche se preferisco le banane o le mele. La sera nella la mia famiglia ceniamo verso le sette.	I am Chinese	and I am 14	I like chocolates	and I drink tea	______________ ______________
	Good evening, my name is Yan	For lunch	but I speak Italian	I usually don't have breakfast	______________ ______________
	vegetables and chicken	we have dinner around 7	because it is big	I always eat rice with	______________ ______________
	bananas or apples	because I do not have time	even if I prefer	In the evening in my family	______________

Unit 14. Talking about food (Part 1): WRITING

1. Split sentences

Amo il pollo [1]	minerale
Odio le verdure perché	arrosto [1]
Preferisco la	è dolce
Questo caffè	sono disgustose
Mi piacciono	saporiti ma malsani
I calamari fritti sono	le mele
Adoro l'acqua	pizza

2. Rewrite the sentences in the correct order

e.g. il amo arrosto pollo = *amo il pollo arrosto*

a. le verdure odio

b. caffè questo amaro è

c. frutta bene fa la alla salute

d. minerale l' preferisco acqua

e. rinfrescanti sono arance le

f. mi sono le piacciono uova perché deliziose

g. piace carne rossa è non mi la ma sana

h. pesce il adoro arrostito

i. la è ricca frutta vitamine di

j. cibo mi piccante il piace

3. Spot the mistake and rewrite the correct sentence (there may be missing words)

a. Mi piace le patate fritte e le gamberi

b. Non piacciono le verdure

c. Il pollo e saporito è picante

d. Adoro il cafe caldo

e. Preferisco la insalada verde

f. Odio a carne e il pescie

4. Anagrams

a. ttela

b. berimga

c. rneca = carne

d. sainlata

e. canpicte

f. dilesozio

g. mineviat

5. Guided writing – write 4 short paragraphs describing the people below using the details in the box [I]

Person	Loves	Quite likes	Doesn't like	Hates
Loretta	pizza because tasty	milk because healthy	red meat	eggs because disgusting
Eddie	chicken because healthy	oranges because sweet	fish	meat because unhealthy
Angela	honey because sweet	fish because tasty	fruit	vegetables because bland

6. Write a paragraph on Sara in Italian [using the third person singular]

Name: Sara

Age: 18

Description: tall, good-looking, sporty, friendly

Occupation: student

Food she loves: chicken

Food she likes: vegetables

Food she doesn't like: red meat

Food she hates: fish

TERM 3 - BRINGING IT ALL TOGETHER – 14

1. Mi chiamo Andrew e ho quattordici anni. Il mio compleanno è il due gennaio. Sono scozzese e vivo ad Edinburgo, la capitale della Scozia, con la mia famiglia. Oggi sono un po' stanco e stressato perché ho troppi *(too many)* compiti.

2. Nella mia famiglia siamo quattro persone: mia sorella maggiore, Skye, mio padre, Angus, mia madre, Isla, ed io. Vado molto d'accordo con mia madre perché è molto paziente e buona, però mio padre è un po' impaziente.

3. Mia sorella maggiore si chiama Skye. A Skye piace leggere libri, scrivere e cantare. Ha vent'anni ed è molto creativa e talentuosa. Il suo compleanno è il sette maggio. Skye ha i capelli castani e gli occhi verdi. Skye é più studiosa *(studious)* di me e a me piace la musica. Sono anche molto sportivo. Faccio sport tutti i giorni.

4. La mia routine quotidiana è molto semplice. Generalmente, mi sveglio molto presto, verso le cinque del mattino. Dopo mi faccio la doccia e mi metto l'uniforme. Dopo, verso le sei, faccio colazione con mia sorella Skye in cucina. Entrambi mangiamo una fetta (a slice) di pane tostato con miele e beviamo un bicchiere *(a glass)* di latte. Dopo mi lavo i denti ed esco di casa. Vado sempre a scuola a piedi. Mi piace andare a scuola a piedi perché vivo molto vicino alla scuola.

5. Che cosa preferisco mangiare? Amo la verdura perché è ricca di vitamine e minerali. La mangio tutti i giorni. Mi piace anche la carne, soprattutto la carne di manzo *(beef)*, perché è molto saporita. Però non è molto sana quindi la mangio solo una volta alla settimana. Adoro anche il pesce ed i frutti di mare *(seafood)*. Non sopporto le uova.

6. Mi piace la mia scuola perché i professori sono bravi e ho molti amici. La mia materia preferita è l'arte perché sono una persona abbastanza creativa. Inoltre, mi piace l' educazione fisica perché adoro fare sport e giocare con i miei amici. Il mio professore di educazione fisica è molto severo, ma anche molto divertente e bravo.

7. Il fine settimana prossimo faccio molte cose. Venerdì vado con i miei amici al centro commerciale. Facciamo shopping e ceniamo in un ristorante italiano. Sabato rimango a casa e guardo un film con mia sorella Skye. Sarà divertente!

---

1. Complete the sentences below based on paragraphs 1-4 in Andrew's text

a. Andrew is _______ years old

b. today he is a bit ________ and stressed

c. his ___________ sister is called Skye

d. Skye enjoys reading books, ________ and singing

e. Skye has ________ hair and green eyes

f. Skye is more __________ than Andrew

g. he does sport ___________

h. Andrew gets up very _________

i. he goes to school _________

---

2. Find the Italian for the following in paragraph 5

a. vegetables: v	i. what: c c
b. I eat: m	j. but: p
c. also: a	k. them: lit *(F)*: L
d. above all: s	l. very: m
e. beef: m	m. of: d
f. tasty: s	n. only: s
g. healthy: s	o. once: u v
h. fish: p	p. eggs: u

---

3. Some of the below statements about Andrew are incorrect. Spot them and correct the inaccuracies

a. today, Andrew has no homework

b. Skye is more studious than Andrew

c. they have breakfast in the dining room

d. he goes to school by bike

e. he only eats meat twice a week

f. his teachers are good

g. his favourite subject is PE

h. his PE teacher is very strict

i. next Saturday he is going shopping

j. he is also watching a movie at the cinema

1. Mi chiamo Angus e ho sedici anni. Il mio compleanno è l'otto ottobre. Sono di Aberdeen, nel nord della Scozia. Vivo qui con la mia famiglia.

2. Nella mia famiglia siamo quattro persone: mia sorella maggiore, Maisie, mio padre, Gordon, mia madre, Olivia, ed io. Vado molto d'accordo con mia madre perché è tranquilla, paziente e divertente. Anche mio padre è molto divertente. Vado molto d'accordo con lui perché mi ascolta sempre.

3. Maisie ama fare sport acquatici. I suoi sport preferiti sono la canoa e lo sci nautico. Ha diciott'anni ed è molto sportiva e forte. Il suo compleanno è il dodici giugno. Maisie ha i capelli biondi e lunghi e gli occhi verdi. Lei è più sportiva di me, ma a me piace la musica piú di lei.

4. Durante la settimana la mia routine quotidiana è uguale tutti i giorni. Generalmente, mi sveglio intorno alle sette di mattina. Dopo mi lavo la faccia e i denti e mi vesto. Poi, alle sette e un quarto faccio colazione con mia sorella Maisie nella sala da pranzo. Mangiamo del pane tostato e dei cereali con latte. Ogni tanto, prendo anche un caffelatte. Vado sempre a scuola in autobus. Mi piace andare a scuola in autobus perché posso chiacchierare con i miei amici.

5. Che cosa preferisco mangiare? Mi piace molto il pollo arrosto perché è saporito e ricco di proteine. Mi piacciono abbastanza anche le uova. Sono sane e ricche di proteine. Mi piace molto la frutta, soprattutto le mele. Sono deliziose e ricche di vitamine. Però non mi piacciono per niente le arance.

6. Mi piace molto la scuola. I professori non sono molto severi e non mi sgridano mai. La cosa più bella è che ho molti buoni amici. La mia materia preferita è la matematica perché sono una persona abbastanza logica. Inoltre, mi piacciono le lezioni di scienze. Il mio professore di scienze è molto severo ma mi piace.

7. Il fine settimana prossimo faccio un sacco *(a loat of)* di cose. Venerdì vado in gita *(on a trip)* in spiaggia con i miei amici. Prendiamo il sole in spiaggia e nuotiamo nel mare. Poi, sabato, vado al parco con la mia famiglia. Facciamo una grigliata *(barbeque)* con i miei zii e i miei cugini. Mangiamo hamburger e insalata. Mia cugina Clara mangia generalmente un hamburger di tofu perché lei è vegetariana. Poi, domenica, rimango a casa per riposare.

4. Translate the following phrases from paragraphs 1 to 3

a. vivo qui

b. mia sorella maggiore

c. tranquilla

d. mi ascolta

e. sport acquatici

f. sportiva e forte

g. i capelli biondi e lunghi

h. più sportiva di me

5. Fix the 10 mistakes in the following English translation of paragraph 4

Every week my daily routine is the same every day. In general, I get up around 7 o'clock in the morning. Then, I wash my hair and teeth and I shave. Afterwards, at seven-thirty, I have breakfast with my sister Maisie in the kitchen. The two of us have toast and cereal with juice for breakfast. I always go to school by bus. I like to go to school by bus because I can mess around with my friends.

6. Answer the questions below about paragraphs 6 and 7 in Italian, as if you were Angus

a. Ti piace la tua scuola? Perché?

b. Qual è la cosa più bella della tua scuola?

c. Perché ti piace la matematica?

d. Com'è il professore di scienze?

e. Dove vai in gita il fine settimana prossimo?

f. Con chi vai?

g. Che cosa fate in spiaggia?

h. Dove fate una grigliata sabato prossimo?

i. Che cosa mangi?

j. Chi è Clara?

k. Perché Clara non mangia gli hamburger?

l. Dove vai domenica prossima?

UNIT 15
My holiday plans
(Talking about future plans for holidays)

In this unit you will learn how to talk about:

- What you intend to do in future holidays
- Where you are going to go
- Where you are going to stay
- Who you are going to travel with
- How it will be
- Means of transport

You will revisit:

- The verb 'andare'
- Free-time activities
- Previously seen adjectives

UNIT 15
My holiday plans

Dove andrai quest'estate?	*Where are you going to go this summer?*		
Come viaggerai?	*How are you going to travel?*		
Quanto tempo passerai lì?	*How long are you going to spend there?*		
Dove starai?	*Where are you going to stay?*		
Che cosa farai durante le vacanze?	*What are you going to do during the holidays?*		

***Quest'estate** *This summer* **Quest'inverno** *This winter* **L'anno prossimo** *Next year* **A Natale** *This Christmas* **Tra due settimane** *In two weeks*	**andrò in vacanza in** *I am going to go on holiday to* **andrà in** *he/she is going to go* **andremo in** *we're going to go to*	**Australia** **Francia** **Italia** **Grecia** **Spagna** **Liguria** **Puglia** **Toscana**	**in aereo** *by plane* **in camper** *by campervan* **in macchina** *by car* **in nave** *by boat* **in treno** *by train* **in pullman** *by coach*	**ballerò** *I will dance* **dormirò** *I will sleep* **farò immersioni** *I will go diving* **farò delle compere** *I will go shopping* **mangerò** *I am going to eat* **non vedo l'ora!** *I can't wait!* **mi riposerò** *I am going to rest* **sarà divertente** *it will be fun* **sarà fantastico** *it will be fantastic* **sarà noioso** *it will be boring*
	passerò *I will spend* **passerà** *he/she will spend* **passeremo** *we will spend*	**una settimana** *one week* **due settimane** *two weeks*	**lì** *there* **con la mia famiglia** *with my family* **solo/a** *alone*	
	starò *I am going to stay* **starà** *he/she will spend* **staremo** *we are going to stay*	**nella casa di famiglia** *in the family home* **in un campeggio** *in a campsite* **in un hotel economico** *in a cheap hotel* **in un hotel di lusso** *in a luxury hotel*		
	mi piacerebbe... *I would like to...* **ci piacerebbe...** *we would like to...*	**ballare** *dance* **fare delle compere** *do shopping* **fare immersioni** *go diving* **fare un giro turistico** *go sightseeing* **mangiare e dormire** *eat and sleep* **prendere il sole** *sunbathe* **riposare** *rest* **suonare l'ukulele** *play the ukulele* **viaggiare** *travel* **uscire in centro** *go out into town*		

Author's notes: a. *Questo/questa means 'this'. When it is followed by a word starting with a vowel it becomes* **quest'** *like in* **quest'estate**. *Elision is very common in Italian :* *l'acqua/ un'insalata...*
b. *Have you noticed the verbs: andrò/ mangerò/ riposerò. What does this ending suggest to you? These verbs in the future can be translated both as 'I will...' or 'I am going to...'*

1. Listen and fill in the gaps

a. Quest'estate __________ in vancanza a Cuba.

b. Andrò in ___________.

c. ___________ una settimana lì.

d. __________ divertente.

e. ___________ in un hotel di lusso.

f. ___________ in discoteca.

g. ___________ shopping.

h. Mi piacerebbe __________ ___________.

i. Ci piacerebbe __________ __________.

2. Spot the differences and correct your text

a. quest'inverno andrò in vacanza in Svizzera

b. passerò tre giorni lì

c. andrò con il mio amico

d. staremo in un hotel caro

e. farò i compiti

f. mia sorella comprerà dei regali

g. andremo in piscina

h. mi piacerebbe vedere il sole

i. mi piacerebbe andare al museo

j. ci piacerebbe comprare delle verdure

3. Multiple choice quiz

	1	2	3
a.	he is Swiss	he is Swedish	he is Russian
b.	he is travelling by train	he is travelling by plane	he is travelling by boat
c.	he is travelling alone	he is travelling with his friend	he is travelling with his family
d.	he is staying in a cheap hotel	he is staying in a three-star hotel	he is staying in a luxury hotel
e.	he is staying there for two weeks	he is staying there for three weeks	he is staying there for ten days
f.	he is going diving	he is going to go clubbing	he is going to eat and sleep
g.	he will also go sightseeing	he will also go shopping	he will also sunbathe
h.	it will be fun	it will be fantastic	it will be expensive

4. Write in the missing words

(a) Quest'estate andrò _____ vacanza a Roma, ___ Italia. (b) _______ in aereo. Passeremo una settimana _____. (c) Staremo ___ un hotel _______ lusso. (d) Andrò _________ discoteca perché ___ _________ ballare.

Mia sorella _________ a fare shopping (e) e mia madre _________ a comprare regali. (f) Inoltre, faremo un giro turistico perché ___ _________ vedere molti monumenti _________.

---

5. Listen, spot and correct the spelling and grammar errors

(a) Questo estate andrà in vacanza aereo. (b) Passero due settimana lì. (c) Andrò con mia tutta famiglia. (d) Staremo in hotel di luso con piscina vicino alla spiagia. (e) La mattina andremo spiaggia. (f) Il pomeriggio andemo a fare shopping e un giro turistico. (g) Verso le otto andremo a cenare in ristoranti locale per mangiare dei piatti tipici. (h) La sera, io e mia sorella andremo a discoteca. (i) Mi piacerebbe anche imparare a ballo tipico. Serà fantastico.

---

6. Listen to Carlo and answer the questions below in English

a. Where is he going on holiday? (two details)

b. When does his holiday begin?

c. How long for?

d. How is he travelling?

e. Who with?

f. Who are they staying with?

g. What is the name of the town where they will stay?

h. What are they going to do there? (4 details)

1.   3.

2.   4.

---

7. Narrow listening: fill in the grid in English

	a. Carolina	b. Beniamino	c. Sandra	d. Matteo
Destination				
Who with				
Departure date				
How long for				
Accommodation				
Location				
Activities				

Unit 15. My holiday plans: VOCABULARY BUILDING

1. Match up

1. andrò	a. I will eat
2. mangerò	b. a campsite
3. starò	c. I'm going to go
4. un hotel economico	d. it will be fun
5. un campeggio	e. I'm going to stay
6. mi piacerebbe	f. to rest
7. riposare	g. a cheap hotel
8. sarà divertente	h. I would like to

2. Complete with the missing word

a. Mangiare e ____________   *To eat and sleep*

b. ____ _____________ tanto   *I will rest a lot*

c. Mi ____________ andare a…   *I would like to go to…*

d. ______ ________ l'ukulele   *I want to play the ukulele*

e. Prenderò ___ _________   *I will sunbathe*

f. _________ noioso   *It will be boring*

g. Passeremo ____ _______________ in Italia
We are going to spend two weeks in Italy

h. Viaggerò in __________
I'm going to travel by plane

i. Staremo in un hotel ___ ___________
We are going to stay in a luxury hotel

3. Translate into English

a. Quest'estate andrò in Grecia

b. Viaggerò in nave

c. Andrò a Cuba in aereo

d. Farò compere

e. Mi piacerebbe fare un giro turistico

f. Mi riposerò tutti i giorni

g. Ci piacerebbe mangiare e dormire

h. A volte farò immersioni

i. Andremo in vacanza in Spagna

4. Complete with the missing words

a. M______________ e dormire   *To eat and sleep*

b. _____________ in un campeggio   *We will stay in a campsite*

c. _____________ in macchina   *I am going to go by car*

d. _________una settimana   *I am going to spend 1 week*

e. Mi______________ andare   *I would like to go to*

f. Andare in______________   *To go to the beach*

g. Fare un giro_______________   *To go sightseeing*

h. _________ il sole   *To sunbathe*

i. Non vedo l'________   *I can't wait*

5. Broken words

a. Andr____________   *I will go*

b. Andre_______   *we will go*

c. Vacan____________   *holiday*

d. Camp__________   *campsite*

e. Immers_________   *diving*

f. Un a____________   *by plane*

g. I__ n__________   *by boat*

h. Ball____________   *to dance*

i. Mang____________   *to eat*

j. Ripos____________   *to rest*

6. Bad translation – spot any translation errors and fix them

a. Il prossimo anno andrò: *Next summer I will go*

b. Andrò a Cuba in aereo: *I am going to go to Cuba by boat*

c. Mangerò e dormirò: *I am going to drink and sleep*

d. Mi piacerebbe riposarmi tanto: *I would like to rest a bit*

e. Staremo in un hotel: *I am going to stay in a hotel*

f. Passerò due settimane lì: *I am going to spend one week here*

g. Viaggeremo in autobus: *I am going to travel by train*

h. Staremo a casa della mia famiglia: *We stay in my family's house*

Unit 15. My holiday plans: READING (Part 1)

Mi chiamo Hugo. Sono spagnolo, di Oviedo ma vivo a Madrid. Quest'estate andrò in vacanza nel sud della Spagna, in Andalusia. Viaggerò in macchina con il mio ragazzo Alejandro. Passeremo quattro settimane lì. Andremo in spiaggia tutti i giorni e mangeremo cibi deliziosi. Non farò un giro turistico, a mio parere è faticoso. Preferisco prendere il sole e ballare!

Mi chiamo Deryk e vivo in Canada. Nella mia famiglia siamo in quattro. Quest'estate andremo in Inghilterra e poi in Quebec, in Canada. Durante le vacanze riposerò e leggerò un libro. Penso che andrò anche a sciare con i miei amici in Canada. Mi piacerebbe mangiare cibi deliziosi, come 'poutine' (simile alle patate fritte con formaggio). Sarà fantastico!

Mi chiamo Dino. Sono italiano ma vivo in Cina. Tra due settimane andrò in Svizzera in aereo. Passerò quindici giorni lì, da solo, e starò in un camper in montagna. Mi piacerebbe vedere il lago di Lemano. Penso che visiterò anche i musei. Non mi piace molto lo sport, preferisco scoprire *[discover]* la cultura del posto. Sarà interessante!

Mi chiamo Diana, sono polacca ma vivo in Germania. Il prossimo anno andrò a Roma con la mia amica, Natasha. Viaggerò in aereo e poi in macchina, perché ho molto tempo. Passerò cinque settimane lì e starò in una casa di famiglia, in campagna. Non vedo l'ora di andare in centro di mattina e visitare il Vaticano. Non mi piace fare delle compere, secondo me è noioso. Preferisco andare a cena fuori, in un ristorante o in una pizzeria.

1. Find the Italian for the following in Hugo's text

a. I am from

b. but I live in

c. I am going to travel by

d. with my boyfriend

e. four weeks

f. we will go

g. in my opinion

h. I prefer to sunbathe

2. Find the Italian for the following in Diana's text

a. next year

b. by car

c. I have a lot of time

d. I don't like to do shopping

e. in the family home

f. in the morning

g. according to me

h. dining out

3. Complete the following statements about Deryk

a. He is from ________________

b. There are ______ people in his family

c. They will travel to ____________ and ____________

d. Deryk is going to ______________ and ___________

e. He thinks that he is going to __________ with his friends

f. "Poutine" is made up of ____________ and ___________

4. List any 8 details about Dino (in 3rd person) in English

1.

2.

3.

4.

5.

6.

7.

8.

5. Find Someone Who…

a. …is going to England this summer

b. …loves learning about culture

c. …prefers sunbathing to sightseeing

d. …is going on holiday to Europe

e. …is going to travel by car

Unit 15. My holiday plans: READING (Part 2)

Mi chiamo Berta. Sono tedesca. Ho una tartaruga in casa. È grossa e molto buffa ed è la mia migliore amica. Quest'estate andrò in vacanza in Italia, con la mia famiglia. Viaggerò in aereo e poi in macchina. Passerò due settimane sul Lago di Garda e starò in un hotel di lusso. Non vedo l'ora! Poi andremo tre giorni a Verona. Penso che vedremo i monumenti famosi, come l'Arena di Verona (un antico anfiteatro romano), dove fanno opera e concerti di musica. Tutti i giorni mangerò tanti cibi deliziosi e gelati. Mi piacerebbe fare compere e comprare vestiti italiani firmati, se avrò **soldi!** *[money]*

Mi chiamo Oliver. Sono di Sydney, in Australia. Il prossimo anno andrò in vacanza in Toscana con mio fratello. Viaggeremo in aereo e passeremo tre settimane lì. In Toscana visiteremo tanti posti. Non vedo l'ora di andare a Firenze, famosa per i suoi musei e i monumenti, e visitare il Duomo. Poi andremo a Siena per vedere il *Palio* (antica corsa di cavalli), penso che sarà emozionante. Infine, riposerò qualche giorno in campagna, in una villa con una piscina e un grande giardino. Sicuramente mangerò tanti cibi locali come la *ribollita* (zuppa di pane, fagioli e verdure) e tanti salumi.

Mi chiamo Catrina, ho dodici anni e vivo a Genova. Quest'estate andrò in vacanza ad Amalfi, nel sud dell'Italia per dieci giorni. Viaggerò in macchina con mio padre e mia nonna. Staremo in un hotel economico, a pochi metri *[a few metres away]* dalla spiaggia. Andrò al mare tutti i giorni e prenderò il sole. La costa lì è spettacolare! Farò lunghe passeggiate e mangerò tanti gelati. Faremo anche un giro turistico a Napoli e andremo a vedere Pompei, famosa per il sito archeologico. Ho un'amica che vive a Sorrento, vicino ad Amalfi, si chiama Anna. Mi piacerebbe giocare con lei e fare immersioni. Sarà divertente, non vedo l'ora!

1. Answer the following questions about Berta

a. Where is she from?

b. What does she say about her pet?

c. Who will she go on holiday with? How will they travel?

d. Where will they stay?

e. What are they going to visit?

f. What is the "Arena" in Verona?

g. What will she do every day?

h. What would she like to buy?

2. Find the Italian in Catrina's text

a. this summer

b. for 10 days

c. the coast

d. long walks

e. famous for

f. I have a friend

g. to go diving

h. I will sunbathe

i. I can't wait

3. Find the Italian for the following phrases/sentences in Oliver's text

a. Next year

b. Famous for its museums

c. Old horse festival

d. It will be exciting

e. Finally

f. A few days in the countryside

g. With a swimming pool

h. Local food

4. Find Someone Who...

a. ...is going to travel south.

b. ...would like to buy Italian clothes.

c. ...has a funny pet.

d. ...is going to be staying in a villa with pool.

e. ...is going to see a spectacular coast.

f. ...is travelling from Australia.

g. ...is going to visit an archeological site.

h. ...is planning to eat ice-cream every day.

Unit 15. My holiday plans: TRANSLATION/WRITING

1. Gapped translation

a. *I am going to go on holiday:* Andrò in ________________

b. *I am going to travel by car:* Viaggerò in ______________

c. *We are going to stay one week there:*
_____________ una settimana _____________________

d. *I am going to stay in a cheap hotel:*
Starò in un hotel ___________________________________

e. *We are going to eat and sleep every day:*
Mangeremo e ______________ tutti i giorni

f. *When the weather is nice I am going to go to the beach:*
Quando farà bel tempo ___ ________ in spiaggia

g. *I am going to go shopping:* Farò ________________

2. Translate to English

a. Mangiare

b. Comprare

c. Riposare

d. Fare un giro turistico

e. Andare in spiaggia

f. Tutti i giorni

g. In aereo

h. Fare immersioni

i. Andare in centro

j. Fare delle compere

3. Spot and correct the grammar and spelling mistakes [note: in several cases a word is missing]

a. faro imersioni

b. passerò una setimana li

c. starò in hotel lusso

d. staremo in un hotel a centro

e. mi piacerebbe farò delle compere

f. viaggerò con aereo e machina

g. andrò vacanza per due settimana

h. suonerò l'ukulele e sara divartento

i. mangerro cibi delizioso

4. Categories: Positive or Negative? Write P or N

a. Sarà divertente: **P**

b. Sarà noioso:

c. Sarà piacevole:

d. Sarà rilassante:

e. Sarà interessante:

f. Sarà terribile:

g. Sarà spettacolare:

h. Sarà faticoso:

i. Sarà affascinante:

j. Sarà impressionante:

5. Translate into Italian

a. I am going to rest

b. I will go diving

c. We will go to the beach

d. I will sunbathe

e. I would like to go sightseeing

f. I will stay in…

g. A cheap hotel

h. We are going to spend two weeks

i. I will go by plane

j. It will be fun

1. Mi chiamo Barri Mock ed ho sedici anni. Il mio compleanno è il ventitré marzo. Sono gallese e vivo a Caerphilly, vicino a Cardiff, la capitale del Galles, con la mia famiglia. Oggi sono molto felice perché la settimana prossima andrò in vacanza in Spagna con la mia famiglia.

2. Nella mia famiglia siamo quattro persone: mia sorella maggiore, Rhiannon, mio padre, Gareth, mia madre, Elin, ed io. Vado molto d'accordo con mia madre perché è molto paziente e simpatica. Però, mio padre è un po' impaziente. Normalmente andiamo d'accordo, ma a volte è un po' antipatico e mi sgrida se non faccio i compiti.

3. La mia routine quotidiana è abbastanza semplice. Generalmente, mi sveglio un po' tardi, verso le otto di mattina. Dopo mi faccio la doccia, mi pettino e mi vesto. Poi, verso le otto e un quarto, faccio colazione con mia sorella Rhiannon in cucina. Entrambi mangiamo *(we both have)* del pane tostato con marmellata e un succo d'arancia.

4. Che cosa mi piace mangiare? Adoro la verdura, come gli spinaci, le carote e le zucchine perché sono ricchi di vitamine e cereali. Però, non mangio la carne perché sono vegetariano. Il mio cibo preferito è il cibo indiano, lo mangio tutte le settimane. Mi piace molto la frutta, soprattutto le fragole.

5. Mi piace la mia scuola perché i professori sono intelligenti e pazienti e spiegano le cose molto bene. La mia materia preferita è il teatro perché sono una persona abbastanza creativa. Inoltre, adoro le lezioni di musica perché mi piace cantare e suonare la chitarra.

6. Il fine settimana prossimo cominciano le vacanze estive. Vado in vacanza in Emilia Romagna, nel nord Italia, con la mia famiglia. Andremo in aereo e dopo in macchina. Visiteremo *(we will visit)* Riccione e staremo in un hotel di lusso. Dopo andremo in macchina a Bologna e vedremo i monumenti famosi, come le due torri e la basilica di San Petronio. Mangerò del cibo delizioso. Faremo anche shopping tutti i giorni e comprerò dellecose belle.

1. True (T), False (F) or Not Mentioned (NM)?

Today, Barri is quite sad	
He doesn't get on well with his mother	
Barri has a girlfriend	
He has breakfast in the dining room	
For breakfast he has toast with honey	
He loves vegetables	
He doesn't eat fish	
He likes Indian food but has it rarely	
He likes strawberries a lot	
He can't stand his school	
He enjoys singing	
He is going on holiday to Southern Italy	
In Riccione he will stay in a luxury hotel	
He will go shopping every day	

2. Find the Italian equivalent for the following phrases/sentences in the text

a. I am very happy (par. 1)

b. I am going on holiday (par.1)

c. I get on well (par. 2)

d. however (par. 2)

e. a bit (par. 2)

f. tells me off (par. 2)

g. I wake up (par. 3)

h. I adore vegetables (par. 4)

i. I don't eat meat (par. 4)

j. they explain things (par. 5)

k. I like singing (par.5)

l. I am going to go (par.6)

m. we are going to spend (par. 6)

n. we are going to go shopping (par. 6)

o. I am going to buy (par. 6)

1. Mi chiamo Federica ed ho diciassette anni. Il mio compleanno è il ventirè giugno. Sono italiana e vivo a San Felice Circeo, un paese piccolo sulla costa del Lazio con la mia famiglia. Oggi sono molto felice perché sono in vacanza con la mia famiglia.

2. Nella mia famiglia siamo quattro persone: mia sorella maggiore Francesca, mio padre Gennaro, mia madre Gabriella, ed io. Mia madre è molto più severa di mio padre. Lui fa ciclismo con i suoi amici tutti i giorni. C'è una montagna vicino a dove vivo. I miei nonni si chiamano Gabriele e Alessia. Gabriele ha ottantatré anni e Alessia ha ottantadue anni. Entrambi sono molto simpatici e affettuosi.

3. Mia sorella maggiore si chiama Francesca. Le piace dipingere e cantare. Ha sedici anni ed è molto creativa e talentuosa. Il suo compleanno è il nove maggio. Francesca è molto bella. Ha i capelli castani e gli occhi azzurri. Francesca è più artistica di me, ma i miei amici dicono che io sono più divertente di lei.

4. Che cosa mi piace mangiare? Amo la verdura, come la lattuga, i pomodori e i cetrioli perché sono ricchi di vitamine e minerali. Il mio cibo preferito è il cibo cinese. Lo mangio due volte alla settimana. Mi piace molto la frutta, soprattutto l'anguria. Odio la carne.

5. Mi piace la mia scuola perché i professori sono molto gentili e divertenti. Mi aiutano sempre quando ho un problema. La mia materia preferita è la musica. Il mio professore di musica suona molto bene la batteria e il pianoforte, ma il suo strumento principale è il violino. Lui suona in un'orchestra di Roma e del Lazio. In futuro mi piacerebbe essere musicista professionista come lui.

6. Il fine settimana prossimo cominciano le vacanze estive. Andremo in vacanza ad Atene, la capitale della Grecia, con la mia famiglia. Andremo lì in aereo e poi in treno. Staremo una settimana ad Atene e staremo in un hotel economico. Sarà molto interessante! Poi andiamo in nave in un'isola che si chiama Santorini. Staremo in una casa tipica, di colore bianco e azzurro. Mangerò dei piatti locali deliziosi e nuoterò in piscina tutti i giorni. Sarà incredibile!

---

3. Read paragraphs 1 to 3 and complete the following statements correctly

a. Federica lives in a _______ town.

b. Federica's dad cycles ______________.

c. There is a mountain near _____________.

d. Her grandparents are called _______ and ______.

e. Her ______ sister is called Francesca.

f. Francesca likes _______ and _______.

g. Federica's friends say she is ______ than Francesca.

---

4. Correct the 14 mistakes in the following translation of paragraphs 4 and 5

What do I like to eat? I like vegetables, such as carrots, tomatoes and mushrooms because they are rich in vitamins and minerals. My favourite is Indian food. I eat it twice a month. I like fruit a lot, apart from pineapple. I hate meat

I love my school because the pupils are very kind and helpful. They often help me when I have a problem. My favourite subject is music. My music teacher plays the guitar and the piano quite well, but his minor instrument is the violin. He plays in the Roma and Lazio orchestra. In the future I would like to be a music teacher like him.

---

5. Answer the questions below in Italian as if you were Federica

a. Dove si trova il tuo paese?

b. Che sport fa tuo padre?

c. Che cosa piace fare a tua sorella Francesca?

d. Com'è Francesca?

e. Qual è il tuo cibo preferito?

f. Che cosa pensi della carne?

g. Come sono i tuoi professori?

h. Che lavoro ti piacerebbe fare in futuro?

i. Che cosa comincia la settimana prossima?

j. Dove vai in vacanza?

k. Come ci vai?

l. Dove starai a Santorini?

m. Che cosa mangerai lì?

TERM 3 - BRINGING IT ALL TOGETHER – QUESTION SKILLS

1. Fill in the missing question words – Daily life

a. _____ _______ _______ ti svegli?

b. _______ _______ ________ la mattina?

c. _____ _________ _______ ____ ____________normalmente?

d. ____ _______ _______ esci di casa?

e. _______ vai a scuola?

f. _______ __________ ______ per il fine settimana prossimo?

g. _______ ti piacerebbe andare?

h. _______ _______ andrai?

i. ____ _______ ___________ ti piacerebbe fare?

2. Sentence Puzzle – Food: listen and re-arrange the sentences

a. cosa mangi Che colazione a?

b. ti cibo Perché piace Quale??

c. pesce piace Ti il?

d. cibo Qual è preferito tuo il?

e. Quale odi cibo?

f. la la Preferisci o carne verdura?

g. la frutta è tua Qual preferita?

3. Tangled translation – Holidays: into Italian

a. **Where** andrai in **holidays** quest' **summer**?

b. Come **will you go**? **Why**?

c. Quanto **time** passerai **there**?

d. Dove **will you stay**?

e. **What** ti piacerebbe **do** lí?

4. Translate, then listen and check

a. Where? e. What do you do?

b. How? f. With who?

c. When? g. Do you like…?

d. At what time? h. How much time?

5. Listen and write in the missing information to the questions: Daily life

a. A _______ ora ti svegli? Mi _______ verso le _______ di ___________.

b. Che cosa _______ la mattina? La mattina, quasi sempre __________ ________ con mia _______ in _______.

c. Che cosa _______ ? Normalmente _______ un succo d' _______ e mangio_______ tostato con _______.

d. A che _______ esci di _______ ? _______ di casa alle _______ e un _______ .

e. _______ vai a _______ ? Vado a _______ a _______ con il mio migliore _______.

f. _______ programmi _______ per il fine _______ prossimo? Questo _______ settimana vado __ __________ con il mio _______ al parco e dopo vado a ___________ un _______.

g. _______ ti _______ andare? Se c'è _______ tempo mi _______________ andare in _______ .

h. _______ _______ andrai? Andrò _________i miei _______ perché mi _______ passare _______ con loro.

6. Listen and write in the missing information to the questions: Food & Holidays

a. _______ cibo ti _______? _______? Mi _______ molto il cibo_______ perché è _______

b. Ti _______ il _______? _______ il _______, ma mi _______ di più i _______ di _______

c. _______ è il tuo cibo _______? Il mio _______ preferito è la _______

d. _______ _______ odi? _______? _______ i _______. Sono _______.

e. _______ andrai in _______ quest' _______? Quest' _______ andrò in __________ in _______

f. _______ andrai? Prima _______ in _______ e poi in _______

g. _______ _______ starai _______? Starò lì _______ settimane

h. _______? _______ in un _______ in ___________

i. ____ _________ti piacerebbe _______ lí? Mi ___________fare _______ e _______ perché mi ___________gli sport all' _______ aperta

TERM 3 - BRINGING IT ALL TOGETHER – QUESTION SKILLS

7. Fill in the grid with your personal information

Question	Answer
1. A che ora ti svegli?	
2. Che cosa fai la mattina?	
3 A che ora esci di casa?	
4. Come vai a scuola?	
5. Che programmi hai per il fine settimana?	
6. Dove ti piacerebbe andare?	
7. Quale cibo (non) ti piace? Perché?	
8. Qual è il tuo cibo preferito?	
9. Quale cibo odi?	
10. Dove andrai in vacanza quest'estate?	
11. Come andrai lì?	
12. Quanto tempo starai lì?	
13. Dove starai?	
14. Che cosa ti piacerebbe fare lì?	

8. Survey one of your classmates using the same questions as above– write down the main information they give you in Italian

Q.	Person 1
1.	
2.	
3.	
4.	
5.	
6.	
7.	
8.	
9.	
10.	
11.	
12.	
13.	
14.	

No Snakes No Ladders

START	1 I get up at seven	2 I get dressed at seven thirty	3 I have breakfast in the kitchen	4 I leave the house at eight	5 I go back home at four	6 Next weekend…	7 I am going to the cinema
15 I like roast chicken because it is delicious	14 I adore cheese because it is tasty	13 What do you like to eat?	12 It will be fun	11 In order to watch a match	10 In order to swim	9 My friend (m) is going to the pool	8 I would like to go to the park
16 Meat is rich in protein	17 I hate oranges!	18 Hamburgers are not healthy	19 I prefer vegetables	20 I am going to go on holidays to Sicily	21 I am going to spend one week there	22 I am going to stay in a cheap hotel	23 I am going to stay in a luxury hotel
FINISH	30 We would like to go sightseeing	29 We would like to go to the beach	28 I would like to go shopping	27 I would like to sunbathe at the beach	26 We are going to go diving	25 We are going to buy souvenirs	24 I am going to eat delicious food

No Snakes No Ladders

PARTENZA	1 Mi alzo alle sette	2 Mi vesto alle sette e mezza	3 Faccio colazione in cucina	4 Esco di casa alle otto	5 Torno a casa alle quattro	6 Il fine settimana prossimo	7 Vado al cinema
15 Mi piace il pollo arrosto perché è delizioso	14 Adoro il formaggio perché è saporito	13 Che cosa ti piace mangiare?	12 Sarà divertente	11 Per guardare una partita	10 Per nuotare	9 Il mio amico va in piscina	8 Mi piacerebbe andare al parco
16 La carne è ricca di proteine	17 Odio le arance!	18 Gli hamburger non sono sani	19 Preferisco la verdura	20 Andrò in vacanza in Sicilia	21 Starò una settimana lì	22 Starò in un hotel economico	23 Starò in un hotel di lusso
ARRIVO	30 Ci piacerebbe fare un giro turistico	29 Ci piacerebbe andare in spiaggia	28 Mi piacerebbe fare shopping	27 Mi piacerebbe prendere il sole in spiaggia	26 Faremo immersioni	25 Compreremo souvenirs	24 Mangerò del cibo delizioso

PYRAMID TRANSLATION

Term 3 - Recap - Holidays

Translate each part of the pyramid out loud with your partner, then write it into the spaces provided below.

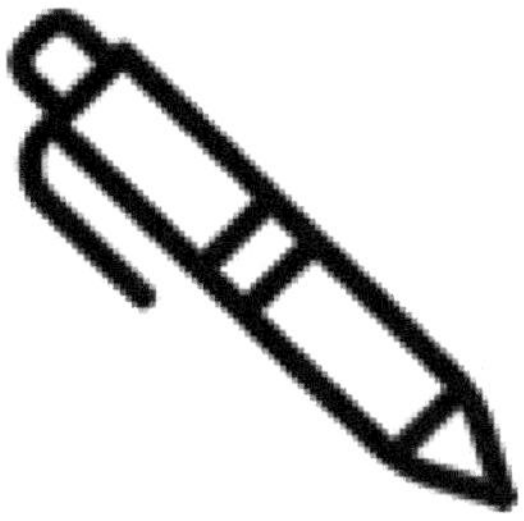

a. This summer

b. This summer I am going to go on holiday with my family.

c. This summer I am going to go on holiday with my family to Italy.

e. This summer I am going to go on holiday with my family to Italy. We are going to spend two weeks there and we are going to stay in a campsite.

f. This summer I am going to go on holiday with my family to Italy. We are going to spend two weeks there and we are going to stay in a campsite. I am going to do sightseeing and go to the beach. It will be fun.

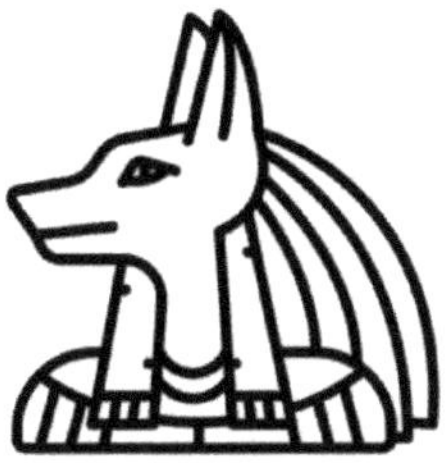

Write your translation here

SOLUTION: *Quest'estate andrò in vacanza con la mia famiglia in Italia. Staremo due settimane lì e staremo in un campeggio. Farò un giro turistico e andrò in spiaggia. Sarà divertente.*

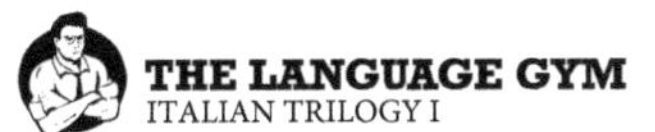

One pen One dice

Play in pairs. You only have 1 pen and 1 dice.
One person has the pen and starts translating the sentence into **English.** The other person rolls the dice until they roll a 6, they swap the pen and translate. The winner is the person who finishes translating all the sentences first.

1. Mi alzo alle otto.	
2. Mi faccio la doccia e mi vesto.	
3. Esco di casa e vado a scuola a piedi.	
4. Il fine settimana prossimo vado al cinema.	
5. Vado in piscina a nuotare.	
6. Mi piace la carne ma non mi piace il pesce	
7. Mi piace l'insalata perché è sana.	
8. Andrò in vacanza in Francia.	
9. Starò una settimana lì.	
10. Comprerò dei regali.	

One pen One dice

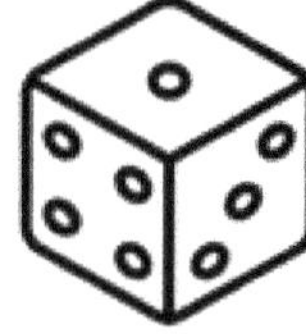

Play in pairs. You only have 1 pen and 1 dice.
One person has the pen and starts translating the sentence into **Italian.** The other person rolls the dice until they roll a 6, they swap the pen and translate. The winner is the person who finishes translating all the sentences first.

1. I get up at eight.	
2. I shower and I get dressed.	
3. I leave the house and go to school on foot.	
4. Next weekend I am going to go to the cinema.	
5. I am going to go to the pool (in order) to swim.	
6. I like meat but I don't like fish.	
7. I like salad because it's healthy.	
8. I am going to go on holiday to France.	
9. I am going to spend one week there.	
10. I am going to buy some presents.	

The End

We hope you have enjoyed using this workbook and found it useful!

As many of you will appreciate, the penguin is a fantastic animal. At Language Gym, we hold it as a symbol of resilience, bravery and good humour; able to thrive in the harshest possible environments, and with, arguably the best gait in the animal kingdom (black panther or penguin, you choose). In Italian, it is also the best example of the gui sound (pronounced like the 'gui' in "penguin"). The same occurs with 'gue' (gue).

Join us again for Italian Sentence Builders – TRILOGY – Part II